THE NEW MASTERS OF CAPITAL

A volume in the series

Cornell Studies in Political Economy

edited by Peter J. Katzenstein

A full list of titles in the series appears at the end of the book

THE
NEW MASTERS
OF CAPITAL

American Bond Rating Agencies
and the Politics of Creditworthiness

TIMOTHY J. SINCLAIR

Cornell University Press

Ithaca and London

First published 2005 by Cornell University Press

Printed in the United States of America

Library of Congress Cataloging-in-Publication Data

Sinclair, Timothy J.
   The new masters of capital : American bond rating agencies and the politics of creditworthiness / Timothy J. Sinclair.
        p. cm. -- (Cornell studies in political economy)
   Includes bibliographical references and index.
   ISBN 0-8014-4328-8 (cloth : alk. paper)
   1. Rating agencies (Finance)--United States.   2. Bonds--Ratings--United States.   3. Credit ratings--United States.   I. Title.   II. Series.
   HG3751.7.S56 2004
   332.63′23′0973--dc22

                                                            2004023503

For the Wilson sisters,
Delphine, Helen, Nancy, and Frances

CONTENTS

TABLES AND FIGURES

PREFACE

Global finance is big business. *Really* big business. The bond rating agencies that are the subject of this book maintain ratings on $30 trillion worth of debt issued in American and international markets. These markets are surely too big for us to ignore if we want to understand how our world works.

Not only is global finance big, but it touches us all. The fortunes of currencies—and of banks and the markets for securities—affect our lives every day. They affect the interest rates we pay for our credit card debt, those for our house mortgage, and the return on our pension fund.

A lot of people are confused by how finance works. It appears very technical. Because finance has this image, many prefer to leave it to "the experts." But we must not allow ourselves to do so. Like war, the institutions and processes of global finance are too important to leave to professionals to figure out. This book is an effort to cross the boundary into expert territory and identify the broader political significance of these seemingly arcane technical institutions.

Sir Robert Muldoon, prime minister and minister of finance of New Zealand, 1975–84, may not be a frequent beneficiary of scholarly thanks, but this book would not exist at all had it not been for him. Although I never met the man, his relations with the bond rating agencies first made me think that understanding these institutions might be important in the post–Bretton Woods era. Muldoon, short of stature and wide of girth, was energetic, intelligent, and truculent. Very little cowed him. Noted exceptions were the rating agencies, which Muldoon seemed to think were very important. He left an impression on rating officials that was still evident

xi

several years after his tenure ended, as I discovered during interviews on Wall Street. Muldoon's views had an impact on me as well.

I was very fortunate in the intellectual and institutional support that came my way as this book developed. Robert Cox, Stephen Gill, and David Leyton-Brown (DLB) all had a major influence. I could not have asked for more challenging scholarly training or better mentoring. I also thank DLB for the generous financial support he provided in connection with research funded by the Social Sciences and Humanities Research Council of Canada, without which my fieldwork in Japan would not have been possible. At York University in Toronto, the faculty and staff of the Department of Political Science, the Faculty of Graduate Studies, Stong College, and the York Centre for International and Security Studies supported this research in many ways, providing office space, fieldwork grants, and conference funding to test my initial ideas.

At the University of Warwick in England, where I have worked since 1995, I am thankful for two research development grants, which allowed me to undertake supplemental fieldwork. I also appreciate the financial support for conference participation generously provided by the Department of Politics and International Studies. The Warwick Center for the Study of Globalisation and Regionalisation provided support for attendance at a conference on rating agencies held at New York University's Stern School in 2001. At Warwick, I have been fortunate to teach a graduate class on the politics of global finance for some years. Many students have offered valuable insights while reading and discussing my journal articles on rating. Joe Horneck and Belkys López are notable among their colleagues for bringing useful documentary sources to my attention. Paola Robotti, a Warwick doctoral candidate, applied her considerable skill to improve my primitive efforts at drawing figures.

During the closing stages of this project, I was fortunate to spend a sabbatical year at Harvard University, as a visiting scholar at the Weatherhead Center for International Affairs. Jeffry A. Frieden and James A. Cooney were instrumental in making this happen and helped make it a most valuable experience. While at Harvard, I was resident at Winthrop House, where Karen Reiber, Martine van Ittersum, David Simms, and Enoch Kyerematen made a big difference to my experience.

Many people in the global academic community helped with this book in one way or another. In Canada, Eric Helleiner, Louis W. Pauly, Chris Robinson, A. Claire Cutler, and Ricardo Grinspun were key. In the United States, I greatly benefited from the interest of James N. Rosenau, Raymond D. "Bud" Duvall, Craig N. Murphy, Rawi E. Abdelal, James H. Mittelman, Timothy J. McKeown, Kenneth P. Thomas, Jeffry A. Frieden, Peter Gourevitch, Richard W. Mansbach, Yale H. Ferguson, Michael Schwartz, Mark Amen, Virginia Haufler, Kathryn Lavelle, and "Skip" McGoun. In Europe, I learned much from Ronen Palan, Jan Aart Scholte, Susan Strange, Dieter Kerwer, Torsten Strulik, Helmut Willke, Oliver Kessler, Philip G. Cerny, Donald MacKenzie, Tony Payne, Marieke de Goede, Peter

Burnham, Henk Overbeek, and Kees van der Pijl. Frank and Patrick McCann provided expert photographic input.

I have many debts to acknowledge for the help I received during my field research. Particularly kind were Leo C. O'Neill and Cathy Daicoff of Standard & Poor's, and David Stimpson of Moody's Investors Service. I met Mr. O'Neill, president of Standard & Poor's, near the start and the end of the project, and at each meeting he was forthcoming and incisive. Most helpful in the final years of my research was David Levey of Moody's. David is a great source of knowledge and good judgment about the rating business and its challenges, as well as a scholar and political economist himself. I learned a great deal from him. Chris Mahoney, also of Moody's, provided important aid. Takehiko Kamo, before his early death a professor in the Faculty of Law at the University of Tokyo, assisted my research in Japan, sponsoring my stay at the International House of Japan. Donald J. Daly, Hiroharu Seki, and Seiji Endo helped with contacts in Japan.

In addition to anonymous reviewers, several scholars read the entire manuscript. I am greatly indebted to Benjamin J. Cohen, Tony Porter, Richard Higgott, Randall Germain, and Edward Cohen for their useful comments. They influenced me in many ways.

Friends and associates also supported me during the research and writing of this work. Especially important were Steve Patten, Graham Todd, Edward Comor, Robert O'Brien, J. Magnus Ryner, Martin Hewson, Liliana Pop, Randall Germain, Peter Burnham, Shirin Rai, and my IPMS Mercia friends in Warwickshire.

Peter J. Katzenstein and Roger Haydon made a major contribution to my thinking about how this book should be organized. Their belief in the project and their practical impact cannot be underestimated.

Finally, my deep thanks go to the Wilson sisters. Delphine, Helen, Nancy, and Frances pushed me to defend my early ideas about politics, most memorably around the gas lamps and dinner tables at Mataikona. They inspired me, although it has taken me thirty years to appreciate fully their significance.

TIMOTHY J. SINCLAIR

Kenilworth, Warwickshire

THE NEW MASTERS OF CAPITAL

CHAPTER ONE

Introduction

> We live again in a two-superpower world. There is the U.S. and there is
> Moody's. The U.S. can destroy a country by levelling it with bombs:
> Moody's can destroy a country by downgrading its bonds.
>
> THOMAS L. FRIEDMAN, *New York Times*, 1995

Contemporary American power is obvious to the casual observer. If you want concrete evidence of U.S. superpower status, take a trip to southern Arizona. Outside the city of Tucson is AMARC, the USAF "boneyard," the greatest collection of mothballed warplanes on Earth.[1] If an airplane was a part of the American war machine during the past thirty years you will probably find it here, patiently awaiting its fate in the blazing Sonoran desert sun, together with some three thousand others. In this place, B-52 Stratofortresses, like those that dropped bombs on Vietnam, Afghanistan, and Iraq, and which were held in readiness for nuclear retaliation during the Cold War, are broken up, their shattered fuselages and wings displayed for the benefit of Russian spy satellites documenting the fulfillment of Strategic Arms Reduction Treaty (START) obligations. A-10 Thunderbolt IIs, the venerable "Warthog" tank-busters of Gulf Wars I and II, now expected to be in the USAF inventory until 2028, stand row upon row in the searing desert heat, quietly awaiting redeployment. Other "hogs," based at nearby Davis-Monthan Air Force Base, fly low overhead, silently circling the University of Arizona campus. In this arsenal, the embodiment of a Tom Clancy or Don DeLillo novel, the basis of America's superpower status could not be clearer.

But things are different when it comes to the "second superpowers," the major bond rating agencies—Moody's Investors Service (Moody's), its competitor, Standard & Poor's (S&P), the smaller and less important Fitch Ratings (Fitch), and the multitude of minor domestic rating agencies around the globe. They operate in a very different world. Their arsenal is an occult one, largely invisible to all but a few

---

1. AMARC—Aerospace Maintenance and Regeneration Center.

1

most of the time.[2] Financial stress expands the size of the group aware of the agencies: in 2002, Europe had its highest-ever level of defaults, up to $15 billion from $4 billion in 2001. To the people directly concerned with matters of financial health—chief financial officers, budget directors, Treasury officials, and increasingly even politicians—rating agencies are well known.[3] In this book the world of these second superpowers is explored: the basis of their power, the nature of their authority in financial markets, and implications of their judgments for corporations, municipal governments, and sovereign states.

In examining this world, I argue that rating agency activities reflect not the "correctness" or otherwise of rating analyses but instead the store of expertise and intellectual authority the agencies possess. Market and government actors take account of rating agencies not because the agencies are right but because they are thought to be an authoritative source of judgments, thereby making the agencies key organizations controlling access to capital markets. It is the esteem enjoyed by rating agencies—a characteristic distributed unevenly in modern capitalism—that this book explores, rather than whether agency ratings are actually valid.

A further claim made here is that this consequential speech has semantic content or meaning. That content, developed within the framework of rating orthodoxy delineated in chapter 3, is not purely technical but is linked to social and political interests. Although it is tempting to suggest that those interests are not related to location, the American origins of the rating agencies are relevant.

Changes on Wall Street and in other global financial centers increased the significance of Moody's and S&P during the 1990s. The destruction of the World Trade Center in 2001 did not reverse this trend.[4] Since the terrorist attacks, international trade and financial transactions have increased.[5] The broad context for the increased role of rating is the process of financial globalization that began in the 1970s.

Financial globalization encompasses worldwide change in how financial markets are organized, increases in financial transaction volume, and alterations in government regulation. As discussed here, the concept is more comprehensive than

2. Rating is not always so invisible. Consider, e.g., the 30 percent slide in the stock price of Tyco International when Moody's and S&P downgraded the corporation in 2002 (Peter Thal Larsen and Gary Silverman, "Tyco Suffers Downgrade and Steep Shares Slide," *Financial Times,* June 8–9, 2002, 1).

3. On defaults in Europe, see Aline van Duyn, "Rating Agencies See More Gloom," *Financial Times,* December 17, 2002, 30. On New York mayor Michael Bloomberg's wariness of the rating agencies as an example of the attitude of elected officials, see Elizabeth Kolbert, "The Mogul Mayor," *New Yorker,* April 22 and 29, 2002, 138–49, esp. 145. Even the U.S. government can be subject to the attentions of the rating agencies. See Päivi Munter, "Credit Rating Agencies Worried by U.S. Debt," *Financial Times,* September 20–21, 2003, M21.

4. Charles Batchelor, "Companies and Regulators Go on Offensive in the Global Ratings Game," *Financial Times,* July 5–6, 2003, M3.

5. On the growth in transactions, see Jon E. Hilsenrath, "Globalization Persists in Precarious New Age," *Wall Street Journal,* December 31, 2001, 1.

Armijo's specification of financial globalization as "the international integration of previously segmented national credit and capital markets."[6] In financial globalization, markets are increasingly organized in an "arms length" way. Institutions that once dominated finance and were politically consequential, as a result, now have other roles.

Cross-border transactions have, of course, massively increased since capital controls were liberalized in most rich countries during the late 1970s and 1980s. The regulation of financial markets has also changed form since then. Though increasingly detailed, regulation is typically implemented by market actors. Government agencies create and adjust the self-regulatory framework as circumstances merit. In this environment, new financial products and strategies emerge frequently. Market volatility is associated with these developments, as is a sense that governments themselves are increasingly subject to the judgments of speculators and investors.

The changes in market organization have been significant. Commercial banks used to be the institutions that corporations, municipalities, and national governments sought out in order to borrow money. Today, in a process known as *disintermediation,* bonds and notes sold on capital markets are displacing traditional bank loans as the primary means of borrowing money. In a related process, *securitization,* mortgages, credit card receivables, and even bank loans are being transformed into tradeable securities that can be bought and sold in capital markets. This does not mean banks are of little importance in global financial markets. It means that judgments about who receives credit and who does not are no longer centralized in banks, as was the case in the past.

Over the past decade, the liberalization of financial markets has made rating increasingly important as a form of private regulation.[7] States have had to take account of private sector judgments much more than in the heavily controlled postwar era.[8] Liberalization of the financial markets have also increased exposure to risk and therefore the importance of information, investigation, and analysis mechanisms. Outside the rich countries, liberalization has been pursued by developing-country governments in Asia and Latin America that have sought to create local capital markets to finance investment in new infrastructure and industrial production. The importance of these new markets is that their operatives want information about the creditworthiness of the corporations and governments that seek to borrow

---

6. Leslie Elliott Armijo, preface to the paperback edition, in Armijo, ed., *Financial Globalization and Democracy in Emerging Markets* (London: Palgrave, 2001), xiii.

7. On private regulation, see A. Claire Cutler, Virginia Haufler, and Tony Porter, eds., *Private Authority and International Affairs* (Albany: State University of New York Press, 1999); and Rodney Bruce Hall and Thomas J. Biersteker, eds., *The Emergence of Private Authority in Global Governance* (Cambridge: Cambridge University Press, 2002).

8. For an example of this transformation, see Malcolm McKinnon, *Treasury: The New Zealand Treasury, 1840–2000* (Auckland: Auckland University Press, 2003), 353.

their money. As things stand, market operatives get some of this information, in the form of bond ratings, from Moody's and S&P.

The two major U.S. rating agencies pass judgment on around $30 trillion worth of securities each year.[9] Of this $30 trillion, around $107 billion worth of debt issued by 196 bond issuers was in default in 2001—a figure up sharply from 2000, when 117 issuers defaulted on $42 billion.[10] Ratings, which vary from the best (AAA or "triple A") to the worst (D, for default), affect the interest rate or cost of borrowing for businesses, municipalities, national governments, and, ultimately, individual citizens and consumers. The higher the rating, the less risk of default on repayment to the lender and, therefore, other things being equal, the lower the cost to the borrower. Rating scales are described in more detail in chapter 2.

The phenomenon investigated here is usually thought of as a technical matter. But this is largely a nontechnical book. An accurate, meaningful understanding of bond rating requires a broader view than the technical, just as an understanding of war cannot be limited to the analysis of military maneuvers or logistics. Hence, this book considers not just how ratings are done but also the purposes attributable to the rating process, the power and authority of the agencies, the implications of rating judgments, and the problems that may bring change to the world of ratings.

Widespread misunderstandings exist about the way capital markets and their institutions work and shape the world. These markets are complex and seemingly arcane. The amount of money involved is titanic and likely awesome to all but the richest inhabitants of the planet. Many think these markets shape economic and political choices in an objective way, much as the laws of physics shape the universe.[11] But the unqualified influence of markets and market institutions in recent years has not always been evident. For a time, during the New Deal era of the 1930s and the years of postwar prosperity in the West, a greater degree of public control tempered these global forces. U.S. and other Western governments developed welfare programs and policy measures to insulate their populaces from the vagaries of capital markets. But the constraints, so the story goes, were artificial and, since the 1970s, have been challenged. Financial markets have again opposed the dictates of elected authorities and voters, to assume their "rightful place" in the scheme of things. Now, we are told by the popular and the scholarly press, there is no escaping these impersonal forces.

9. Moody's Investors Service, "Introduction to Moody's," in "About Moody's," available at www.moodys.com, accessed October 15, 2001.

10. Alex Berenson, "Junk Bonds Still Have Fans Despite a Dismal Showing in 2001," *Wall Street Journal*, January 2, 2002, C9.

11. See, e.g., Clive Crooks, "Globalization and Its Critics: A Survey of Globalization," *Economist*, September 29, 2001; William Greider, *One World, Ready or Not: The Manic Logic of Global Capitalism* (New York: Simon & Schuster, 1997); or Richard B. McKenzie and Dwight R. Lee, *Quicksilver Capital: How the Rapid Movement of Wealth Has Changed the World* (New York: Free Press, 1991).

As an explanation of financial globalization, this sort of mechanistic view is not adequate. A technical understanding of the forces that constrain our economic and political choices is necessarily limited. This view assumes markets develop in ways beyond the influence of citizens, that people should simply allow things to take their "natural" course—financial globalization is inevitable. This is a key point. Much that is written about financial markets, even by people who recognize the political consequences of these markets, misses the fundamentally social character of what happens inside the markets and their institutions.[12]

The assumption in established texts is that markets reflect fundamental economic forces, which are not subject to human manipulation. But this view does not take account of the fact that people make decisions in financial markets in anticipation of and in response to the decisions of others.[13] In this book, the social nature of global finance gets particular emphasis. The social view of finance suggests that in situations of increased uncertainty and risk, the institutions that work to facilitate transactions between buyers and sellers have a central role in organizing markets and, consequently, in governing the world.[14] Financial markets are more social—and less spontaneous, individual, or "natural"—than we tend to believe.

The role of rating agencies is not mechanistically determined, either. Many financial markets survived and flourished in the past without them. Typically, banks assumed the credit risk in the relationship between those with money to invest and those wishing to borrow. Alongside banks, traditional capital markets relied on borrowers who were well known and trusted names in their communities. But rating has increasingly become the norm as capital markets have displaced bank lending and as the trust implicit in these older systems has broken down. Rating serves a purpose in less socially embedded capital markets, where fund managers are under pressure to demonstrate they are not basing their understanding of the creditworthiness of investment alternatives on implicit trust in names but use a recognized, accepted mechanism.

At least three other ways of doing the existing work of the rating agencies can be imagined. The first is self-regulation by debtors. Much like the professional bodies for physicians, architects, and lawyers, a debtor-based system of credit information could provide data to the markets. Although this system might not be independent,

12. For a sustained critique of the orthodox view, see Jens Beckert, "What Is Sociological about Economic Sociology? Uncertainty and the Embeddedness of Economic Action," *Theory and Society* 25 (1996): 803–40.

13. Increasingly, economists recognize the importance of social interaction in markets. Paul Krugman's *The Return of Depression Economics* (New York: Norton, 2000) is a persuasive example, esp. chapter 6. For a more sustained conceptual exploration, see Edward Fullbrook, ed., *Intersubjectivity in Economics* (New York: Routledge, 2002).

14. Similar processes can be seen in many other fields. A recent example is the dietary supplement industry, where third-party certification is of growing importance in the absence of government regulation (Marian Barros, "It's on the Label, But in the Tablet?" *New York Times*, January 2, 2002, D1).

collective self-interest would mitigate the tendency to self-serving outputs, much as is the case with professional self-regulation. Second, nonprofit industry associations could undertake or coordinate creditworthiness work. Good precedents already exist in countries where nonprofits enforce some national laws, such as in the case of animal welfare. The nonprofit model offers to eliminate some conflict of interest tensions implicit in charging debtors for their ratings. Third, governments could collectively take on the job, perhaps in the form of a new international agency. The International Organization of Securities Commissions (IOSCO) is already involved in discussions about rating standards and codes of conduct.[15] The World Bank, the International Monetary Fund (IMF), and regional development banks could encourage local rating agencies in emerging markets to issue ratings. Such an arrangement would be independent of particular debtors and less subject to conflict of interest concerns, especially if not funded by rating fees.

John Moody, a muckraking journalist, Catholic convert, and credit analyst, published *The Masters of Capital* in 1919. In this volume he chronicled the construction of the railroad and steel trusts in the United States, and the links between these interests and Wall Street during the "robber baron" years, the era between the end of the Civil War and 1914.[16] Moody investigated the capitalism of his day by looking at great entrepreneurs. Here, twenty-first-century capitalism is examined through analysis of institutions rather than the actions of "great men," an ontology more appropriate to present conditions.[17]

Within contemporary capitalism, rating agencies do not represent the only institutionalization of power, nor are they all-seeing, all-knowing, all-powerful. This volume is not an account of a conspiracy. The issue of power and authority inside capitalism today is its focus, just as Moody sought insight into the business power of his time. Ironically, however, the watchdogs of his day are the subject here.

Characteristics of the Rating Agencies

Rating agencies are some of the most obscure institutions in the world of global finance. Everyone knows what a bank is. Most people can explain what an insurance company does or offer a rough outline of an accountant's activities. But rating agencies are specialist organizations whose purpose and operations are little known outside their immediate environment.

15. "Report on the Activities of Credit Rating Agencies," September 2003, available at www.iosco.org.

16. John Moody, *The Masters of Capital: A Chronicle of Wall Street* (New Haven: Yale University Press, 1919). Moody's book has been reprinted several times, most recently in 2002.

17. For a comparison of the power over markets exercised by the robber barons with the rating agencies, see Eric Helleiner, "Sovereignty, Territoriality and the Globalization of Finance," in David A. Smith, Dorothy J. Solinger, and Steven C. Topik, eds., *States and Sovereignty in the Global Economy* (New York: Routledge, 1999), 138–71.

The discussion is not concerned with the merits of the agencies from an economic or policy perspective, to determine whether they are "good" or "bad." The purpose, based on the agencies' growing impact, is to evaluate their role in financial globalization. The agencies are influential mechanisms of financial globalization, shaping what governments (at all levels) do and corporate behavior, too. Hence, an understanding of the motivations, objectives, and constraints on these institutions is worthwhile.

Although they are often confused with Moody's and S&P, institutions such as Dun and Bradstreet, which undertake the mercantile rating of retailers for suppliers, are excluded from the analysis. Also excluded are corporations that issue credit ratings on individual consumers, such as Experian.[18] Many of the broader processes identified here are evident in these institutions, but these other raters are not central to the organization of capital markets. Rating agencies are examined in the context of their work with institutions in the capital markets, including municipalities, corporations and sovereign states, because that is where rating has the most impact.

What do the raters actually do? The agencies claim to make judgments on the "future ability and willingness of an issuer to make timely payments of principal and interest on a security over the life of the instrument."[19] Ostensibly, this is a narrow remit. The more likely it is that "the borrower will repay both the principal and interest, in accordance with the time schedule in the borrowing agreement, the higher will be the rating assigned to the debt security."[20] The agencies are adamant about what a debt rating is *not*. According to Standard & Poor's, a rating is "not a recommendation to purchase, sell, or hold a security, inasmuch as it does not comment as to market price or suitability for a particular investor," because investors' willingness to take risks varies.[21] In other words, a credit rating should form just part of the information investors use to make decisions. Rating agencies themselves do not claim to provide more than some of the information investors need.

As noted, financial globalization has widened the scope of the agencies' work. The prevailing objective, for both major agencies, is to achieve globally comparable ratings. If an AA on a steel company in South Korea is equivalent in credit-risk terms to AA on a pulp mill in British Columbia or to a similar rating on a software

18. On mercantile credit rating, see *World Development Report 2002: Building Institutions for Markets* (Washington, D.C.: World Bank, 2002), 94–96; also see Rowena Olegario, "Credit Reporting Agencies: Their Historical Roots, Current Status and Role in Market Development," paper presented to the World Bank workshop "The Role of Credit Reporting Systems in the International Economy," Washington, D.C., March 1–2, 2001, available at www.worldbank.org, accessed May 25, 2002; and Margaret J. Miller, ed., *Credit Reporting Systems and the International Economy* (Cambridge: MIT Press, 2003).

19. *Moody's Investors Service: Consistency, Reliability, Integrity* (New York: Moody's Investors Service, n.d.), 3.

20. George Foster, *Financial Statement Analysis*, 2nd ed. (Englewood Cliffs, N.J.: Prentice-Hall, 1986), 498.

21. Standard & Poor's, *Ratings Handbook*, 1, no. 5 (August 1992): 183.

producer in California, investors can make global choices. In recent years, the agencies have also sought to provide ratings that are comparable within specific national contexts. New York, however, very much remains the analytical center, where rating expertise is defined and reinforced internally through the agencies' established training cadres and standard operating procedures.

The agencies produce ratings on corporations, financial institutions, municipalities, and sovereign governments in terms of long-term obligations, such as bonds, or short-term ones like commercial paper.

Once issued, rating officials maintain surveillance over issuers and their securities. They warn investors when developments affecting issuers—their tax base, say, or their market—might lead to a rating revision, either upward or downward. As will be seen, this surveillance aspect of rating work is a key one, just as Pauly has shown in the context of International Monetary Fund monitoring.[22] Rating agency surveillance shapes the thinking and action of debt issuers. It also shapes the expectations of investors, who want the agencies to forensically scrutinize issuers and who complain vociferously when this scrutiny seems less than they think it ought to be. Investors seem to expect rating agencies to play the role of the prison guards in Bentham's perfect penitentiary, the panopticon.[23]

What product do the agencies sell? They purvey both professional, expert knowledge in the form of analytical capacities and local knowledge of a vast number of debt security issuers. The disintermediation process heightens the role of bond rating agencies. It increases their analytical and local specialization absolutely, because they now rate more issues in more locations, and relatively, because with the growth of capital markets, comparable specialists (bank credit analysts are the obvious example) have become less important as gatekeepers.[24]

Both Moody's and S&P are headquartered in New York. Both global agencies have numerous branches in the United States, Europe, and emerging markets. A distant third in the market is Fitch Ratings, a unit of Fimalac SA of Paris. Domestically focused agencies have developed in OECD countries and in emerging markets since the mid-1990s.[25]

22. See Louis W. Pauly, *Who Elected the Bankers? Surveillance and Control in the World Economy* (Ithaca: Cornell University Press, 1997), chap. 6.

23. For an incisive analysis of the panopticon concept, which explores how Bentham's idea relates to contemporary capitalism, including rating agencies, see Stephen Gill, "The Global Panopticon? The Neoliberal State, Economic Life, and Democratic Surveillance," *Alternatives* 20, no. 1 (January–March 1995): 1–49.

24. Circumstances have increased the importance of rating and, at the same time, made rating agencies a target for discontent. Criticism of the agencies as unresponsive and backward-looking includes Margaret A. Elliott, "Rating the Debt Raters," *Institutional Investor* (December 1988): 109–12, and "OK, So What Is Quality?" *Euromoney Supplement* (September 1991): 36–44; Batchelor, 2003. These issues are examined in chapter 7.

25. Susan Greenberg, "New Rating Agency Causes a Stir," *Guardian*, February 13, 1993. A comprehensive listing of the new agencies can be found at www.everling.de. Also see Andrew Fight, *The Ratings Game*, (Chichester, U.K.: Wiley, 2001) 90–99.

Public panics or crises about rating miscalls are the most significant challenge the agencies face. Crises erode and even threaten to shatter the reputational assets the agencies have built up since the interwar period. The 1990s and the first years of the new millennium saw more of these events, when volatility grew along with financial globalization. Threatening events included Mexico's financial crisis of 1994–95, Asia's financial crises of 1997–98, and Russia's default in 1998. Derivatives and other innovations stimulated corporate and municipal scandals and financial collapses in the United States, including the bankruptcy of Enron Corporation in late 2001. The new millennium was marked by the $141 billion sovereign debt default of Argentina in 2001–02.[26]

Two main strategies characterize the agencies' responses to these legitimacy crises. Like other financial industry institutions, the agencies try to keep up with financial innovation, spending large sums on staff training and hiring. They push development of their own products. The agencies have created new symbols to indicate when, for example, ratings are based on public information only and do not reflect confidential data (in the case of Standard & Poor's). The agencies, especially Moody's, have sought to change their cloistered, secretive corporate cultures and, since 1997, have become more willing to set out a clear rationale for their ratings. That strategy may have much to do with managing public expectations of the agencies.

How do the agencies relate to governments? Despite assumptions to the contrary, the work of rating agencies, in terms of their criteria and decision-making, is not regulated seriously anywhere in the developed world. Indeed, tight regulation would potentially destroy the key thing agencies have to sell: their independent opinion on market matters. However, some process by capital market regulatory agencies of "recognizing" rating agencies' activities is customary around the world.[27] This recognition is especially significant in the United States, where many states have laws governing the prudential behavior of public pension funds.[28] In these cases, the agencies' outputs are recognized as benchmarks limiting what bonds a pension fund can buy.

A central feature of United States and other countries' processes of governmental recognition is regulators' reliance on wide market acceptance of a firm's rating. In turn, the agencies resist recurrent efforts to develop more invasive forms of

26. Daniel Altman, "A Country in Chapter 11? Yes, But . . .," *New York Times*, January 6, 2002, sec. 3, 1, 9.

27. On the use of ratings in regulation around the world, see Asian Development Bank, "Development of Credit Rating Agencies," background paper for the Second Workshop on the Development of CRAs in the APEC Region (Manila: Asian Development Bank, 2001), sec. 13, available at www.adb.org, accessed August 4, 2001. Also see table 4, chap. 2.

28. For details on use of ratings in U.S. regulation, see table 3 in chap. 2, and Richard Cantor and Frank Packer, "The Credit Rating Industry," *Federal Reserve Bank of New York Quarterly Review* 19, no. 2 (Fall 1994): 6. See chap. 2 for further discussion.

regulation and hold up the public standard of market acceptance as the best test of their quality. They also oppose deeper incorporation of their ratings as benchmarks in law. Developing country governments often make ratings of domestic debt issues compulsory as a way of promoting the development of liquid, transparent capital markets.

Increasingly, ratings are key elements in transnational financial regulation. In 2001, the Bank for International Settlements proposed replacing established capital adequacy standards with a new system in which ratings play a significant role in estimating the risk exposure of banks.[29]

Rating and Politics

Nuances of power and authority heighten the significance of rating. Rating agencies do possess, via rating downgrades, the capacity at times to coerce borrowers eager to obtain scarce funds. But relations between rating agencies and other institutions are more often about changing world views and influence than "power wielding." On the one hand, the influence of the rating agencies grows as new borrowers look to raise funds in lower-cost capital markets rather than borrow from banks in the traditional way. In this environment, the number of agency branches is expanding, and the role of Moody's and Standard & Poor's is more significant: the agencies put a price on the policy choices of governments and corporations seeking funds.

On the other hand, many government administrations, particularly in the developing world and Japan, have encouraged the formation of national bond rating agencies. These initiatives are intriguing. They suggest that the loss of government policy autonomy implied in the establishment of rating has not been imposed on governments but is actually something states have sought, even promoted. Hence, a view of rating simply as a coercive force does not capture the whole story. Consideration also must be given to where rating shapes, limits, and controls—often in connection with the generation of authority—rather than the brute application of power. Elaborating this consideration is a key focus of this book.

Analytical Approach

In this book specific institutions and associated "micropractices" at the core of contemporary capitalism are examined, in particular the "reconfiguring" effect these

29. Basel Committee on Banking Supervision, *Overview of the New Basel Capital Accord* (Basel: Bank for International Settlements, January 2001), available at www.bis.org; also see Michael R. King and Timothy J. Sinclair, "Private Actors and Public Policy: A Requiem for the New Basel Capital Accord," *International Political Science Review* 24, no. 3 (July 2003): 345–62.

institutions and practices have on global economic and political life within sovereign states.[30] Natural science seeks to establish universal laws and considers specific events in terms of these laws. The objective is always generalization, and many social scientists have followed this path. Here, the purpose is similar to "process tracing," the historical development of interpretive frames actors use to understand the world.[31]

Specific events, institutions, and ways of thinking are associated with rating agencies. The focus on particular aspects of rating agencies—rather than on the positing of universal laws about agencies "in general"—means that the research design of this book is "realistic" and inductive. The design does not aspire to the "hypothetico-deductive mode of theory construction" that dominates much of social science.[32] One way of viewing this book is as an exploration or probe that may help to create the basis for future hypothesis testing.

Substantively, this investigation is concerned with the veracity of different approaches, or general theoretical orientations, to motivation and action that are the subject of contemporary debate in the field of international political economy (IPE). These general theoretical orientations offer heuristics, in the form of relevant variables and causal patterns that provide guidelines for research.

IPE has been dominated by rationalist approaches such as realism and liberalism, informed by economics, in which the heuristic is the struggle of rational actors with fixed preferences around scarce resources. This heuristic can be applied to any number of problems as a guiding set of assumptions about what likely motivates an action.[33] Here, this dominant rationalist lens is compared and contrasted with a very different general theoretical orientation.

This second approach draws on economic and organizational sociology and on the social sciences, other than economics. Rationalist approaches adopt the assumption that there is a one-to-one match between imputed material interests and social action. The constructivist approach can complement the instrumental cause-effect focus of rationalism. The heuristic focuses on processes through which the preferences and subsequent strategies of actors (such as corporations and states) are socially constructed, varying over time and space, and defining the identity or nature of the actors in relation to others.[34] The norms, identity, knowledge, and culture that

30. John Gerard Ruggie, "What Makes the World Hang Together? Neo-Utilitarianism and the Social Constructivist Challenge," introduction to Ruggie, *Constructing the World Polity: Essays on International Institutionalization* (New York: Routledge, 1998), 27.

31. Ronald L. Jepperson, Alexander Wendt, and Peter J. Katzenstein, "Norms, Identity, and Culture in National Security," in Katzenstein, ed., *The Culture of National Security: Norms and Identity in World Politics* (New York: Columbia University Press, 1996), 67.

32. Ruggie, 1998, 34.

33. Peter J. Katzenstein, Robert O. Keohane, and Stephen D. Krasner, "*International Organization* and the Study of World Politics," *International Organization* 52, no. 4 (Autumn 1998): 645–68, 646.

34. Ibid., 681–82.

comprise intersubjective structures—things held constant in rationalism—are among the things that constitute or regulate actors in this general theoretical orientation.[35]

Both rationalism and constructivism are, as it is seen in subsequent chapters, essential for understanding bond rating agencies. The constructivist lens has, however, so far been neglected in IPE, to our detriment.[36] In part, this book is an effort to correct that omission and to demonstrate the analytical contribution constructivist social science can make to IPE research.

International political economy started as a study of foreign economic policy, mainly of the United States and the European powers. These origins have led to IPE being dominated by the view that markets are very different from the typical institutionalized manifestations of politics, like political parties and government bodies such as houses of representatives. Unlike most economists, many IPE specialists have been interested in the interaction of the economic and political spheres (understood as different motivations), which scholars with diverse approaches have thought were neglected.

Only through an analysis of this interaction could an understanding of international economic relations be formed, one that included many more variables than those economists have focused on. This area of analysis has contributed much to our understanding of the developing global order since World War II, especially of the creation and decay of the Bretton Woods regime. But global markets have developed and states have changed in form and behavior during the three decades since the end of that regime. Consequently, the strict separation of IPE subject matter, into a "states" category on the one hand and "markets" on the other, has become problematic. Increasingly, IPE thinkers have been concerned with intermediary institutions that are neither states nor markets but interact with both.[37] Some scholars have also looked at the economic sphere, to reappraise inherited notions of what markets are and how they work.[38]

Economic sociology offers an alternative theoretical source for analytical insight.[39] The prime benefit it offers in abstract terms is to ground the agentcentric

35. Ibid., 679–80. Also see Peter J. Katzenstein, "Alternative Perspectives on National Security," introduction to Katzenstein, ed., 1996, 5–6.

36. A pioneering effort to utilize a constructivist lens and to link this to rationalist understandings are the essays in Jonathan Kirshner, ed., *Monetary Orders: Ambiguous Economics, Ubiquitous Politics* (Ithaca: Cornell University Press, 2003).

37. See Cutler, Haufler, and Porter, 1999; Hall and Biersteker, 2003.

38. Charles W. Smith, *The Mind of the Market: A Study of Stock Market Philosophies, Their Uses, and Their Implications* (Totowa, N.J.: Rowman and Littlefield, 1981); Mitchel Y. Abolafia, *Making Markets: Opportunism and Restraint on Wall Street* (Cambridge: Harvard University Press, 1996); Charles W. Smith, *Success and Survival on Wall Street: Understanding the Mind of the Market* (Lanham, Md.: Rowman and Littlefield, 1999).

39. For an introduction, see Neil J. Smelser and Richard Swedberg, "The Sociological Perspective on the Economy," in Smelser and Swedberg, eds., *The Handbook of Economic Sociology* (Princeton: Princeton University Press and Russell Sage Foundation, 1994).

understanding (of states, of companies, of individuals) implicit in traditional IPE in a structure emerging from social relations. Waltz and international relations Neorealism offered a sense of structure. But that structure did not encompass market relations and tended to minimize the role of actors other than states, even if the formal account of the approach gave space to other agents.[40]

By contrast with the Neorealist vision of an anarchy of self-regarding units, the notion of "embeddedness" Granovetter identified—a key concept in economic sociology—sought to link institutions to the social relations in which they existed.[41] In this understanding, economic life was not separate from society like a free-standing machine but was linked to historical and cultural circumstances and, therefore, variable over time and space.[42] However, despite embeddedness, economic and institutional sociology has produced "evidence of global cultural homogenization."[43] This process of change is linked to pervasive myths or mental frameworks, which legitimate specific organizational forms (and negate others).

Mental or intersubjective frameworks are just as consequential as other social structures. As W. I. Thomas noted in 1928, "If men [sic] define situations as real, they are real in their consequences." Thomas claimed that people respond not just to objective things, like mountains and automobile accidents, "but also, and often mainly," to their collective attribution of meaning to the situation. As Coser points out, if people think witches are real, "such beliefs have tangible consequences."[44]

The importance of mental frameworks is reflected within institutions. Meyer and Rowan argue that organizations and how they are structured reflect not the efficient undertaking of their function but the myths or mental frameworks that depict a public story about the organization.[45] Internal rules and organizational forms within institutions reflect "the prescriptions of myths." These rules and organizational forms demonstrate that the organization is acting "in a proper and adequate manner." By conforming to the myth, the organization protects itself from interrogation. The key process is identifying elements of the myth and then reconfiguring the organization around them. Organizations, Meyer and Rowan suggest, typically face

40. On Waltz and Neorealism, see Robert O. Keohane, ed., *Neorealism and Its Critics* (New York: Columbia University Press, 1989).

41. Mark Granovetter, "Economic Action and Social Structure: The Problem of Embeddedness," in Granovetter and Richard Swedberg, eds., *The Sociology of Economic Life* (Boulder, Colo.: Westview Press, 1992), 53.

42. Frank R. Dobbin, "Cultural Models of Organization: The Social Construction of Rational Organizing Principles," in Diana Crane, ed., *The Sociology of Culture: Emerging Theoretical Perspectives* (Cambridge, Mass.: Blackwell, 1994.

43. Martha Finnemore, "Norms, Culture, and World Politics: Insights from Sociology's Institutionalism," *International Organization* 50. no. 2 (Spring 1996): 325.

44. W. I. Thomas with Dorothy Swaine Thomas, *The Child in America* (New York: Alfred A. Knopf, 1928), cited by Lewis A. Coser, *Masters of Sociological Thought: Ideas in Historical and Social Context*, 2d ed. (New York: Harcourt Brace Jovanovich, 1977), 521.

45. John W. Meyer and Brian Rowan, "Institutionalized Organizations: Formal Structure as Myth and Ceremony," *American Journal of Sociology* 83, no. 2 (September 1977): 340–63.

dilemmas between the prescriptions of these elements and their internal, shared sense of what they are really supposed to be about, and also between diverse competing myths held by different parts of society, such as government, interest groups, and market associations.[46]

Professional judgment and analysis—and public expectations about its development and standards—is a key, societally legitimated rationalized element of the rating agencies' mental framework. One conception of how this framework can be understood in its wider social context is through what Peter Haas and his fellow contributors have called epistemic communities.[47] Haas defines epistemic communities as "networks of knowledge-based experts" that address complex, seemingly technical problems. The "recognized expertise and competence" of these professionals give them an authoritative claim to offering good advice, and their control of expertise is "an important dimension of power."

Haas suggests four features of epistemic communities: a shared set of normative and principled beliefs, shared causal beliefs, shared notions of validity in the area of expertise, and a "common policy enterprise" connected to enhancing human welfare. Epistemic communities neither guess nor produce data but interpret phenomena. The major role of the communities lies in ostensibly "less politically motivated cases," where they introduce a range of policy alternatives.[48] The communities differ from the concept of profession in that they share normative commitments but such commitments may develop within professions (for example, the subset of economists concerned with economic inequalities).

A normative element also distinguishes epistemic communities from other concepts such as policy entrepreneur.[49] Haas argues that the communities do not behave as rational choice or principal-agent theory would predict because of the central role attributed to their beliefs. Epistemic communities are important in themselves because they "convey new patterns of reasoning" to policymakers and "encourage them to pursue new paths of policymaking," with unpredictable outcomes.[50]

The concept of epistemic communities is relevant to this book's focus on patterns of reasoning, on the politics of technical expertise, and on the power that emanates from knowledge. However, this book parts company with epistemic communities over the key concept of normative beliefs. A subset of raters may share a conscious commitment to such beliefs, but this commitment is a defining element of epistemic communities. The notion of epistemic communities may be useful to the analysis of

46. Ibid., 349, 352, 355.
47. Peter M. Haas, "Introduction: Epistemic Communities and International Policy Coordination," *International Organization* 46, no. 1 (Winter 1992): 1–35.
48. Ibid., 2, 3, 4, 16.
49. Michael A. Mintrom, *Policy Entrepreneurs and School Choice* (Georgetown: Georgetown University Press, 2000).
50. Haas, 1992, 20, 21.

particular elements within the rating world to be examined in future work. An alternative concept—embedded knowledge networks—is elaborated below.

Embedded Knowledge Networks

Embedded knowledge networks are analytical and judgmental systems that, in principle, remain at arms length from market transactions. "Embedded" does not mean that the networks are locked in and, thus, simply resistant to change. "Embedded" should not convey the idea of inertia, path dependency, or vested interests. Instead, it is supposed to suggest that actors view embedded knowledge networks as endogenous rather than exogenous to financial globalization. The networks are, therefore, generally considered legitimate rather than imposed entities by market participants.

How the networks construct and reinforce this collective understanding of themselves is of great interest. Where institutions that are embedded knowledge networks in one society attempt to transplant themselves into others, they risk losing their embedded knowledge network status, unless they recognize the necessity of getting the market actors in these other places to recognize their endogeneity. To return to the discussion of myth and mental frameworks, rating agencies must adapt themselves to public expectations of what they should be doing, as they expand from their American home base. Achieving endogeneity and, hence, legitimacy has been easier in some places than others for the major U.S. bond rating agencies.

The role of knowledge in investment decision-making is at the heart of embedded knowledge network activity. Market actors are overwhelmed with data about prices, business activity, and political risk. A typical form of knowledge output is some sort of recommendation, ranking, or rating, which ostensibly condenses these forms of knowledge. This knowledge output becomes a benchmark around which market players subsequently organize their affairs. Market actors can and do depart from the benchmarks, but these still set the standard for the work of other actors, providing a measure of market success or failure. In this way, embedded knowledge network outputs play a crucial role in constructing markets in a context of less-than-perfect information and considerable uncertainty about the future.

Rating agencies, acting as embedded knowledge networks, can be thought to adjust the "ground rules" inside international capital markets, thereby shaping the internal organization and behavior of institutions seeking funds. The agencies' views on what is acceptable shape the actions of those seeking their positive response. This anticipation effect or structural power is reflected in capital market participants' understanding of the agencies' views and expectations. In turn, this understanding acts as a base point from which business and policy initiatives are developed. The coordination effect of rating agencies therefore narrows the expectations of creditors and debtors to a well-understood or transparent set of norms, shared among all parties. Thus, the agencies do not just constrain the capital markets but actually provide significant pressures on market participants, contributing to their internal constitution.

Counterfactual Method

How might rationalist and constructivist analytical lenses be deployed in this substantive discussion of rating institutions? Since the objective is to understand the implications of the particular rather than establish general laws, we need a suitable method of thinking through the implications of rating. For the type of cases described in this book, counterfactual analysis is an appropriate approach.[51] In counterfactual analysis, the factor or variable thought most likely to be causal is subsequently excluded from an alternative scenario the researcher constructs.[52] Given this modification of what Weber terms the "causal components," we have to think through whether, in these changed conditions, the "same effect" would be expected empirically.[53] If, in the imaginative construct established, the supposition is that the effect would probably be different, we have likely isolated an adequate cause in the initial scenario and can feel confident about the analysis. But, as Weber cautions, causal significance of this sort always suggests a range of degree of certainty about causation.[54]

One objection to counterfactual scenarios is, as Ferguson notes, the notion that "there is no limit to the number which we can consider." But the reality is quite different. "In practice," suggests Ferguson, "there is no real point in asking most of the possible counterfactual questions" that can be imagined.[55] Plausibility is key, as in all analysis. We are interested in what happened or could have happened, not what could not have happened. Our focus should be on "possibilities which seemed probable." Accordingly, there is a plausible set of counterfactuals, not an infinite number of alternatives for any situation. Even if we grant that this plausible set is always open to critique, by requiring us to rethink our arguments, the posing of counterfactuals is, as Ferguson suggests, a useful "antidote to determinism."[56]

51. James D. Fearon, "Counterfactuals and Hypothesis Testing in Political Science," *World Politics* 43 (January 1991): 169–95, 194; Niall Ferguson, "Virtual History: Towards a 'Chaotic' Theory of the Past," introduction to Ferguson, ed., *Virtual History: Alternatives and Counterfactuals* (London: Picador, 1997), 81; Gary King, Robert O. Keohane, and Sidney Verba, *Designing Social Inquiry: Scientific Inference in Qualitative Research* (Princeton: Princeton University Press, 1994), 10.

52. Fearon, 1991, 169.

53. Max Weber, "Objective Possibility and Adequate Causation in Historical Explanation," in Edward A. Shils and Henry A. Finch, trans. and eds., *The Methodology of the Social Sciences* (New York: Free Press, 1949), 171.

54. Ibid., 181.

55. Ferguson, 1997, 83.

56. Ibid., 84, 85, 89.

In the substantive chapters of this book, a rationalist account of rating agency effects is constrasted with a constructivist one inspired by economic sociology. The purpose is to demonstrate the utility of a constructivist-economic sociology analysis of rating agencies and, thus, of IPE problems more generally. Since constructivist accounts are not always better than rationalist ones, the working assumption is that the constructivist-economic sociology heuristic complements the rationalist account. In some cases, the most plausible explanation may be rationalist rather than constructivist.

Central and Supporting Arguments

Economists have been keenly interested in the question whether bond ratings actually add new information to markets and thus affect market behavior. The central argument of this book concerns the intersubjective effect of rating, that is, how rating affects the social context in which corporate and government policy plans are made. Specific attention is given to the power and authority of the agencies, and the implications of rating for private and public life.

Rating agencies are not the neutral, technical, detached, objective arbitrators they are assumed to be among people who see them as merely transmitting market views to investors. Capital markets (and other markets) are actually organized, coordinated, or "made" by processes of information gathering and judgment forming the rating agencies exemplify. These processes reflect particular ways of thinking and reject or exclude other ways.[57] The judgments produced acquire the status of understood facts in the markets—even when analysis shows they are at times faulty—because of the authoritative status market participants and societies attribute to the agencies. These particular ways of thinking, which are hegemonic in the Western world and which the agencies enforce increasingly internationally, are referred to here as the *mental framework of rating orthodoxy*.

Most broadly, it is argued, the work of the agencies integrates further elements of economic and political organization around the world, pushing these toward a prevailing institutional pattern. In this emerging order, norms are increasingly shared, and policy converges around characteristically American "best practice."[58] American ideas have become the most important transnational ones.[59] Rating agency

57. A recent exploration of this theme can be found in Abolafia, 1996.

58. On Americancentric internationalization processes, see Robert W. Cox, "Social Forces, States, and World Orders: Beyond International Relations Theory," in Robert W. Cox with Timothy J. Sinclair, *Approaches to World Order* (Cambridge: Cambridge University Press, 1996), 107–111.

59. Some events define the major rating agencies as U.S. institutions. In June 2002, Moody's Investors Service withdrew its rating on the Islamic Republic of Iran, citing U.S. economic

judgments contribute to this process, as does the work of other institutions like the IMF and World Bank.[60]

Three supporting or mid-range arguments about the increasing importance of rating agency judgments are developed.

Supporting Argument I: Investment

The first argument is concerned with investment, a central feature of any modern society that produces an economic surplus. Many economists, in the tradition of Hayek, assume that investment happens automatically if certain basic conditions hold.[61] But investment may also be understood as an implicitly coordinated social process. Investment has its own history and particular constraints. It is therefore necessary to understand the context in which investment choices are made.

In current circumstances, the increasing importance of capital markets alters the basis on which investment is undertaken. As banks are displaced as key investment sources, gatekeeper power is concentrated in the hands of the small number of rating agencies. Rating judgments are more important today and this trend will continue into the future, because less investment capital in the form of loans is being allocated by banks. This change in the character of investment has significant consequences for corporations and governments seeking access to resources. Rating has become a key means of transmitting the policy orthodoxy of managerial best practice. Much more of the world is now open to the consequences of rating judgments than was the case during the Cold War.

Centralization of investment judgment is the essential element of the first mid-range argument. This argument is supported by evidence from the relationship between corporate ratings and the cost of debt, Michael Milken's activities, and the rating of the automobile industry. Municipal rating adds further evidence of gatekeeping. The spread of the U.S. agencies and the emergence of local agencies in new markets also supports this first mid-range argument.

---

sanctions. The withdrawal was a first for Moody's, according to David Levey, managing director of sovereign risk at the agency (Reuters, "Moody's, Citing U.S. Concern, Cancels Ratings on Iran Debt," *New York Times*, June 4, 2002, W7). The *Wall Street Journal* reported that the U.S. Treasury had raised the matter with Moody's in 2001. The *Journal* noted that Moody's rating, which was unsolicited, produced no revenue for Moody's, which did not have a commercial relationship with the Iranian government (Angela Pruitt, "Moody's Credit Rating on Iran Roils the U.S.," *Wall Street Journal*, June 5, 2002, B12). On Iranian issuance plans, see Arkady Ostrovsky and Guy Dinmore, "Iran Prepares International Bond Issue," *Financial Times*, July 3, 2002, 31.

60. Analyses of these other institutions are discussed in Pauly, 1997.

61. On Hayek's spontaneous view of economic life, see Andrew Gamble, *Hayek: The Iron Cage of Liberty* (Cambridge, U.K.: Polity, 1996), 68.

Supporting Argument II: Knowledge

The second argument is about knowledge. Knowledge is usually thought of as something that transcends particular situations or times. In fact, certain forms of knowledge are more typical of some eras and places than others. Like the investment process, knowledge is a social creation, an arena in which particular understandings of the world compete for control over what is accepted as a basis for action and policy. Politically, the key thing about knowledge is the moment when an idea changes from being an individual idiosyncratic view to one widely or intersubjectively held and collectively consequential. Rating judgments are not objective.

A specific form of knowledge at the heart of the rating phenomenon has consequences for what we think of as legitimate knowledge elsewhere in the policy process. The knowledge form that dominates rating tends to be analytical, to focus on how things do or should function in our world, in a cause-effect fashion. What this analytical form excludes is an explanation of origins: how institutions develop and also their potential for future transformation. Rating reinforces knowledge based on the assumption of a fundamentally unchanging world, one in which economic markets, for example, are thought to perform the same function today as "always."

Where did this specific form of knowledge originate? Sorel suggested the static, unhistorical way of thinking about knowledge is a technique linked to monetary accumulation.[62] It eschews reflection and puts a premium on instrumental understanding in the here and now. Capitalism is premised on such a knowledge form. But a static form of knowledge, under the changing conditions created by financial globalization, makes the capacity to anticipate the events of September 11, 2001, for example, inconceivable. Bond rating certainly did not create the static knowledge form, but rating agencies are transmitting and reinforcing this type of knowledge globally—with consequences for public and private policy around the world and, therefore, the daily lives of billions.

In the corporate world, the growth of the rating advisory industry and the rating of telecommunication firms support these claims. Problems with quality of life variables provide evidence from municipal rating. The creation of Japanese rating agencies, discussed in chapter 6, also supports the claims.

Supporting Argument III: Governance

Ironically, perhaps, rating forces change in how we govern our lives because it spreads the static, instrumental form of knowledge, thus challenging established ways of thinking and acting. Governance is about how institutions or processes are

---

62. Georges Sorel, *Reflections on Violence*, trans. T. E. Hulme and J. Roth (New York: Collier, 1961), 141.

organized in hierarchies and how these structures shape our lives as citizens and consumers. Sometimes, the existence of these governance structures is obvious, such as in the case of representative democracy. Other governance structures are quite diffuse. They operate in society much as operating systems do in computers, beneath the surface of things. The third mid-range claim made in this book is that established, historically derived norms and practices regarding governance are challenged by the judgments of rating agencies: the views of appropriate constitutional arrangements and corporate governance approaches that the agencies promote are often derived from U.S. experience. Rating agencies did not invent these governance structures but act as interpreters, advocates, and enforcers of them around the world. When put in place, these patterns shape the nature of working life and the limits of democracy, making the former more insecure and competitive and the latter less inclusive and meaningful.

In chapter 4, the problems in Japanese banks support this mid-range argument. New York City's financial problems provide evidence from the municipal world. Additional evidence from controversies over sovereign ratings, for both rich countries such as Japan, Australia, and Canada, and developing countries, is given in chapter 6.

Plan of the Book

The three supporting arguments are developed in the chapters where the implications of rating processes in particular contexts are investigated. First, however, in chapters 2 and 3, the book looks at the agencies: their internal organization, important features of their processes for creating ratings, and the relation between rating and regulation. Next to be examined is the power and authority of rating agencies, which underpin the mid-range issues. The key question asked is from what is rating power derived, and what are its limits? The context is development of the arguments about investment, knowledge, and governance to be investigated in subsequent chapters.

In chapters 4, 5, and 6, the discussion concerns corporate rating, municipal rating, the sovereign rating of national governments, and the growth of rating agencies outside the United States. These accounts are organized in terms of the arguments about investment, knowledge, and governance that are developed in chapter 3.

This book focuses on more than one level of analysis, such as sovereign states. The politics of rating pervades the world order, requiring that we consider the effects on municipal government and private corporations as well as national states. In chapter 7, recent rating "failures" are explored. Why did these failures happen, what marks them as failures, and to what degree have they undermined rating authority? Just how resilient are the reputational assets the agencies possess?

Ironically, the financial crises of the 1990s and of the early years of the new millennium may have actually enhanced the power of rating agencies: capital market financing has come to be seen as less risky than traditional bank lending, especially in emerging markets. Underlying market trends may be rescuing the rating agencies from their critics, even as the increasing importance of rating motivates further criticism.

The concluding chapter examines the significance of the discussion, in particular the degree to which authority and power take on new forms in globalized conditions and how the agencies affect people in their everyday lives. What are some ways of responding effectively to the heightened role of the new masters of capital?

CHAPTER TWO

Good, Bad, or Indifferent:
The Emergence of Rating

All mentally competent individuals are engaged in an almost continual
course of judging, of weighing, of rating. The choice of food, of cloth-
ing, and of activity are made chiefly as the result of judgments . . . All
stimuli coming to the attention of the individual are being judged,
either consciously or subconsciously, as good, bad, or indifferent. Such
is the essential nature of rating.

GILBERT HAROLD, *Bond Ratings as an Investment Guide,* 1938

The increasing role of capital markets in global finance has given rating agencies power and authority that has important implications for both developed
societies and emerging markets. These claims are historical and situational rather
than universal. The historical development of rating agencies examined here highlights how the power and authority of the agencies came to be established. The subsequent investigation of the rating process specifies what rating is, how it works, and
how its impact is experienced. This information serves as background to the conceptual exploration and substantive analysis in the following chapters. In the last
part of this chapter, the focus is on the ways in which rating has become a feature of
the post–Bretton Woods regulation of financial markets. The dynamic between rating agency outputs and governments suggests that state–rating agency relationships
are not purely conflictual or dichotomous.

Emergence of the Agencies

The appraisal of creditworthiness is, in itself, nothing new. It is a key feature of borrowing and lending throughout history and a prime activity banks undertake as part
of the loan business. What is intriguing is how this financial function has come to be

separated into distinct institutions, the significance and implications of this separation, and the growth of rating institutions beyond their U.S. home.

What do we know or need to know about the emergence of the rating agencies? Rather than a history of bond rating activity, this book considers how the agencies have changed over time, to help us understand the basis of their power and authority. Debt security rating had its beginnings in the early part of the last century, during the public controversy and market turbulence created by failed railroads, dubious Florida land schemes, and other property deals in the newly opened lands of the western United States.[1]

Rating agencies evolved from market surveillance mechanisms that had developed over many years. From around mid-century until World War I, American financial markets experienced an information explosion. *Poor's American Railroad Journal* appeared in the mid-1850s.[2] This was followed by Henry V. Poor's *History of the Railroads and Canals of the United States of America* in 1860.[3] His book detailed the track length of railroads, enumerated investors' share capital, and provided a record of the railroads' profit and loss, among other things. Many of these highly detailed records gave a useful picture of investment in American infrastructure. As Poor noted, "The need of such a work" had long been felt:

> There is not in this country as in most others, a central point at which the more important companies are either domiciled, or at which all are required to present annual statements of their affairs, for the reason that they derive their existence and powers from the legislatures of the several States.[4]

In 1868, Poor's produced the first *Manual of the Railroads of the United States*. By the early 1880s, this publication had five thousand subscribers.[5]

John Moody saw that while information on the railroads was available, there was a poverty of useful data on the emerging industrial combinations. At the time, "A high percentage of corporation securities had to be bought on faith rather than knowledge."[6] According to Moody, "One bright morning the thought flashed through my mind: 'Somebody, sooner or later, will bring out an industrial statistical manual, and when it comes it will be a gold mine. Why not do it myself?' "[7] Moody

---

1. Interview with Leo C. O'Neill, president, Standard & Poor's Ratings Group, New York City, August 18, 1992.

2. Edward C. Kirkland, *Industry Comes of Age: Business, Labor and Public Policy, 1860–1897* (New York: Holt, Rinehart and Winston, 1961), 233.

3. See "History of Standard & Poor's," www.standardandpoors.com, accessed January 25, 2002.

4. Henry V. Poor, *History of the Railroads and Canals of the United States of America* (New York: John H. Schultz, 1860), v.

5. Kirkland, 1961, 233.

6. John Moody, *The Long Road Home: An Autobiography* (New York: Macmillan, 1933), 90.

7. Ibid., 90.

first began publishing his *Manual of Industrial Statistics* in 1900. His prediction turned out to be accurate. This publication did indeed prove to be a "gold mine."[8]

The transition between issuing compendiums of information and actually making judgments about the creditworthiness of debtors occurred between the 1907 financial crisis and the Pujo hearings of 1912. The 1907 crisis was every bit as threatening as the Asian financial crisis. It changed attitudes toward financiers, destroyed public confidence in how American finance was regulated, expanded demand for information free from conflicts of interest, and helped to bring about the founding of the Federal Reserve system.

The crisis was so severe it forced Moody to sell his manual business, John Moody & Company. He returned with a business assessing creditworthiness in 1909, based in part on the mercantile credit rating of retail businesses and wholesalers by companies like R. G. Dun and Company.[9] In a speech he made in 1950, Moody noted that the idea of securities ratings "was not entirely original with me" but "the idea of actually doing it was my own."[10] Elsewhere, Moody claimed to have been inspired by bond rating activities in Vienna and Berlin, codified in what he called the *Austrian Manual of Statistics.*[11] Americans Roger Babson and Freeman Putney, Jr. separately invented debt ratings in 1901, but neither exploited the concept before Moody.[12] Poor's, following Moody, issued their first rating in 1916, followed by the Standard Statistics Company in 1922.[13] According to Harold, "Security ratings were first published on 'hunch.' " Many traders were hostile to ratings at the time, as a factor potentially limiting future market fluctuations of bond prices.[14]

Ratings developed in a haphazard way in the early years of the twentieth century. One of the things Moody's Investors Service had to attend to in the 1920s was the legacy of John Moody & Company. Roy W. Porter became editor of Moody's manuals after Moody lost control of the company in 1908.[15] Porter bought the company in 1914 (a year after Moody's Analyses Publishing Company became Moody's Investors Service) and five years later merged it with Poor's Railroad Publishing Company, forming Poor's Publishing Company. Ironically, then, part of contemporary S&P was built on the basis of John Moody's original bond information

8. Kirkland, 1961, 234.

9. "Moody's History," in "About Moody's," www.moodys.com, accessed January 25, 2002.

10. John Moody, "A Fifty Year Review of Moody's," speech given in early 1950; supplied by Moody's Investors Service, cited by Richard S. Wilson, *Corporate Senior Securities: Analysis and Evaluation of Bonds, Convertibles, and Preferreds* (Chicago: Probus, 1987), 358.

11. Gilbert Harold, *Bond Ratings as an Investment Guide: An Appraisal of Their Effectiveness* (New York: Ronald Press, 1938), 11. No trace of the Austrian book has been found.

12. Ibid., 9.

13. "History," www.standardandpoors.com, accessed January 25, 2002. Harold distinguishes the dates of the start of rating at the separate Poor's and Standard Statistics companies (1938, 13).

14. Harold, 1938, 14.

15. Wilson, 1987, 322.

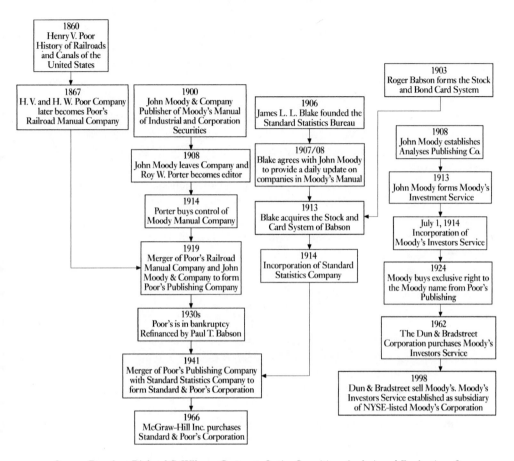

Figure 1. Origins of Moody's and Standard & Poors

Source: Based on Richard S. Wilson, *Corporate Senior Securities: Analysis and Evaluation of Bonds, Convertibles and Preferreds*, (Chicago: Probus, 1987), p. 323.

company. The historical links between the two contemporary rivals are displayed in figure 1.

Strangely, as it seems now, after 1919, Poor's had the legal right to use the Moody's name. As Moody's observed in 1950, "For long years this was a matter of great confusion in our markets; people were always confusing Poor's publications as ours and naturally enough this was a factor in limiting our sales."[16] In 1924, Moody's bought back the rights for $100,000, selling preferred stock to fund the purchase. Interestingly, the complicated lineage of what we know today as Moody's and S&P has rarely been mentioned in print and seems little known among rating agency staff.

16. Moody cited in Wilson, 1987, 18.

Moody's effort to buy back his name seems to have eliminated the confusion he noted in 1950.

The growth of the bond rating industry subsequently occurred in several distinct phases. Up to the 1930s, before the separation of the banking and the securities businesses in the United States with passage of the Glass-Steagall Act of 1933, bond rating was a fledgling activity, carried out as a supplement to the data compendiums. Rating entered a period of rapid growth and consolidation with this legally enforced separation and institutionalization of the securities business after 1929. Rating became a standard requirement for selling any issue in the United States, after many state governments incorporated rating standards into their prudential rules for investment by pension funds in the early 1930s.

A series of defaults by major sovereign borrowers, including Germany, made the bond business largely a U.S. sphere from the 1930s to the 1980s, dominated by American blue chip industrial firms and municipalities.[17] During this time, foreign borrowers usually had to obtain funds from U.S. or domestic banks at relatively higher interest rates.

The third period of rating development began in the 1980s, as a market in low-rated, high-yield (junk) bonds developed. This market—a feature of the newly released energies of financial globalization—saw many new entrants into capital markets.

The categories of issuers the agencies cover have changed over time. Initially, the focus of rating activity was railroads, industrial corporations and financial institutions in the United States. After World War I, U.S. municipalities and foreign governments sought ratings. As we have seen, with the defaults of the 1930s and the creation of the Bretton Woods system, rating firms retreated to U.S. municipalities and higher-rated U.S. industrial firms. In this era of rating conservatism, sovereign rating coverage was reduced to a handful of the most creditworthy countries. During the Bretton Woods era, the rating agencies did not significantly alter the way they did business, aside from introducing fees for issuers in the late 1960s and early 1970s. There were no competitors to a comfortable oligopoly, and the rating institutions took on a gravitas in keeping with the nature of their task. Significant barriers to entry existed for possible competitors, and events like the collapse of New York City's finances in the mid-1970s did not give rise to fundamental change.

With the end of the Bretton Woods system of capital controls and the liberalization of financial regulation in the 1970s and 1980s, the narrowness and exclusivity of the system that had prevailed since the 1930s was challenged by a vibrant junk bond market. For the first time, lower-rated companies were able to raise capital by selling bond debt. In this new market, ratings helped to distinguish between issues

---

17. Alvin Toffler, *Powershift: Knowledge, Wealth, and Violence at the Edge of the Twenty-first Century* (New York: Bantam, 1990), 43–57.

and price debt, rather than simply exclude issuers from the market altogether, as had been the case in the era of rating conservatism.

The Contemporary Rating Industry

The most obvious feature of current rating growth is internationalization. As is discussed in chapter 3, cheaper, more efficient capital markets now challenge the role of banks in Europe and Asia. Ratings have been a standard feature of European bond issues since the mid-1990s, and the rating agencies are expanding to meet the demand for their services.

A second major feature is innovation in financial instruments. Derivatives and structured financings, among other things, have stressed existing analytical systems and outputs, and the agencies have been developing new rating scales and expertise in response. The demand for timely judgments is greater than ever, and agency resources reflect this demand. Compared to the hundreds of staff today, in the mid-1960s, as Wilson notes, S&P had "three full-time analysts, one old-timer who worked on a part-time basis, a statistical assistant, and a secretary in the corporate bond rating department."[18]

A third feature is competition in the rating industry, developing for the first time since the inception of the industry. The basis for this competition lies in niche specialization (e.g., Fitch Ratings in municipalities and financial institutions) and in "better treatment" of issuers by smaller, newer rating firms in developing countries. The global rating agencies, especially Moody's, have been characterized as high-handed or, in other ways, unresponsive.[19] This perception has not yet produced any really significant change, but after the Asian financial crisis of 1997–98, Moody's corporate culture became less secretive. Enron's bankruptcy in 2001–2002 accelerated this switch at Moody's, prompting the previously guarded institution to "invite comment" from market stakeholders on proposed improvements in the rating process.[20]

Both Moody's and S&P are headquartered in lower Manhattan's financial district. Moody's was sold off in 1998 as a separate corporation by Dun and Bradstreet, the information concern that had owned Moody's since 1962. S&P remains a subsidiary of publishers McGraw-Hill, owners since 1966.[21] As table 1 shows, both

18. Wilson, 1987, 327.

19. See, e.g., Ann Monroe, "Rating the Rating Agencies," *Treasury & Risk Management,* July 1995, unpaginated; U.S. Department of Justice, "DOJ Urges SEC to Increase Competition for Securities Ratings Agencies," press release, Washington, D.C., March 6, 1998; also see surveys by Cantwell & Company, at www.askcantwell.com/iscr_survey.htm.

20. Jenny Wiggins and Peter Spiegel, "Enron's Fall May Spark Credit Rating Rethink," *Financial Times,* January 19–20, 2002, 1.

21. Paul Abrahams, "Dun & Bradstreet Opts for Divorce," *Financial Times,* November 1, 1996, 26. Also see Moody's Corporation, *2001 Annual Report* (New York: Moody's Corporation, 2002).

Table 1. Moody's and S&P: Branch Establishment

Region/Office	Moody's Investors Service	Standard & Poor's
U.S. and Canada		
Canada (Toronto)	1994	1993
U.S. (Boston, Massachusetts)		1994
U.S. (Chicago, Illinois)		1994
U.S. (Dallas, Texas)	1993	1996
U.S. (New York)	1909	1941
U.S. (San Francisco)	1989	1989
U.S. (Washington, D.C.)		1994
Europe		
France (Paris)	1988	Affiliation 1990; acquired 1995
Germany (Frankfurt)	1991	1992
Italy (Milan)	1999	1999
Spain (Madrid)	1993	Affiliation 1992; acquired 1994
Ireland (Dublin)	2000	
Czech Republic	Affiliation 2000	
Sweden (Stockholm)		Affiliation 1988; acquired 1990
UK (London)	1986	1984
Other		
Israel (Tel Aviv)		Affiliation 1998
Cyprus (Limassol)	1995	
Russia (Moscow)		1998
South Africa (Johannesburg)		Affiliation 1997
Asia Pacific		
China (Beijing)	2001	
Australia	(Sydney) 1988	(Melbourne) 1990
Hong Kong	1994	1994
India	ICRA, Affiliation 1998	(Bombay) Affiliation 1996
Indonesia (Jakarta)		Affiliation 1996
Japan (Tokyo)	1985	1985
Philippines (Manila)		Affiliation 1999
Singapore	1995	1996
Korea	KIS, Affiliation 1998	
Taiwan (Taipei)		Affiliation in 1997
Latin America		
Argentina (Buenos Aries)	Humphreys, Affiliation 1999	Affiliation 1995; acquired 1997
Brazil (Sao Paulo)	1997	1998
Chile (Santiago)	Humphreys, Affiliation 1999	Affiliation 1996
Mexico (Mexico City)	2000	Acquired 1993

Source: Moody's Investors Service and Standard & Poor's web pages.

agencies have numerous branches in the United States, other developed countries, and several emerging markets. S&P is well known for the S&P 500, the benchmark U.S. stock index listing around $1 trillion in assets.[22] Unlike Moody's, S&P also offers stocks analysis.

Third in the market is the French-owned Fitch Ratings. It has forty branch, subsidiary, and affiliate offices worldwide.[23] IBCA (International Bank Credit Analysts) merged with Euronotation of France in 1995, in what was then rumored to be the first step toward the creation of a "true European rating agency."[24] The subsequent merger of IBCA with Fitch creates the potential for a truly international agency. Fitch has a long way to go to achieve the eminence of Moody's and S&P, however.

Domestically focused agencies have developed in OECD countries (including Japan, after 1985, and in Germany during the late 1990s) and, especially since the mid-1990s, in emerging markets (including China, India, Malaysia, Indonesia, Thailand, Israel, Brazil, Mexico, Argentina, South Africa, and the Czech Republic).[25]

In the late 1960s and early 1970s, raters began to charge fees to bond issuers to pay for ratings. Today, at least 75 percent of the agencies' income is obtained from such fees.[26] In Canada, the Dominion Bond Rating Service (DBRS) gets more than 80 percent of its revenue from rating fees. Before being purchased by Moody's in the late 1990s, the Canadian Bond Rating Service (CBRS) made 50 percent of its revenue this way.[27] It has been suggested that charging fees to bond issuers constitutes a conflict of interest. This may indeed be the case with some of the smaller, lower-profile firms desperate for business. With Moody's and S&P, "grade inflation" does not seem to be a significant issue. Both firms have fee incomes of several hundred million dollars a year, making it difficult for even the largest issuer to manipulate them through their revenues. Moody's Corporation (owner of Moody's Investors Service) reported revenue of $602 million in 2000, $796.7 million in 2001, and $1.02 billion in 2002.[28] Revenue figures for S&P are not broken out from McGraw-Hill data but likely are similar. The real constraint is that any hint of corruption in ratings would diminish the reputation of the major agencies—and reputation is the very basis of the rating franchise.

22. Interview with Joanne W. Rose, vice president and general counsel, Standard & Poor's, New York City, February 1993.

23. See "Company Description," in "About Fitch," at www.fitchibca.com, accessed January 25, 2002.

24. Rupert Bruce, "Debt-Rating Agencies Fill the Gap," *International Herald Tribune,* November 14–15, 1992, 11.

25. Susan Greenberg, "New Rating Agency Causes a Stir," *Guardian,* February 13, 1993. A comprehensive listing of the new agencies can be found at www.everling.de.

26. Interview with Rose, February 1993.

27. Lynne Kilpatrick, "Debt-Rating's Flaws," *Financial Times of Canada,* March 30–April 5, 1992, 1.

28. Moody's Corporation, *2002 Annual Report,* 1; see "Shareholder Relations," in www.moodys.com, accessed September 23, 2003.

In the case of rating agencies in Japan and the developing world, financing typically comes from ownership consortia, which often include financial institutions and government agencies. Within local financial communities, this arrangement casts some doubt on the independence of the agencies' work. It remains to be seen whether ownership of Moody's Corporation stock raises conflict of interest issues.

Rating Process

> It's the same type of credit analysis that you would do if you were in a bank . . . there's really no magic to it . . . The differences come because there [is] clearly, after you get to your basic analysis, much qualitative interpretation.
>
> BRIAN I. NEYSMITH, Montréal, June 1992

How do raters do what they do? Debt rating is a process that begins with information inputs, both quantitative and qualitative. The next steps are the analytical determination itself, the output of the process, and the surveillance after a rating is done. The rating universe is treated here in an undifferentiated manner. In other words, the differences between the rating of, say, municipalities and corporations are left out of the picture, because the core judgment processes are sufficiently similar. The rating process in simplified terms is illustrated in Figure 2.

Information

The rating process in the United States may be initiated by either the issuer or the rating agency, after the filing of an SEC registration statement on the bonds for sale. Moody's has rated "without request," to the irritation of many in the financial markets, attracting investigation by the U.S. Justice Department.[29]

For first-time securities issuers, typically there is a meeting with rating officials on the agencies' information requirements.[30] However, S&P and Moody's organize public seminars with the same intent.[31]

---

29. Interview with Charles S. Prescott, IBCA Ltd., London, December 8, 1992, and with various Japanese rating agency officials in Tokyo, May 1994. The Justice Department investigation did not lead to prosecution.

30. Moody's Investors Service, *Moody's Introduction* (New York: Moody's Investors Service, 1989), 6.

31. See Hyman C. Grossman, "Introduction to the Debt Rating Process," presentation to the Standard & Poor's seminar, Institute for Professional Development, New Jersey Law Center, New Brunswick, N.J., August 7, 1992. During the 1990s, the Euromoney Institute of Finance frequently organized credit-analysis training workshops, which featured Moody's analysts speaking on the influence, scope, and methods of rating agencies.

Figure 2. Outline of the rating process

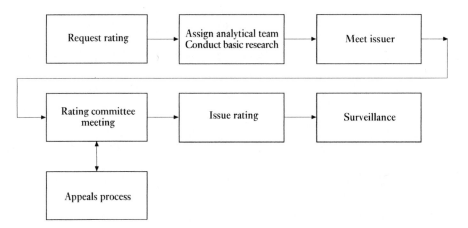

Source: Standard & Poor's Corporation, *S & P's Corporate Finance Criteria* (New York: Standard & Poor's Corporation, 1992), p. 9.

Hawkins, Brown, and Campbell note that the rating process incorporates information on (a) quantitative data from the issuer about its financial position; (b) quantitative data the agency gathers on the industry, competitors, and the economy; (c) legal advice relating to the specific bond issue; (d) qualitative data from the issuer about management, policy, business outlook, and accounting practices; and (e) qualitative data the agency gathers on such matters as competitive position, quality of management, long-term industry prospects and economic environment.[32]

The rating agencies indicate they are most interested in data on cash flow relative to debt service obligations.[33] They want to know how liquid a company is and whether timing problems are likely to hinder repayment. So, fluctuations in the flow of cash into the entity are important, as are the timing of major obligations.[34] Other information may include five-year financial projections, including income statements and balance sheets, analysis of capital spending plans, financing alternatives, and contingency plans.[35] This information may not be publicly known. It is supplemented by agency research into the value of current outstanding obligations, stock valuation, and other publicly available data that allow for an inference

32. David F. Hawkins, Barbara A. Brown, and Walter J. Campbell, *Rating Industrial Bonds* (Morristown, N.J.: Financial Executives Research Foundation, 1983), 38; also see Hugh C. Sherwood, *How Corporate and Municipal Debt Is Rated: An Inside Look at Standard & Poor's Rating System* (New York: John Wiley, 1976), 21–26.

33. Jan Konstanty, *Moody's Starts with the Basics* (London: Moody's Investors Service, 1991), 1.

34. David Stimpson, ed., *Global Credit Analysis* (London: Moody's Investors Service/IFR Books, 1991), 98.

35. Standard & Poor's, *S&P Corporate Finance Criteria*, (New York: Standard & Poor's, 1992), 9.

of the corporation's quantitative basis for future debt repayment. The major agencies have invested in up-to-date information resources to facilitate this research.[36] As became evident with Enron, none of the rating agencies conduct independent audits themselves.[37]

Social science can be important in rating decisions. An example is the calculation of the size of the future tax base of the city of Detroit. In 1992, Moody's formed a negative view of the future prospects of the city repaying its obligations based on, among other things, the expectation that the population is expected to shrink to less than half the current figure of around 1 million persons by 2012, had very high tax rates when compared to other U.S. cities, and an unemployment rate twice the U.S. average.[38]

The rating agencies are also interested in legal information relevant to the status of the issue, to determine the degree of protection provided to the holder of the debt security, relative to unsecured creditors. Accordingly, agencies insist on being provided with the indenture or contract between issuer and bondholder. This contract must cover such considerations as (a) the type of bond for sale; (b) the amount of the issue; (c) what collateral or assets are pledged, if any; (d) the nature of protective covenants, including provisions for sinking funds in which the issuer deposits principal repayments prior to their final repayment to the holder; (e) the working capital or liquidity position of the issuer; and (f) redemption rights or call privileges on the bond.[39]

This legal work is an underrated, vital activity of rating agencies. In the United States, because of SEC disclosure regulations, indentures tend to be voluminous, running to thousands of pages, and written in very specialized language. These documents are crucial in what are called "structured deals," where a particular asset or pool of assets acts as collateral for bonds. As a result, "Smaller purchasers typically rely not on the prospectus but on the rating supplied by the rating agency." Accordingly, in the legal literature, bond rating agencies have been recognized as gatekeepers (along with underwriting investment banks).[40] Significant inaccuracies have been reported in the agencies' gatekeeping function for bond indentures, based on comparisons of published agency information in *Moody's Industrial Manual* and actual prospectuses. When comparing the actual terms of 171 bonds with Moody's

36. Interview with Douglas Green, reference librarian, Business Information Center, Standard & Poor's Corporation, New York City, August 13, 1992.

37. Canadian Bond Rating Service, *The CBRS Method of Rating* (Montreal: Canadian Bond Rating Service, 1989), 13.

38. Barbara Presley Noble, "A Downgraded Detroit Cries Foul," *New York Times*, November 3, 1992, C1.

39. On provisions of an indenture, see John Downes and Jordan Elliot Goodman, *Dictionary of Finance and Investment Terms*, 5th ed. (New York: Barron's, 1998), 273.

40. John C. Coffee, Jr., "The Bondholder Puzzle," *New York Law Journal*, March 22, 1990, 5, 7, 8.

version, Coffee found Moody's to be inaccurate in 36 out of the 171 cases, or 21 percent of the time.

Issuers provide to the agencies qualitative information about their policy choices and strategic plans. This information is taken very seriously by rating officials, as it informs their judgments about management capacities.[41] This information is usually provided as part of the issuer's formal presentation, which includes the quantitative information mentioned above. Typically, these meetings cover (a) background on the company or other government; (b) corporate strategy or philosophy; (c) operating position (competitive position, manufacturing capacity, distribution and marketing networks); (d) financial management and accounting policies (in the case of a non-U.S. issuer, their accounting standards and whether they use GAAP, Generally Accepted Accounting Principles); and (e) topics of concern, such as risk of additional government regulation, major investment plans, and litigation.[42]

The major agencies also gather qualitative information about the issuer and the issuer's business environment. In the case of non-U.S. issues in the "Yankee" market—the huge U.S. domestic market where bonds are issued in dollars—relevant information includes the foreign issuer's economic and political environment. Other things deemed pertinent are industry risk, or the viability of the issuer's industry.[43] Many factors, the agencies suggest, might affect industry growth, stability, or decline: technological change, labor unrest, and regulatory shifts.[44] Like others in the financial markets, rating agency officials pay close attention to what the news services are carrying about the institutions the agencies rate.

Analytical Determination

How is an analysis undertaken and ratings determined? The agencies assemble analytical teams that undertake research, meet with issuers, and prepare a report containing a rating recommendation and rationale. The teams present their view to a rating committee of senior agency officials, which makes the final determination in private. These decisions are usually subject to appeal by the issuer.

Next to the confidential information flows, the most secretive aspect of the rating business is the analytical process for producing bond rating judgments.[45] Historically, there was some variation between the major agencies on this issue. Moody's, true to its history of a more conservative and secretive corporate culture, tended to be much less revealing about its ratings criteria than its major rival. The reason, according to one Moody's representative, is that publishing rating criteria

41. Interview with Brian I. Neysmith, president, Canadian Bond Rating Service, Montréal, June 16, 1992.
42. Moody's, 1989, 7.
43. Standard & Poor's, 1992, 15.
44. Ibid., 15.
45. The author has not had access to documents used for specific rating determinations.

that indicate, for example, acceptable financial ratios for particular industries, were thought potentially to distort expectations among issuers. Criteria based on quantitative information tend to "confuse people" when their issue does not achieve the expected rating for qualitative reasons.[46] Moody's gradually abandoned this position during the 1990s. *Moody's Rating Methodology Handbook*, issued in February 2000, contains financial ratio appendices.[47]

S&P publishes a great number of criteria books that contain guidelines on appropriate financial ratios for different types of credits. What are these ratios? In the case of sovereign credits (a country and its national government), a typical assessment of the debt-bearing capacity of the country begins with the evaluation of the current debt burden.

S&P's Corporate Finance Criteria contains a section that links ratios with specific ratings. For example, a utility company distributing gas and seeking an AA rating needs to ensure that "funds flow interest coverage,"—the number of times cash flow into the business covers interest payments out—equals 4.25 or better. For a BBB rating, the company needs to ensure coverage is in the range of 2.25 to 3.5. To issue junk bonds in the upper ranges, anything under 2.5 was considered adequate by S&P at the time.[48]

Ratios are important in analytical determination. Certainly, rating officials referred to them at length in interviews. However, as a Moody's analyst commented, "Ratios really are a starting point. . . . All a ratio gives you is a historical look at a company. Where a company has been. And by the time an account comes out, it is old anyway."[49] Raters' comments support the idea that rating mixes qualitative and quantitative data, producing a fundamentally qualitative result—a judgment[50] But they are quick to use the objectifying cloak of economic and financial analysis and, as it were, hide behind the numbers when it is easier than justifying what may, in fact, be a difficult judgment to a potentially hostile issuer.

The Detroit case again provides an example. Although he acknowledged that the rating process for a municipality includes so-called quality of life factors, such as crime and homelessness, the leader of the Moody's rating team claimed that his report to the rating committee (where the rating determination was actually made)

46. Interview with Susan D. Abbott, associate director, Corporate Department, Moody's Investors Service, New York City, August 21, 1992.

47. Moody's Investors Service, *Moody's Rating Methodology Handbook* (New York: Moody's Investors Service, February 2000); see, e.g., 174–75.

48. Standard & Poor's, 1992, 65.

49. John Diaz, quoted in Rupert Bruce, "Debt-Rating Agencies Fill the Gap," *International Herald Tribune*, November 14–15, 1992, 11.

50. See, e.g., Standard & Poor's, 1992, 15; where S&P notes that "there is no formula for combining these [quantitative and qualitative] scores to arrive at a rating conclusion." The judgments are therefore by nature "highly subjective. Yet that is at the heart of every rating."

"was based on the kinds of objective numbers the agency had always used to provide information to investors."[51]

The rating agencies know that public views of the ratings process tend to revolve almost exclusively around the numbers. The prevailing assumption seems to be that quantitative indicators are *the* form of data incorporated into the rating determination and that the process is therefore technical rather than judgmental. This view certainly seems to be behind Detroit city officials' frustration with bond raters. The officials insisted that Moody's ought to have considered whether Detroit paid its debts and controlled its budget, rather than make judgments about the future population base or quality of life in the jurisdiction. Such matters would usually be subjects for political judgment, social science, or speculation.[52] The intersubjective belief that quantitative data is the only criterion of credit rating, *or that it should be,* has fostered research into variables that would help an issuer secure a higher rating and therefore access to cheaper credit.[53]

Outputs

Typically, at the end of the rating committee meeting, a rating is established. A variety of rating scales are available for different financial instruments. The debt ratings on bonds are the most commonly recognized, but S&P also has scales for commercial paper, preferred stock, certificates of deposit, money market funds, mutual bond funds, and insurance company claims-paying ability. S&P and Moody's bond rating scales are given in table 2, along with brief definitions of these ratings.

In the scales, an important distinction is made between investment and speculative "grades." These grades, which neatly cleave the rating scale in two, are a result of securities legislation passed during the 1930s, which permits fiduciaries such as pension funds and insurance companies to invest only in bonds above a level deemed prudent. Over the years this distinction has become a market convention and serves to define the demarcation between speculative, high-yield, or junk bonds and those considered acceptable for investment.[54]

Ratings have a greater role in the investment process than raters publicly acknowledge. Smith has discussed the ways in which knowledge comes to be "objectified"

---

51. Paul Devine, quoted in Noble, 1992, c1.

52. Ibid.

53. See, e.g., George S. Cluff and Paul G. Farnham, "A Problem of Discrete Choice: Moody's Municipal Bond Ratings," *Journal of Business and Economics* 37 (1985): 277–302; also see Paul G. Farnham and George S. Cluff, "The Bond Rating Game Revisited: What Information Can Local Officials Use?" *Journal of Urban Affairs* 6, no. 4 (Fall 1984): 21–37.

54. Despite the label, "investment grade" ratings "are not recommendations to buy, hold or sell a security" on the part of the rating agencies (interview with Leo C. O'Neill, president, Standard & Poor's Ratings Group, New York City, August 18, 1992).

Table 2. Bond rating symbols and definitions

Grade	S&P[a]	S&P Definitions[b]	Moody's[c]	Moody's definitions[d]
Investment	AAA	An obligation rated AAA has the highest rating assigned by Standard & Poor's. The obligor's capacity to meet its financial commitment on the obligation is extremely strong.	Aaa	Bonds and preferred stock which are rated Aaa are judged to be of the best quality. They carry the smallest degree of investment risk and are generally referred to as "gilt edged." Interest payments are protected by a large or by an exceptionally stable margin and principal is secure. While the various protective elements are likely to change, such changes as can be visualized are most unlikely to impair the fundamentally strong position of such issues.
Investment	AA+ AA AA−	An obligation rated AA differs from the highest rated obligations only in small degree. The obligor's capacity to meet its financial commitment on the obligation is very strong.	Aa1 Aa2 Aa3	Bonds and preferred stock which are rated Aa are judged to be of high quality by all standards. Together with the Aaa group they comprise what are generally known as high-grade bonds. They are rated lower than the best bonds because margins of protection may not be as large as in Aaa securities or fluctuation of protective elements may be of greater amplitude or there may be other elements present which make the long-term risk appear somewhat larger than the Aaa securities.
Investment	A+ A A−	An obligation rated A is somewhat more susceptible to the adverse effects of changes in circumstances and economic conditions than obligations in higher rated categories. However, the obligor's capacity to meet its financial commitment on the obligation is still strong.	A1 A2 A3	Bonds and preferred stock which are rated A possess many favorable investment attributes and are to be considered as upper-medium-grade obligations. Factors giving security to principal and interest are considered adequate, but elements may be present which suggest a susceptibility to impairment sometime in the future.

Table 2—cont.

Grade	S&P[a]	S&P Definitions[b]	Moody's[c]	Moody's definitions[d]
Investment	BBB+	An obligation rated BBB exhibits adequate pro-	Baa1	Bonds and preferred stock which are rated Baa are considered as
	BBB	tection parameters. However, adverse eco-	Baa2	medium-grade obligations (i.e., they are neither highly protected
	BBB–	nomic conditions or changing circumstances are more likely to lead to a weakened capacity of the obligor to meet its financial commitment on the obligation. Obliga-tions rated BB, B, CCC, CC, and C are regarded as having significant speculative characteris-tics. BB indicates the least degree of specula-tion and C the highest. While such obligations will likely have some quality and protective characteristics, these may be outweighed by large uncertainties or major exposures to adverse conditions.	Baa3	nor poorly secured). Interest payments and principal security appear adequate for the present but certain protective elements may be lacking or may be charac-teristically unreliable over any great length of time. Such bonds lack outstanding investment char-acteristics and in fact have specu-lative characteristics as well.
Speculative	BB+	An obligation rated BB is less vulnerable to non-	Ba1	Bonds and preferred stock which are rated Ba are judged to have
	BB	payment than other speculative issues. How-	Ba2	speculative elements; their future cannot be considered as well
	BB–	ever, it faces major on-going uncertainties or exposure to adverse business, financial, or economic conditions which could lead to the obligor's inadequate capacity to meet its financial commitment on the obligation.	Ba3	assured. Often the protection of interest and principal payments may be very moderate, and thereby not well safeguarded dur-ing both good and bad times over the future. Uncertainty of posi-tion characterizes bonds in this class.

Table 2—cont.

Grade	S&P[a]	S&P Definitions[b]	Moody's[c]	Moody's definitions[d]
Speculative	B+ B B–	An obligation rated B is more vulnerable to non-payment than obliga-tions rated BB, but the obligor currently has the capacity to meet its financial commitment on the obligation. Adverse business, financial, or economic conditions will likely impair the obligor's capacity or willingness to meet its financial commitment on the obligation.	B1 B2 B3	Bonds and preferred stock which are rated B generally lack charac-teristics of the desirable invest-ment. Assurance of interest and principal payments or of mainte-nance of other terms of the con-tract over any long period of time may be small.
Speculative	CCC+ CCC CCC–	An obligation rated CCC is currently vulnerable to nonpayment, and is dependent upon favor-able business, financial, and economic conditions for the obligor to meet its financial commitment on the obligation. In the event of adverse busi-ness, financial, or eco-nomic conditions, the obligor is not likely to have the capacity to meet its financial commitment on the obligation.	Caa	Bonds and preferred stock which are rated Caa are of poor standing. Such issues may be in default or there may be present elements of danger with respect to principal or interest.
Speculative	CC	An obligation rated CC is currently highly vul-nerable to nonpayment.	Ca	Bonds and preferred stock which are rated Ca represent obligations which are speculative in a high degree. Such issues are often in default or have other marked shortcomings.
	C	A subordinated debt or preferred stock obliga-tion rated C is currently highly vulnerable to	C	Bonds and preferred stock which are rated C are the lowest-rated class of bonds, and issues so rated can be regarded as having

Table 2—cont.

Grade	S&P[a]	S&P Definitions[b]	Moody's[c]	Moody's definitions[d]
		nonpayment. The C rating may be used to cover a situation where a bankruptcy petition has been filed or similar action taken, but payments on this obligation are being continued. A C also will be assigned to a preferred stock issue in arrears on dividends or sinking fund payments, but that is currently paying.		extremely poor prospects of ever attaining any real investment standing.
	D	An obligation rated D is in payment default. The D rating category is used when payments on an obligation are not made on the date due even if the applicable grace period has not expired, unless Standard & Poor's believes that such payments will be made during such grace period. The D rating also will be used upon the filing of a bankruptcy petition or the taking of a similar action if payments on an obligation are jeopardized.		

Source: "Rating Definitions" at www.standardandpoors.com and www.moodys.com, accessed June 13, 2002; various Moody's and S&P publications; Richard Cantor and Frank Packer, "The Credit Rating Industry," *Federal Reserve Bank of New York Quarterly Review* 19, no, 2 (Summer-Fall 1994), 1–26, 3.

[a] According to S&P, "The ratings from 'AA' to 'CCC' may be modified by the addition of a plus or minus sign to show relative standing within the major rating categories."

[b] "Issue Credit Rating Definitions," at www.standardandpoors.com, accessed June 13, 2002.

[c] According to Moody's, "Moody's appends numerical modifiers 1, 2, and 3 to each generic rating classification from Aa through Caa. The modifier 1 indicates that the obligation ranks in the higher end of its generic rating category; the modifier 2 indicates a mid-range ranking; and the modifier 3 indicates a ranking in the lower end of that generic rating category" ("Rating Definitions" at www.moodys.com, accessed August 6, 2004).

[d] "Rating Definitions," at www.moodys.com, accessed June 10, 2002.

and acquires "authority" in the process of its creation.[55] Her argument is that knowledge, once produced, loses its concrete social origins. One way in which the information output of the rating process acquires this objective status is through its frequent publication in many different forms. A perusal of Standard & Poor's *Canadian Focus* indicates that S&P regularly produces forty-four different serial products in hard copy, CD-ROM, real-time online news, and fax.

The rating agencies' outputs are used by key capital market actors—pension funds, investment banks, other financial institutions, and government agencies. Moody's has four thousand clients for its publications, and the company estimates that around thirty thousand people read its output regularly.[56] Annual subscription fees range from $15,000 to $65,000 for heavier users, who also have the opportunity to talk to analysts directly. Increasingly, outputs are produced for the Internet. "Relationship-level clients" may attend conferences and take part in other events related to credit quality. Moody's actively puts its analysts in front of journalists and, like Standard & Poor's, issues regular press statements on credit conditions. Standard & Poor's produces an even wider range of products, in both traditional and digital format. Their core weekly publication, *CreditWeek,* has some 2,423 subscribers. *Global Sector Review* is bought by 2,988 clients.[57]

The rating product becomes "externalized" through these means, and opinions acquire "facticity," as a consequence.[58] O'Neill underscored this when he observed that "what makes our ratings such a strong factor in the market is that they take into account all the factors that surround a debt obligation and *reduce it to a letter symbol which is easily understood.*"[59] McGuire observed, in congressional testimony on junk bonds, that "when you're on a symbol system you inherently suppress some information and the simplicity of the rating system and its usefulness around the world depends on that simplicity."[60] The clarity of ratings as measures of performance has made them important in the U.S. corporate planning process.[61] The effectiveness of ratings in communication has led to their use in advertising. When they were AAA institutions, the Union Bank of Switzerland and Credit Suisse used

55. Dorothy E. Smith, *The Conceptual Practices of Power: A Feminist Sociology of Knowledge* (Toronto: University of Toronto Press, 1990).

56. Email to the author from Andrew Chmaj, senior vice president/marketing, Moody's Investors Service, London, July 31, 2000.

57. "Standard & Poor's Ratings Services/Subscription Services," memorandum prepared for the author by Standard & Poor's, New York, courtesy of the president, November 13, 2000.

58. Smith, 1990, 66.

59. Interview with O'Neill, August 18, 1992; author's emphasis.

60. Statement of Thomas J. McGuire, executive vice president, Moody's Investors Service, "High Yield Debt Market/Junk Bonds," hearing before the subcommittee on telecommunications and finance of the Committee on Energy and Commerce, House of Representatives, 101st Cong., 2nd sess., March 8, 1990 (Washington, D.C.: U.S. Government Printing Office, 1990), 54.

61. Interview with Edward Z. Emmer, executive managing director, Corporate Finance, Standard & Poor's Ratings Group, New York, August 11, 1992.

ratings in print advertisements, most notably in the *Economist*. One of these adver-tisements, for Union Bank, began with the line, "There are three standards for measuring banks: Moody's, S&P's and our clients." Ratings have even been used in television commercials.[62]

Surveillance

Surveillance of issuers' financial condition is a key aspect of the rating agencies' work, because creditworthiness is a dynamic condition. Economic circumstances do not stand still. Wars break out, and enterprises strategize for good or ill. The qual-ity of any rating output immediately starts to deteriorate as new events impinge on the issuer. Accordingly, the agencies place great emphasis on the ongoing monitor-ing of issuers.

This monitoring allows agencies to react to events and give appropriate signals about the issuer to the market. A major criticism of the agencies has been the back-ward or historical focus of their credit analysis.[63] Hence, attention to surveillance presumably increases analysts' proactive capacity, based on deeper knowledge of the institutions they are rating and their likely risks. The willingness of firms and gov-ernments to subject themselves to this monitoring has been heightened by SEC Rule 415, which instituted "shelf registration," allowing issuers to file with SEC to sell a given amount of securities when market conditions seemed favorable.[64] Conse-quently, issuers have increasingly placed a premium on keeping the agencies informed so that their ratings are always current.

Surveillance should be thought of as the continuation and extension of the links between issuers, raters, and investors. Information can hasten (or preclude) disci-pline, should it reveal a break in the understanding—the basis for rating—that underpins the relationship.[65] The relationship is important to the issuer to the degree the debt markets are attractive places to raise funds. Discipline may take the form of a rating change or a listing on Moody's "Watchlist" and S&P's "CreditWatch," sig-naling positive rating trends or, more usually, negative rating concerns prior to a downgrade. S&P emphasizes that credibility is gained when the "record demon-strates" an issuer's actions are consistent with plans. This credibility may carry an

62. "Independent Bond Rating Agencies Judge Canada Trust as Safe as the Major Banks," advertisement aired on the Canadian Broadcasting Corporation television network, Toronto, Jan-uary–March 1992.

63. On this concern, see Coffee, March 22, 1990; Margaret A. Elliott, "Rating the Debt Raters," *Institutional Investor,* December 1988: 109–12; and Fran Hawthorne, "Rating the Raters," *Institu-tional Investor* 24, no. 9 (July 1990): 121–27; also see "OK, So What Is Quality?" *Euromoney* sup-plement, September 1991, 36–44 (esp. 40).

64. Standard & Poor's, 1992, 9.

65. For a discussion of surveillance in these terms, see Christopher Dandeker, *Surveillance, Power and Modernity: Bureaucracy and Discipline from 1700 to the Present Day* (New York: St. Mar-tin's Press, 1990), 39–40.

issuer over a rough patch, because "once earned, credibility can support the continuity of a particular credit rating," despite, say, short-term liquidity problems.[66]

Ratings and Regulation

Ratings have been incorporated into government regulation since 1931. Government regulation of rating agencies, which in the United States began in the 1970s, reinforced an oligopolistic ratings market and made it harder for new entrants to launch ratings businesses.

The sharp decline of credit quality the Depression produced and the consequent problems of domestic financial institutions led the U.S. Office of the Comptroller of the Currency (OCC) to rule in 1931 that bank holdings of publicly rated bonds had to be rated BBB or better to be carried on bank balance sheets at their face or book value. Otherwise, the bonds were to be written down to market value, imposing losses on the banks.[67] Many state banking departments subsequently adopted this rule. New OCC rules in 1936 prohibited banks from holding bonds not rated BBB by the two agencies. This condition had far-reaching consequences, because 891 of 1,975 listed bonds were rated below BBB at the time. The high-yield or junk bond market was effectively closed for the next forty years, until the end of the 1970s. The bond business and bond rating became quiet, predictable occupations.

Nationally Recognized Statistical Rating Organizations

In 1975, the SEC further pulled ratings into the regulatory system through Rule 15c3-1, the net-capital rule. This rule created a major barrier to entry for new rating agencies in the United States. Under 15c3-1, brokers who underwrote bond issues had to maintain a certain percentage—a "haircut"—of their securities in reserves. However, the rule gave "preferential treatment" to bonds rated investment-grade by at least two 'nationally recognized statistical rating organizations' (NRSROs), who would get a "shorter haircut."[68] The SEC did not define the substance of an NRSRO in any detail.

The NRSRO concept has since been incorporated into many regulatory initiatives. Subsequently, "state authorities, self-regulatory organizations, and great swathes of the U.S. mutual fund industry have adopted ratings to define, control and advertise risk."[69] The NRSRO concept remains vague and unspecified in law but

---

66. Standard & Poor's, *S&P's Structured Finance Criteria* (New York: Standard & Poor's, 1988), 16–17.

67. Richard Cantor and Frank Packer, "The Credit Rating Industry," *Federal Reserve Bank of New York Quarterly Review*, 19, no. 2 (Summer–Fall 1994): 1–26, 6.

68. Ben Edwards, "Will the Agencies Be SEC Puppets?" *Euromoney*, November 1994, 26–27.

69. Ibid., 27.

Table 3. Ratings in U.S. regulation

Year adopted	Ratings-dependent regulation	Minimum rating	Number of ratings?	Regulator/ regulation
1931	Required banks to mark-to-market lower-rated bonds[a]	BBB	2	OCC and Federal Reserve examination rules
1936	Prohibited banks from purchasing "speculative securities"	BBB	N.A.	OCC, FDIC, and Federal Reserve joint statement
1951	Imposed higher capital requirements on insurers' lower rated bonds	Various	N.A.	NAIC mandatory reserve requirements
1975	Imposed higher capital haircuts[b] on broker/dealers' below-investment-grade bonds	BBB	2	SEC amendment to Rule 15c3–1: the uniform net capital rule
1982	Eased disclosure requirements for investment grade bonds	BBB	1	SEC adoption of Integrated Disclosure System (Release #6383)
1984	Eased issuance of nonagency mortgage-backed securities (MBSs)	AA	1	Secondary Mortgage Market Enhancement Act, 1984
1987	Permitted margin lending against MBSs and (later) foreign bonds	AA	1	Federal Reserve Regulation T
1989	Allowed pension funds to invest in high-rated asset-backed securities	A	1	Department of Labor relaxation of ERISA Restriction (PTE 89–88)
1989	Prohibited S&Ls from investing in below-investment-grade bonds	BBB	1	Financial Institutions Recovery and Reform Act, 1989
1991	Required money market mutual funds to limit holdings of low-rated paper	B1	1[c]	SEC amendment to Rule 2a-7 under the Investment Company Act, 1940
1992	Exempted issuers of certain asset-backed securities from registration as a mutual fund	BBB	1	SEC adoption of Rule 3a-7 under the Investment Company Act, 1940
1994	Imposes varying capital charges on banks' and S&Ls' holdings of different tranches of asset-backed securities	AAA & BBB	1	Federal Reserve, OCC, FDIC, OTS Proposed Rule on Recourse and Direct Credit Substitutes
1998	Department of Transportation can only extend credit assistance to projects with an investment grade rating	BBB	1	Transport Infrastructure Finance and Innovation Act 1998

Table 3—cont.

Year adopted	Ratings-dependent regulation	Minimum rating	Number of ratings?	Regulator/ regulation
1999	Gramm-Leach-Biley Act of 1999, Title I, p. 91. Restricts the ability of national banks to establish financial subsidiaries	A	1	Gramm-Leach-Biley Act of 1999
2000	Agencies exempted from Regulation FD requirement to disclose investment-relevant information to public. As long as information is for purposes of making a rating	Entity's rating must be public	N.A.	SEC Rule 100 (b) (2)

Sources: Cantor and Packer, "The Credit Rating Industry," 1994, 6; Arturo Estrella et al., "Credit Ratings and Complementary Sources of Credit Quality Information," Basel Committee on Banking Supervision, Working Paper No. 3, August 2000 (Basel, Switzerland: Bank for International Settlements, 2000), 54; testimony of Jonathan R. Macey, Cornell Law School, before the Committee on Governmental Affairs, U.S. Senate, March 20, 2002, 2 (available in the online archives of the Committee at http://gov-aff.senate.gov/032002witness.htm, accessed August 6, 2004).
[a] Mark-to-market involves recording the price or value of a security on a daily basis.
[b] If a bond is rated by one NRSRO, one rating is adequate. Otherwise, two ratings are required.
[c] If a bond is rated by one NRSRO, one rating is adequate. Otherwise, two ratings are required.

significant in practice. The most explicit statements of the NRSRO criteria are contained in SEC "no action" letters to Fitch Investors Service, Thomson Bankwatch, and IBCA. The letters indicate the SEC would take no enforcement action if ratings from these agencies were used to satisfy the requirements of Rule 15c3–1.

The elements the SEC mentioned in these letters are conflict of interest scrutiny; appropriate institutional separations, to avoid mixing investment advice and rating; adequate financial resources; adequate staff; sufficient training.[70] "Adequate" and "sufficient" are not defined. Moody's and S&P were deemed NRSROs. The SEC's control limits NRSRO designation to agencies that can demonstrate they are "nationally recognized." But there is no codified process for demonstrating this recognition to the SEC.

The NRSRO constraint made life difficult in the 1990s for Canadian agencies, which were denied the status, even though harmonization of securities disclosure laws between the United States and Canada under NAFTA meant that Canadian bonds could be sold in the United States without passing through SEC procedures. However, such sales are contingent on issues being rated by two NRSROs. The SEC was sympathetic but had concerns about the credibility of Canadian (and other foreign) agencies.[71] Finally, in February 2003, the SEC changed its view and issued a

70. Interview with Joanne W. Rose, vice president and general counsel, Standard and Poor's, New York City, August 1992.
71. Interview with SEC official, Washington, D.C., March 31, 1994; also see Lynne Kilpatrick, "Debt-Rating's Flaws," *Financial Times of Canada*, March 30–April 2, 1992, 1. Amendments to the U.S.-Canadian multijurisdictional disclosure system (MJDS) became effective January 1, 1994.

"no action" letter to Dominion Bond Rating Service, stating that it "will not recommend enforcement action," just as the SEC had done with the U.S. agencies years before.[72]

In August 1994, the SEC took the first steps toward changing the NRSRO system. It issued a "concept release" seeking comment on the use of NRSRO ratings in SEC regulation, the process of becoming an NRSRO, and SEC regulation of NRSROs.[73] This release was at the initiative of middle-level SEC officials, who were trying to get the commission to take a stand on the issue.[74] Lobbying was subsequently intense, as the established rating agencies attacked this effort to create formal procedures for designating and monitoring NRSROs.

They invoked the market recognition test of ratings as the most appropriate means for keeping rating accurate and suggested that future regulatory uses of ratings be considered carefully, on a case-by-case basis.[75] However, the current system "clearly favors incumbents," as Cantor and Packer observe, because new entrants to the rating business cannot hope to become "nationally recognized" without NRSRO status.[76] White also opposed the NRSRO designation, advocating adoption of a regulatory framework rather than certification of raters, which he argued limits competition.[77]

In 1997, SEC issued a proposed rule change to the Securities Exchange Act of 1934. This rule set forth a "list of attributes," couched in very broad terms, for the SEC to consider in designating NRSROs and in the NRSRO application process.[78]

These recognized the ratings of agencies recognized by Canadian securities regulators. See *Federal Register* 59, no. 2 (January 4, 1994), n.p., as cited in a letter from Mr. Michael J. Simon, of the law firm Milbank, Tweed, Hadley, and McCloy, to Mr. Walter J. Schroeder of Dominion Bond Rating Service Limited, January 5, 1994; letter supplied by Dominion Bond Rating Service. It still took nearly a decade for the SEC to issue a "no action" letter to Dominion.

72. Letter from Annette L. Nazareth, SEC director, Re: Dominion Bond Rating Service Limited, February 24, 2003, available at http://www.sec.gov/divisions/marketreg/mr-noaction/dominionbond022403-out.pdf, accessed August 12, 2003.

73. Securities and Exchange Commission, "Nationally Recognized Statistical Rating Organizations," release no. 33–7085 (Washington, D.C.: SEC, August 31, 1994).

74. Interviews with Rose, February 1993, and SEC official, March 31, 1994.

75. Standard and Poor's, "S&P Opposes Regulatory Intervention in Rating Activity," *Standard & Poor's Canadian Focus*, January 1995, 6–7. Also see Moody's, *Ratings in Regulation: A Petition to the Gorillas* (New York: Moody's Investors Service, June 1995), and letter from Matthew C. Molé, vice president and general counsel, Moody's Investors Service, to Jonathan G. Katz, secretary, Securities and Exchange Commission, Re: Proposal to Define the Term "NRSRO," March 2, 1998.

76. Cantor and Packer, 1994, 8.

77. Lawrence J. White, "The Credit Rating Industry: An Industrial Organization Analysis," paper presented to the Conference on Rating Agencies in the Global Financial System, New York University Salomon Center, Leonard N. Stern School of Business, New York, June 1, 2001.

78. Securities and Exchange Commission, "Rating Agencies—NRSROs," at www.sec.gov/answers/nrsro.htm, accessed January 27, 2002; Securities and Exchange Commission release no. 34–39457; file no. 57–33–97, "Capital Requirements for Brokers or Dealers under the Securities Exchange Act of 1934," at www.sec.gov/rules/proposed/34-39457.txt, accessed August 10, 2004.

The proposed rule has lingered on the shelf since. But the Enron bankruptcy has revived the NRSRO issue and the question of rating agencies' performance in the corporate bankruptcies of 2001 and 2002.[79]

The initiative to make NRSRO status more transparent reflects intensified competitive conditions within global finance. The emphasis is on removing barriers to entry and the U.S. need to reciprocate where S&P and Moody's have been incorporated into foreign rating agency regulations, such as in Japan or Mexico.

Financial regulation is becoming more codified, institutionalized, and juridified. Rules are more elaborate and formal, with fewer tacit understandings.[80] This tendency both devolves state activities onto nominally private institutions such as the rating agencies, which find themselves increasingly bound by disclosure rules, and establishes the framework for these institutions to operate.[81] In these circumstances, governments actively set the "limits of the possible" for rating agencies. From public scrutiny, the agencies potentially emerge in a strengthened position, with the conviction that they are socially sanctioned judges of prudent economic and financial behavior.

The use of ratings in financial regulation is most developed in the United States, but over the past twenty years ratings have increasingly become a key regulatory tool outside the United States, as depicted in table 4.

The latest and most significant example of ratings used as a regulatory tool internationally is the Basel II capital adequacy proposals, mandating ratings for less sophisticated banks as a means of specifying these institutions' risk exposure. The much-delayed proposals have been controversial and the object of considerable lobbying.[82]

Conclusions

We have seen the key stages in rating history, the workings of the rating process, and the use of ratings in public regulation. Delineating these purposes demonstrates that rating knowledge is very much a social phenomenon. Rating involves an admixture of quantitative and qualitative data, and it is thus inherently a process of judgment.

---

79. See the testimony to the U.S. Senate Committee on Governmental Affairs, by Macey, Reynolds, Schwarcz, and Hunt, March 20, 2002, available at www.senate.gov/~gov_affairs/hearings.htm, accessed June 5, 2002; also see Leslie Wayne, "Credit Raters Get Scrutiny and Possibly a Competitor," *New York Times*, April 23, 2002, C1.

80. Michael Moran, *The Politics of the Financial Services Revolution* (London: Macmillan, 1991), 13.

81. Ibid., 14.

82. "The Basel Perplex," *Economist*, November 10, 2001, 65–66; also see Michael R. King and Timothy J. Sinclair, "Private Actors and Public Policy: A Requiem for the New Basel Capital Accord," *International Political Science Review*, 24, no. 3 (July 2003): 345–62.

The form of knowledge that dominates the rating process is narrowly analytical and largely avoids long-run issues of development.

The inherent tentativeness of the rating process is not something the agencies publicize. The agencies assert that rating determinations are opinions but simultaneously seek to objectify and offer their views as "facts." To understand the social foundations of the rating agencies and what they do, we now return to the mid-range arguments about investment, knowledge and governance.

Table 4. Ratings in financial regulation in selected OECD and APEC countries

Country	Details of the regulation
Argentina	Banks and financial companies must seek a rating from an authorized rating agency. The rating reflects the ability of the financial institution to repay its medium and long-term liabilities. Although the rating scales are identical to those used by international rating agencies, the ratings do not encompass the country risk analysis. In the case of branches of foreign banks or subsidiaries wholly owned by foreign banks whose headquarters guarantee the obligations of their subsidiaries irrevocably, there is an alternative ratings system. Financial institutions must provide copies of the reports to customers who request them free of charge. However, they cannot be used in advertising campaigns or printed documents.
	The central bank prepares a list of banks that can receive time deposits from institutional investors (pension funds). Banks with weak ratings are excluded from this list.
	The Comision Nacional de Valores (CNV), the stock-market watchdog, does not extend authorization for the public offer of a security unless its issuer has sought two ratings. In addition, pension funds are not allowed to invest in assets that do not exceed a certain rating threshold, which is set at BBB for domestic credit ratings and B for ratings issued by international agencies on securities of resident issuers.
	The same provisions are extended to the insurance industry. In this case, the insurance industry is being asked to invest in rated securities with a minimum rating, and also to seek a rating as policies issued by them increasingly are being sold to pension funds.
Australia	Prudential statement C1: Recognizes mortgage insurance for risk-weighting loans secured by residential mortgages where the lenders' mortgage insurer carries a credit rating of A or higher from an approved credit rating agency.
	Prudential statement C2: Covers securitization and funds management, and also makes references to credit ratings.
	Prudential statement C3: Capital Adequacy for Banks, ratings are used to determine the capital requirement for specific risk for interest rate risk in the trading book.
Belgium	CAD [Capital Adequacy Directive] / Market risk amendment.
	Prudential reporting: the descriptive tables relating to the composition of a bank's securities portfolio require information on securities' ratings and the agencies which issued the ratings.

Table 4—cont.

Country	Details of the regulation
Canada	Market risk amendment
Chile	Overseas securities must have a minimum rating otherwise Chilean institutions are not permitted to invest in overseas securities.
France	CAD/Market risk amendment
Germany	No
Hong Kong	Liquidity regime: The statutory minimum liquidity ratio, expressed as a percentage of liquefiable assets to qualifying liabilities, is 25 percent of all Authorized Institution's (AI's). AI's holdings of marketable debit securities may be regarded as liquefiable assts for the calculation of the liquidity of ratio if the debt securities satisfy the qualifying credit rating.
	Capital adequacy regime: Debt securities in a trading book that satisfy the minimum ratings may be included in a 'rated' category. Rated securities carry lower risk weightings compared with "unrated" securities.
	Discount Window: Three types of securities are eligible for the Discount Window operated by the HKMA:
	1. Exchange Fund paper
	2. The existing Specified Instruments
	3. Other HK dollar securities with long-term ratings higher than the minimum acceptable ratings.
Indonesia	One credit rating agency in Indonesia.
	Regulations from Bank of Indonesian requiring ratings for bonds and commercial papers have stimulated the demand for ratings.
Italy	CAD/Market risk amendment
Japan	Market risk amendment
South Korea	Three credit rating agencies operating in South Korea that are supervised by the Korean SEC.
	The SEC requires issuers of unguaranteed bonds and debentures to obtain ratings from at least two agencies, while any bond issued overseas are required to have a rating.
	Guaranteed bonds do not require ratings. Only companies rated A or higher are allowed to issue unguaranteed bonds.
Luxembourg	CAD/Market risk amendment
Malaysia	In 1992, Malaysia introduced a restriction that no private debt securities be issued unless they were rated BBB or higher for long-term debt, or P3 (using the scale given by Rating Agency Malaysia) or MARC-3 or higher for-short term debt.
	From July 1, 2000, while the rating requirement is retained, the minimum credit rating requirement for issuance of private debt securities was removed, i.e. below investment grade private debt securities can be issued.
	The mandatory rating requirement does not apply to the issue of unredeemable convertible loan stocks.
Mexico	No. See page 123.
Netherlands	CAD/Market risk amendment

Table 4—cont.

Country	Details of the regulation
New Zealand	A registered bank is required to disclose ratings in its quarterly disclosure statement if it has a credit rating on its senior unsecured long-term New Zealand dollar debt payable in New Zealand.
	Information to be disclosed must include:
	1. Name of the rating agency 2. Date of the rating 3. Nature of the rating nomenclature used 4. Changes to ratings over the previous two years
	In the event that a bank does not have a rating of specified debt obligations, this fact is required to be stated in its quarterly disclosure statements.
Philippines	The SEC requires issuers of long-term commercial paper to obtain a rating from the local rating agency.
Sweden	CAD/Market risk amendment
Switzerland	Market risk amendment
	Credit risk: some risk-weights depends on whether the counterparty is located within an OECD country. Where OECD countries are defined as full members of the OECD, or countries that have concluded special credit agreements with the IMF in connection with the General Agreements on Credit of the latter, excluding those which have re-scheduled their external debts during the previous 5 years, or have a lower rating than investment grade on its long-term foreign currency debt (where it has no rating, its yield to maturity and remaining duration must not be incomparable with those of long-term liabilities with investment grade ratings).
	Investment funds: fund managers are restricted with whom they may conclude certain derivative transactions, dependent on the counterparty's credit rating.
Thailand	There is one local credit rating agency, Thai Rating and Information Services.
	To ensure independence, no single shareholder is allowed to own more than 5 percent of TRIS.
	Current ownership is divided almost equally among commercial banks, finance companies, securities companies and other firms/organizations (including the ADB and the Ministry of Finance).
	The SEC is pursuing some reforms such as the creation of another credit rating agency and an increase in the variety of debt issues.
	Unsecured debt issues must be rated.
United Kingdom	CAD/Market risk amendment
	Liquidity reporting guidelines for non-clearing banks.

Source: Working Group of the Basel Committee on Banking Supervision, "Credit Ratings and Complementary Sources of Credit Quality Information," Working paper no. 3, August 2000 (Basel Switzerland: Bank for International Settlements, 2000), 42–43; Asian Development Bank, "Development of Credit Rating Agencies: Background Paper for the Second Workshop on the Development of CRAs in the APEC Region," 2001, 154–55 (available at www.adb.org/Projects/APEC/Cra/default.asp, accessed August 6, 2004).

CHAPTER THREE

Unconscious Power

Mr. Untermyer:	You and Mr. Baker control the anthracite coalroad situation, do you not, together?
Mr. Morgan:	No; we do not.
Mr. Untermyer:	Do you not?
Mr. Morgan:	I do not think we do. At least, if we do, I do not know it.
Mr. Untermyer:	*Your power in any direction is entirely unconscious to you, is it not?*
Mr. Morgan:	It is sir, if that is the case.

Pujo congressional hearings, 1912

Investment judgments, as we have seen, are increasingly centralized in rating agencies, rating knowledge is a social phenomenon becoming increasingly instrumental, and governance is assuming new forms more conducive to private interests and increasingly less subject to democratic intervention. In the following analysis of unconscious power, the conceptual and, in some cases, empirical basis of the mid-range arguments about rating and investment, knowledge, and governance are developed. From these arguments and the conceptual exploration undertaken here, a mapping of the norms that underpin rating work can be derived. This "map," or mental framework of rating orthodoxy, sets out the assumptions implicit in rating agency judgments, offering an organized understanding of rating norms and practices. Along with assumptions that comprise the dominant mental framework, the map also sets out opposites of these orthodox principles, to make the orthodoxy approximate contestable claims rather than fixed characteristics. The mental framework of rating orthodoxy is subsequently used in the empirical explorations of chapters 4–6, which consider corporate, municipal, and global rating.

All models of how to think about the world are vulnerable to the criticism that they are arbitrary.[1] The focus on investment, knowledge, and governance reflects a view that these things matter in the conditions of early twenty-first century capitalism, when considering the role and implications of rating agencies' judgments.

Investment

Investment is changing in form, and this transformation increases the potential power and influence of rating agencies. In chapter 1, it was argued that the centralization of investment judgment is a key development underpinning rating power and authority. The basis of this centralization is considered here in three parts. One is the growth of disintermediation. Another concerns the forms of investment bond rating encourages. But before these points can be made, foundational arguments about the significance of bond rating should be examined, along with criticisms of these views and the case for a political-economy understanding of the agencies and what they do.

The views about rating that circulate in financial markets can be gleaned from many different sources, such as newspapers, other media, and surveys of market participants.[2] Bond traders and pension fund managers have seemingly contradictory views of rating agencies. They are at times critical of the agencies' work. As Scott suggests regarding the public roles played by the powerful and the powerless, separate from a positive public discourse about the dominant is typically a "hidden transcript," a critique of power existing as a sort of back-chat, spoken out of sight of the dominant.[3] Back-chat only becomes public, suggests Scott, in times of crisis or unusual stress. But back-chat is just that. Financial market actors take the rating agencies seriously. Market participants usually treat the rating agencies and their views as matters of considerable interest. What the raters think is important to people in the capital markets, because people in the markets believe that the rating agencies know what they are talking about.

In addition to respect for the agencies' reputation, there is also an awareness of the markets' influence on the agencies.[4] As Gary Jenkins, head of credit research at Barclays Capital, London, observed, "Love them or loathe them, if they did not

---

1. The ontology used here is based on work by Cox; see his "Social Forces, States, and World Orders: Beyond International Relations Theory," in Robert W. Cox with Timothy J. Sinclair, *Approaches to World Order* (Cambridge: Cambridge University Press, 1996), 85–123.

2. For example, the surveys undertaken by Cantwell and Company since 1997 (interview with Joseph E. Cantwell, New York City, March 2000); also see www.askcantwell.com.

3. James Scott, *Domination and the Arts of Resistance: Hidden Transcripts* (New Haven: Yale University Press, 1990), xii.

4. A recent confirmation of the growing importance of ratings can be found in the Japan Center for International Finance's 2001 survey on attitudes to bond rating, "Characteristics and Appraisal of Major Rating Companies (2001 ed.), 1; see www.jcif.or.jp/e_index.htm.

exist, we would have to invent them."[5] Even if a trader or a bond issuer does not respect a particular judgment, they might anticipate the effect of the agencies' judgment on others and may act on that expectation, rather than on their own views of the actual quality of the judgment. The intersubjective process described here is sometimes termed "Keynes' beauty contest," after J. M. Keynes' discussion of the similarities between financial market behavior and the tabloid newspaper beauty contests of the 1930s. In these competitions, the objective was not to guess who was the most attractive young woman but to approximate who was *generally thought to be* the prettiest by all competition entrants. On professional investment, Keynes argued, "We have reached the third degree where we devote our intelligences to anticipating what average opinion expects the average opinion to be."[6]

Rating agency outputs comprise an important part of capital market infrastructure. They are key benchmarks in the cognitive life of these markets—features of the marketplace—which form the basis for subsequent decision-making by participants. In this sense, rating agencies are important not so much for any particular rating they produce but for the fact that they are a part of the internal organization of the market. So, we find traders referring to a company as an "AA company," or to some other rating category, as if this were a fact, an agreed and uncontroversial way of describing and distinguishing companies, municipalities, or countries.[7]

The rationalist way to think about what rating agencies do is to see them as serving a function in the economic system. In this view, rating agencies solve the problems that develop in markets when banks no longer sit at the center of the borrowing process.[8] Rating agencies serve as "reputational intermediaries," like accountants, analysts, and lawyers, who are "essential to the functioning of the system" and monitor managers through a "constant flow of short-term snapshots."[9]

Another way to think about the agencies' function is to suggest they establish psychological "rules of thumb" that make market decisions less costly for participants.[10]

5. Jenkins quoted in Charles Batchelor, "Companies and Regulators Go on Offensive in the Global Ratings Game," *Financial Times*, July 5, 2003, 3.

6. John Maynard Keynes, *The General Theory of Employment Interest and Money* (London: Macmillan, 1936), 156.

7. In a 1992 interview, President Leo O'Neill of Standard & Poor's explained how bond traders would, on the one hand, dispute particular ratings with S&P and, on the other, refer to companies unproblematically as AA, A, and so on. Ratings were the common sense of the markets.

8. See, e.g., Richard S. Wilson, *Corporate Senior Securities: Analysis and Evaluation of Bonds, Convertibles, and Preferreds* (Chicago: Probus, 1987), 321–59; also see L. Macdonald Wakeman, "The Real Function of Bond Rating Agencies," in Joel M. Stern and Donald H. Chew, Jr., eds., *The Revolution in Corporate Finance*, 3rd ed. (Oxford: Blackwell, 1997), 25–28.

9. Peter Gourevitch, "Collective Action Problems in Monitoring Managers: The Enron Case as a Systemic Problem," *Economic Sociology—European Electronic Newsletter* 3, no. 3 (June 2002); 1, 11, available at www.siswo.uva.nl/ES, accessed June 12, 2002.

10. Jeffrey Heisler, "Recent Research in Behavioral Finance," *Financial Markets, Institutions and Instruments* 3, no. 5 (December 1994): 78; also see Jens Beckert, "What Is Sociological about Economic Sociology? Uncertainty and the Embeddedness of Economic Action," *Theory and Society* 25 (1996): 803–40.

A functionalist historical analogy can be drawn with the law merchant, who dispensed commercial law in medieval times. The role of the law merchant developed as a means of enforcing contracts through judgments on trade disputes and record-keeping of these actions made available for scrutiny by those engaging in intra-European trade. This mechanism backed up the reputation of traders when their names were not well known to potential new trade partners in geographically distant places, enabling, for example, a Burgundian trader in ribbons to sell to a Catalan haberdasher. Rating agencies share the information-provision and disciplinary characteristics of the law merchant. They, too, can be interpreted as part of a system that keeps an eye on who is violating the prevailing norms of financial and commercial practice.[11]

Serving a "function" does not mean the institutions are free of criticism. Kerwer has suggested that the enforcement function evident in the work of rating agencies complements prevailing "standards"—or expertise-based voluntary rules—about creditworthiness. But this only works when the standard-enforcer is also accountable, he points out. Because rating agencies are not themselves seriously regulated, an "accountability gap" exists in rating.[12] Kerwer concludes that there are insufficient incentives to maintain the agencies' functional focus.

The rating agencies have a strong interest in developing and preserving their eminence as sources of judgment. This interest gives the agencies incentives to be as helpful as possible to investors. Paradoxically, they also have an interest in avoiding full disclosure of their information sources and ways of forming judgments. The agencies seem intent on preserving a sense of mystery surrounding the rating process in general—and any rating in particular—so as to reinforce their role in the capital markets.

Purely functional explanations for the existence of rating agencies are potentially deceptive. Attempts to verify (or refute) the idea that rating agencies must exist because they serve a purpose have proven inconclusive. Rating agencies have to be considered important actors because people view them as important and act on the basis of that understanding—even if it proves impossible for analysts to actually isolate the specific benefits the agencies generate for these market actors.

Investors often mimic other investors, "ignoring substantive private information."[13] People may collectively view rating agencies as important, irrespective of

11. Paul R. Milgrom, Douglas C. North, and Barry R. Weingast, "The Role of Institutions in the Revival of Trade: The Law Merchant, Private Judges, and the Champagne Fairs," *Economics and Politics* 2, no. 1 (March 1990): 1–23; also see A. Claire Cutler, "Locating 'Authority' in the Global Political Economy," *International Studies Quarterly* 43, no. 1 (1998): 59–81, and *Private Power and Global Authority: Transnational Merchant Law in the Global Political Economy* (Cambridge, UK: Cambridge University Press, 2003).

12. Dieter Kerwer, "Rating Agencies: Setting a Standard for Global Financial Markets," *Economic Sociology—European Electronic Newsletter* 3, no. 3 (June 2002): 5.

13. David S. Scharfstein and Jeremy C. Stein, "Herd Behavior and Investment," *American Economic Review* 80, no. 3 (June 1990): 465.

what "function" the agencies are thought to serve. Markets and debt issuers therefore have strong incentives to act *as if* participants in the markets take the rating agencies seriously. In other words, the significance of rating is not to be estimated like a mountain or national population, as a "brute" fact that is true (or not) irrespective of shared beliefs about its existence, nor do the "subjective" facts of individual perception determine the meaning of rating.[14]

What is central to the status and consequentiality of rating agencies is what people believe about them and act on collectively, even if those beliefs are demonstrably false. Indeed, the beliefs may be quite strange to the observer, but if people use them as a guide to action (or inaction) they are significant. Dismissing such collective beliefs, as structural Marxists once did, as "false consciousness" misses the fact that actors must take account of social facts in considering their own action. Reflection about the nature and direction of social facts is characteristic of financial markets on a day-to-day basis. In investment, rating agencies are important most immediately because there is a collective belief that says the agencies are important and that people act on. Whether rating agencies actually add new information to the process does not negate their significance, understood in these terms.

Disintermediation

Changes in the financial markets have made people think the agencies are increasingly important. What banks do has undergone transformation under pressure from financial globalization.[15] A pattern of disembedded investment has increasingly emerged, at least for "large and respectable borrowers."[16]

What is disintermediation? Bank loans have traditionally been the dominant means through which funds were borrowed and lent. Banks acted as financial intermediaries in that they brought together suppliers and users of funds. They borrowed money, in the form of deposits, and lent money at their own risk to borrowers. Those who deposited money in banks and those who borrowed from them did not establish a contractual relationship with each other but with the bank.[17]

---

14. John Gerard Ruggie, *Constructing the World Polity: Essays on International Institutionalization* (New York: Routledge, 1998), 12–13; Ruggie draws on John Searle, *The Construction of Social Reality* (New York: Free Press, 1995). See also Peter L. Berger and Thomas Luckmann, *The Social Construction of Reality: A Treatise in the Sociology of Knowledge* (New York: Anchor, 1966).

15. See Franklin R. Edwards and Frederic S. Mishkin, "The Decline of Traditional Banking: Implications for Financial Stability and Regulatory Policy," *Federal Reserve Bank of New York Economic Policy Review* 1, no. 2 (July 1995): 27–45.

16. Daniel Verdier, *Moving Money: Banking and Finance in the Industrialized World* (Cambridge: Cambridge University Press, 2003), 17.

17. On the concept of disintermediation, see Graham Bannock and William Manser, *The Penguin International Dictionary of Finance*, 4th ed. (London: Penguin, 2003), 86; Timothy J. Sinclair, "Disintermediation," in R. J. Barry Jones, ed., *Routledge Encyclopedia of International Political Economy* (New York: Routledge, 2001), 355–56.

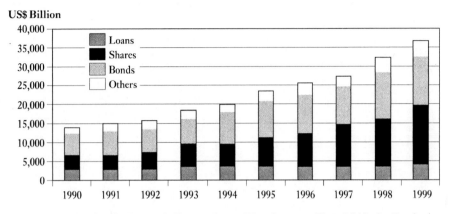

Figure 3. Trends in financial assets of institutional investors

Source: Organization for Economic Cooperation and Development, *Financial Market Trends*, No. 80, September 2001, p. 52.

Disintermediation has occurred on both sides of the balance sheet. Depositors are finding more attractive things to do with their money, just as borrowers have increasingly sought investment funds from sources other than banks. Mutual funds, which sweep depositors' money directly into financial markets, now contain $2 trillion in assets—not much less than the $2.7 trillion held in U.S. bank deposits.[18] In 1994, 28 percent of American households owned a mutual fund, up from 6 percent in 1980. However, the proportion of household assets held in bank deposits fell from 1980 to 1990, from 46 to 38 percent.

The shift on the borrowing side is just as marked. In 1970, commercial lending by banks made up 65 percent of the borrowing needs of corporate America. By 1992, the banks' share had fallen to 36 percent, with the balance made up of various securities.[19] Globally, bank lending decreased from 37 percent of total capital movements in the 1977–81 period to 14 percent in 1982–86. Portfolio investment, as opposed to direct forms of investment in plant and machinery, grew from 36 percent in 1972–76, to 65 percent of total investment in 1982–86. Most of this was funded through securities offerings.[20]

18. "Recalled to Life: A Survey of International Banking," *Economist*, April 30, 1994, 11.

19. Ibid.

20. These figures are taken from the International Monetary Fund, *Balance of Payments Yearbook* (Washington: International Monetary Fund, various years), as cited in Randall D. Germain, "From Money to Finance: The International Organization of Credit," paper presented to the 1992 annual meeting of the Canadian Political Science Association, Prince Edward Island, Canada, June 1992, 14.

Emerging markets were traditionally dominated by bank-intermediated financial systems.[21] But a surge in domestic corporate bond issuance has taken place, especially in Asia and Latin America since 1997. As the March 2003 *Global Financial Stability Report* noted, "Domestic corporate bond issuance rose from 5 percent of total corporate domestic and international funding in 1997–99 to 31 percent in 2000–01."[22] Domestic bank lending fell from 52 percent of corporate finance in 1997–99, to 40 percent in 2000–01. The authors of the report concluded that the trend to disintermediation is continuing.[23] In developing countries, the efficiency of capital market financing is strongly promoted by World Bank and IMF officials.[24]

While the tendency in financial markets is toward disintermediation, the speed of this process varies widely throughout the world.[25] Because of the shift from bank loans, stimulated in part by the advent of the Euro, the value of French corporate bonds grew from €2.5 billion in 1993 to €64 billion at the end of 2002.[26] In some places, despite the continued reliance on bank loans, "the trend is toward a disintermediated, liquid, securitized structure."[27] Even in Germany, the center of bank lending traditionalism, change is taking place.

In the 1990s, German banks tried to avoid the negative implications of global disintermediation for their market share by buying investment banks in London, through which they could participate in securities underwriting and trading. German companies are finding traditional bank lending inside Germany more expensive as local state-backed banks have had access to cheap capital "dramatically curtailed," making German credit more expensive.[28] In this liberalized financial market, German companies have to seek capital market funding (or go without).

21. International Monetary Fund, *Global Financial Stability Report: Market Developments and Issues*, March 2003 (Washington, D.C.: IMF, 2003), 75.

22. Ibid.

23. Ibid., 75, 11.

24. On the World Bank's encouragement of capital market growth in emerging markets, see Clemente del Valle, "Government and Private Bond Markets: 'The Virtuous Circle,' " paper presented to the 4th OECD/World Bank Bond Market Workshop on Developing Corporate Bond Markets, Washington, D.C., March 7, 2002; for the IMF, see Gerd Häusler, "The Globalization of Finance," *Finance & Development* 39, no. 1 (March 2002), available at www.imf.org, accessed April 28, 2003.

25. E.g., see Reinhard H. Schmidt, Andreas Hackethal, and Marcel Tyrell, "Disintermediation and the Role of Banks in Europe: An International Comparison," Working Paper no. 10, January 1998, J. W. Goethe University, Frankfurt, Fachbereich Wirtschaftswissenschaften.

26. Kevin J. Delaney, "France Inc. Is Fuming at Top Rating Agencies," *Wall Street Journal Europe*, November 20, 2002, M1.

27. International Monetary Fund, *International Capital Markets: Developments, Prospects, and Policy Issues* (Washington, D.C.: IMF, 1992), 2–3.

28. James Sproule, "What's Putting the Crunch on Germany?" *Wall Street Journal Europe*, September 1, 2003, A7.

With the trend to disintermediation, "the largest banks have shifted into other lines of business."[29] Banks are not withering away, but they are increasingly engaged in other financial services.[30] Banks remain banks in name, but the actual activities that define a bank are changing.[31] Today, bank lending is a small feature of the work of diversified financial services companies.[32] Thousands of banks that once made lending decisions on wholesale credit are now better described as financial market participants rather than market authorities. As the *Economist* suggested, "Banks have become increasingly market-based."[33] Banks "bundle assets (loans) into securities and trade them; increasingly, they earn income from fees as well as from interest."

Investment Forms

What is the significance of this new way of borrowing and lending capital depicted in figure 4? It produces norms and practices that tend to encourage a specific investment structure, at the same time raising the profile of the agencies and making them a focus of controversy.[34] Variation across nations has historically characterized investment forms. Zysman identifies three major sets of postwar financial arrangements.[35] The first of these, what he calls the capital market form, is typified by competitive price allocation, arm's length relations between government and industry, company-led market strategies, and the absence of conscious development policy. The second form, credit-based with government-administered prices, is designed to facilitate government intervention and state-led industrial adjustment. The last system Zysman identifies is a variant on the credit-based system, in which financial institutions use market power to influence industrial investment decisions by corporations. Zysman sees the United States as the best example of the first system, Japan and France as exemplifying the second, and Germany as an expression of the third.

29. Charles Gaa, Robert Ogrodnick, Peter Thurlow, and Stephen A. Lumpkin, "Future Prospects for National Financial Markets and Trading Centres," *Financial Market Trends* no. 78 (March 2001): 37–72, 52.

30. Biagio Bossone, "Do Banks Have a Future? A Study on Banking and Finance as We Move into the Third Millennium," *Journal of Banking and Finance* 25 (2001): 2239–76, 2260.

31. Banks increasingly seek to earn income from fees for services and the development of new analytical products rather than traditional lending activity. Rebecca Bream, "Banks at Forefront of Rise in Credit Products," *Financial Times*, December 29, 2000, 21.

32. "Crisis? What Crisis?" in "Capitalism and Its Troubles: A Survey of International Finance," *Economist*, May 18, 2002, 6.

33. "The Trouble with Banks," in "A Cruel Sea of Capital: A Survey of Global Finance," *Economist*, May 3, 2003, 12–14.

34. Timothy J. Sinclair, "Synchronic Global Governance and the International Political Economy of the Commonplace," in Martin Hewson and Timothy J. Sinclair, eds., *Approaches to Global Governance Theory* (Albany: State University of New York Press, 1999); and Delaney, November 20, 2002.

35. John Zysman, *Governments, Markets, and Growth: Financial Systems and the Politics of Industrial Change* (Ithaca: Cornell University Press, 1983), 18, 94.

Figure 4. Financing methods: Intermediation and disintermediation

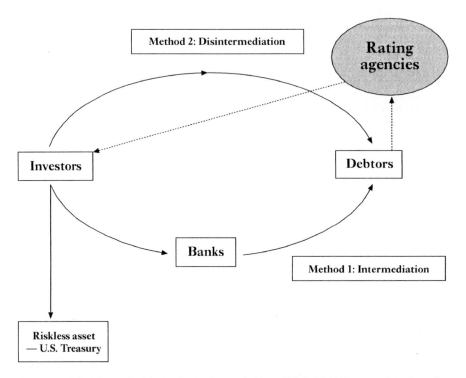

Source: Modified from Arie L. Melnik and Steven E. Plaut, "High-Yield Debt as a Substitute for Bank Loans," in Edward I. Altman (ed.) *The High-Yield Debt Market: Investment Performance and Economic Impact* (Homewood, IL: Dow Jones-Irwin, 1990), p. 211.

Within these sets of arrangements, two broad forms of investment can be identified: the *synchronic* and the *diachronic.* Saussure distinguishes the synchronic from the diachronic in his study of language.[36] The synchronic refers to the logic of a language, or the relations of coexistence among its elements. The diachrony of language seeks the origins and processes of language development.

These ideas were subsequently applied to social analysis by Sorel and, later, Piaget. Sorel linked the prominence of the synchronic study of all things with the maximizing proclivities of the newly emerging middle classes of his time.[37] Synchronic thought, Sorel argued, is best understood as a technology of accumulation.[38]

36. Ferdinand de Saussure, *Course in General Linguistics* (La Salle, Ill.: Open Court, 1983).
37. Georges Sorel, *Reflections on Violence,* trans. T. E. Hulme and J. Roth (New York: Collier, 1961), 141.
38. Piaget makes the case for understanding both the synchronic and the diachronic. But he argues that one does not necessarily follow the other, though the two are interconnected. (Jean Piaget, *Sociological Studies* [London: Routledge, 1995], 50).

The synchronic form is characteristically concerned with the short term and with the profits that can be accumulated in financial markets. The diachronic investment form links financial activity directly to investment in productive assets that improve the social stock of material capabilities. In broad terms, the United States, Britain, and other English-speaking countries fall into the synchronic category. Most European and emerging market countries are best characterized in diachronic terms. Rating agencies promote the tendency toward convergence around synchronic investment norms and, therefore, to a consolidation of the investment practices Zysman identifies.[39]

Zysman underestimates the degree to which the capital market is actually organized. The ascendant financial type can best be described as the *institutionalized capital market form*, in which rating agencies and related institutions construct an analytical basis for market transactions. These institutions promulgate synchronic norms. Market interactions that take place via the institutionalized capital market form typically reflect synchronic norms and thus are relevant in adapting policy frameworks in corporations, municipalities, and sovereign governments. Centralization of investment judgments is characteristic of institutionalized capital markets, even if a comparison of bank lending and capital markets at first suggests a less centralized system than a bank-dominated one. With this substantive centralization, operating assumptions are premised on synchronic norms.

Knowledge

Knowledge is a key element in the political economy of rating. Rating agencies produce knowledge that is socially and politically partial, and then objectify this knowledge, making it authoritative. In turn, rating knowledge takes on a particular, instrumental form consequential for all.

People think of knowledge as separate from social relationships, as neutral and abstract. But knowledge—its creation and the particular forms it assumes in different times and places—is a product of conflicts between social interests.[40] Research on epistemic communities, discussed in chapter 1, has highlighted the extent to which the intellectual work these communities undertake, such as problem identification and policy advice, represent efforts at social control over knowledge.[41]

39. On convergence (and the resilience of national capitalist models), see Suzanne Berger and Ronald Dore, eds., *National Diversity and Global Capitalism* (Ithaca: Cornell University Press, 1996).

40. See the discussion of science as an ideology in Jorge Larrain, *The Concept of Ideology* (Athens: University of Georgia Press, 1979), 14.

41. Peter M. Haas, "Epistemic Communities and International Policy Coordination," *International Organization* 46, no. 1 (Winter 1992): 2. The political significance of this activity is clarified by Diane Stone, *Capturing the Political Imagination: Think Tanks and the Policy Process* (London: Frank Cass, 1996).

Strange is also concerned with knowledge, how it is made and who benefits from it. She argues that a "knowledge structure" exists at the heart of the world economy, alongside other major structures associated with finance, production, and security.[42] Her view implies that rating knowledge becomes significant as knowledge, not so much because of its quality or informational value—but because it addresses issues that powerful social interests consider important.

Valuable knowledge—powerful knowledge—is so because it is socially validated. Knowledge is not inherently valuable or powerful but only when it is instrumental to, say, a specific phase of capitalist development. That is why knowledge of the Internet was valuable to young IT graduates in the mid-1990s but after the "dot.com" crash of the late 1990s, much less so. The knowledge itself did not change. How that knowledge fitted into capitalism did—dramatically.

Instrumental Knowledge

Rating agencies fit into a specific capitalist knowledge structure. Market participants view rating agencies as endogenous (rather than exogenous) to global finance.[43] Rating agencies are therefore seen by market participants as legitimate rather than imposed entities. In chapter one, we referred to this specific understanding of the nature and role of the agencies as embedded knowledge networks, the bigger set of mechanisms to which the rating agencies belong. How rating agencies construct, reinforce, and reconstruct this collective view of rating agencies as embedded knowledge networks is a crucial feature of global finance. The risk is that embedded knowledge networks lose their embedded identity as they move into new territories. As we will see, this is a constraint on the expansion of the major U.S. agencies into emerging markets (as it was for them in Europe).

The specific form of knowledge promoted by rating agencies is instrumental in character, focused on immediate gain rather than growth based on sustainable social reproduction. The instrumental form of knowledge is linked to a synchronic understanding of the world.

What are the characteristic elements of the synchronic, instrumental form of knowledge? There are two central principles. The first principle is the universalization of self-regulating markets and the exoticization of other modes of social interaction. Although never realized in the concrete, the notion of a self-regulating market, a market free from state interference and redistributive costs, has become a

---

42. Susan Strange, *States and Markets* 2nd ed. (London: Pinter, 1994), 30.

43. Granovetter, writing against the assumptions of the New Institutional Economics, emphasized endogeneity. He suggested that economic action is "embedded in ongoing networks of personal relations rather than carried out by atomized actors." In these circumstances, economic institutions (like all institutions) do not develop spontaneously but are constructed (Mark Granovetter, "Economic Institutions as Social Construction: A Framework for Analysis," *Acta Sociologica* 35 [1992]: 3–11, 4).

central organizing focus in Western societies since the 1970s. Other forms of social organization are, it seems, increasingly to be judged against this norm. The resurgence of the self-regulating market norm makes any sense of intentional community action open to question not on its merits but, more important, in principle.

The second principle of synchronic, instrumental knowledge is its tendency to identify time and space merely as obstacles, of no value, and therefore as problems to be overcome. Synchronic, instrumental knowledge is centrally concerned with faster turnover, just-in-time practices, the application of financial analysis tools such as the capital asset pricing model (CAPM), and the maximization of efficiency gains. However, the evaluation of investment opportunities using techniques like CAPM or discounted cash flow (DCF) analysis, to the exclusion of other types of information and forms of judgment, perhaps undervalues "less quantifiable strategic benefits," such as the acquisition of market share.[44]

Knowledge is a key dimension of the rating world. Rating knowledge is partial and political. Some knowledge is validated and considered a source of influence yet is represented as objective. The form of knowledge rating agencies use is synchronic and instrumental. The utilization of this knowledge form, when linked to the gatekeeping role of the agencies, is consequential. Those seeking the acclamation of the agencies have strong incentives to adopt the synchronic instrumental knowledge form, with attendant consequences.

Governance

> Most Americans think that the large, well-known credit rating organizations like Moody's and Standard & Poor's are purely private enterprises: they are unaware of the fact that these organizations are, in fact, more properly viewed as quasi-governmental entities.
>
> JONATHAN R. MACEY, U.S. Senate, March 20, 2002

It is one thing to claim that rating agencies are consequential at some times and in some places. It is another to claim that they are political in nature. How are ratings politically important? Macey's argument about the agencies' quasi-governmental status is significant here. But politics also influence the rating process.

Rating is not the technical activity it is thought popularly to be. Instead, it is highly indeterminate, qualitative, and judgment laden. Rating is, first and foremost, about creating an interpretation of the world and about the routine production of practical judgments based on that interpretation. This interpretation is made within the terms of the socialization and interests of rating agency officials, who are part of a wider financial and analytical community. The authoritative rather than persuasive

---

44. Michael T. Jacobs, *Short-Term America* (Boston: Harvard Business School Press, 1991), 179.

nature of bond rating conceals the qualitative processes of rating determination. Those processes, if widely known, would perhaps lead to a more skeptical use of rating information by investors.

Rating agencies do not limit their analysis to quantitative debt or income data, as people typically assume. Their view of management structure, policy, and the wider context of the issuer—all of which are contestable issues—make the credit rating process inherently a nondeductive matter. This judgment process implies gatekeeping, and gatekeeping is—even when not intended explicitly—manifestly political. Moreover, as discussed earlier, the bond rating agencies tend to promote specific frameworks of investment practices, knowledge forms, and governance systems. In any other context, these views would be readily recognizable as instances of political ideology.[45]

This book does not claim that rating agencies are biased or conspiratorial in their operations, although this may be the case at times. The argument is that the logic of rating is linked to a particular form of social organization and set of interests. It does not represent a universally beneficial system, as might be otherwise assumed. Raters try to avoid any hint of partiality and seek to appear as scientific as they can. Nor, for the most part, are rating officials cynical about this. As one senior rating official said, the "true believers" in the rating agencies think they really are neutral and objective. The "pragmatists," the informant observed, see what they are doing much more in terms of judgment and are skeptical about the potential for a truly objective or scientific view.[46] Certainly, raters are no more cynical than other groups who have sought to professionalize themselves and thereby acquire social standing and a bigger share of resources.[47]

Even if the work of rating agencies involved no interpretation or judgment, it would still not be "objective" in a wider sense. The rating mode of thought is premised on the assumptions of the given social and economic order. The significance of the cognitive frame used in credit rating becomes clearer in the context of international capital mobility. Credit rating serves as a vetting and surveillance system for capital mobility, allowing mobility to occur "securely" across geographic and cultural space. The agencies can be thought of as representing the interests of international or external capital to sovereign countries and corporations seeking capital. Andrews has argued that international capital mobility is a structure, which states encounter and must respond to, as they do the international

45. *Ideology* is used not in the sense of bias, untruth, or distorted ideas. The meaning adopted here follows Larrain, who suggests interests mobilize different ways of thinking. There is no universal or pan-social interest or knowledge. (Larrain, 1979).

46. Senior rating official, confidential source, New York City, April 2002.

47. On professionalization (and its links with knowledge), see Andrew Abbott, *The System of Professions: An Essay on the Division of Expert Labor* (Chicago: University of Chicago Press, 1988); and Harold Perkin, *The Third Revolution: Professional Elites in the Modern World* (New York: Routledge, 1996).

system of states.[48] In this structure, rating agencies serve an important policing role enforcing the needs of the structure and clarifying its signals to states, corporations, and municipalities.

There is a second sense in which we need to take rating agencies seriously in political terms, premised on this first argument about the partiality of rating judgments. That is, the judgments raters make have important distributional consequences for society. The agencies' output influences the global distribution of money, jobs, and economic opportunity. Hence, they are highly consequential actors in the global economy. What they say and do is too important for our collective global welfare to be considered nonpolitical. The "who gets what, when, how" questions of distribution are the sort of political questions that cannot be separated from a broader consideration of bond rating.[49] An insistence that rating agencies are not political is really an assertion that the market should be above social intervention. The partiality of such an affirmation needs little emphasis.

If rating agencies are political, do they also exercise power or something like power in their work? Rating agencies do, at times, exercise power in the common-sense definition of the term: A gets B to do what B would not otherwise do.[50] A less-understood feature of this power is the ability to define a situation as a crisis of creditworthiness, when the facts are really a matter of interpretation.[51] The relational form of power is complemented by a second, more significant form of power, which is structural. This exists when the perceived relational power of the agencies is anticipated by others who act in advance of the agencies' explicit judgments, to avoid any actual exercise of power. The idea of structural power does not capture the full extent of rating agency influence, however.

An altogether more hidden form of social control than either relational or structural power resides in the agencies' authority. The concept of authority is often used in a narrow, legal context to describe the legitimate, lawful status of an entity. That is not the usage here.

A key distinction in the concept of authority is between the epistemic authority of technical experts, scholars, and professionals, who are "an authority," and executive authority, of political leaders, military officers, and police forces, who are "in authority."[52] What both have in common characterizes the *auctoritas* of Roman law,

48. David M. Andrews, "Capital Mobility and State Autonomy: Toward a Structural Theory of International Monetary Relations," *International Studies Quarterly* 38, no. 2 (June 1994): 193–218.

49. Harold D. Lasswell, *Politics: Who Gets What, When, How* (Cleveland: World Publishing, 1958).

50. On power, see Steven Lukes, *Power: A Radical View* (London: Macmillan, 1974); John Scott, *Power* (Cambridge: Polity, 2001); and Sallie Westwood, *Power and the Social* (New York: Routledge, 2002).

51. On this process of crisis definition, see Davita Silfen Glasberg, *The Power of Collective Purse Strings: The Effect of Bank Hegemony on Corporations and the State* (Berkeley: University of California Press, 1989), 19.

52. Bruce Lincoln, *Authority: Construction and Corrosion* (Chicago: University of Chicago Press, 1994), 3–4.

namely, they produce "consequential speech" that quells doubts, winning the trust of audiences. Lincoln argues that the consequentiality of authoritative speech actually has little to do with the form or content of what is said. There is a hierarchy that allows some speakers to command not just audience attention but also their confidence, respect, and trust.

Lincoln concludes that historical circumstances are crucial to identifying the existence of authority. Authority is best understood as an effect of these circumstances, rather than as an entity or a characteristic of an actor or institution. Its existence is therefore not functional, easily understood through a rationalist lens, but always contingent on time, place, and circumstance. Capacities for producing these effects are central to understanding authority, as are understandings of who—what actors—have the capacity for producing the effect at specific times in particular places.[53]

The notion of authority, or epistemic authority, may suggest to some a system of relations in which no opposition is possible, in which the rating agencies control the views and actions of all who need their services. This is not the intention in using the concept. The authority of rating agencies is ambiguous and shifting, like other norms. In writing about the Italian-American community of East Harlem, Orsi discussed the role of the southern Italian notion of *rispetto*. Orsi suggested rispetto was "above all . . . a posture of obedience to authority."[54] Respect and fear were bound up together in the notion. But rispetto was a public posture, which often concealed disagreement. This private hostility Scott has called the "hidden transcript."[55] The important thing is that disagreement was rarely aired publicly, and the mask of rispetto was maintained. Rispetto is a good approximation of the fear-respect relations that exist between rating agencies and those dependent on their judgments.

Authority is not persuasion. The major rating agencies do not seek to persuade others to agree with their views. Indeed, as Lincoln suggests, "The exercise of authority need not involve argumentation and may rest on the naked assertion that the identity of the speaker warrants acceptance of the speech."[56] Persuasive efforts (and coercion, too) reveal a lack of authority. As Hannah Arendt observed, authority can be defined in contrast to both coercion and persuasion.[57] Persuasion and coercion are implicit within authority but are actualized only when authority itself is in jeopardy. Their explicit actualization gives a signal that, at least temporarily, authority is negated.[58]

53. Ibid., 10.
54. Robert Anthony Orsi, *The Madonna of 115th Street: Faith and Community in Italian Harlem, 1880–1950* (New Haven: Yale University Press, 1985), 93.
55. Scott, 1990, xii.
56. Lincoln, 1994, 5.
57. Arendt cited in David Miller, "Authority," in Miller, ed., *The Blackwell Encyclopaedia of Political Thought* (Oxford: Blackwell, 1991), 29. Arendt sets out her ideas about authority in *Between Past and Future: Six Exercises in Political Thought* (London: Faber and Faber, 1954).
58. Lincoln, 1994, 6.

Epistemic authority is not impermeable. The authority of rating agencies (or at least its scope) has expanded with the growth of capital markets and the decline of banks as major allocators of resources. Rating agencies have moved from a more persuasive role into that of epistemic authority, or embedded knowledge network. Persuasion implies a range of levels of respect. Epistemic authority is bivariate: authority either exists or is absent. By its very nature, it is hard to budge once generated, because market participants tend to discount the "mistakes" or epistemic failures of the agencies, given their identity as authorities. Of course, these resources could be overwhelmed by a persistent record of perceived failure or by a change in the relationship between raters and those who use ratings—a change in the structure of capitalism.

Rating agencies, especially Moody's and Standard & Poor's, worked hard to create a reputation for impartiality. In situations where people surrender their powers of judgment to an institution or to a group, the surrender may be quite fragile, as in the case of a fad or fashion.[59] Or, as the notion of rispetto suggests, it may be largely a public posture. The circumstances, including the longevity of the rating agencies, make their particular authoritative niche more resilient than that of most other nonstate institutions. Their position within the capital markets gives them considerable epistemic resources. Moreover, even if individuals do become skeptical about rating agencies, as often happens, they cannot necessarily assume others in the markets have, too. This risk gives skeptical individuals incentives to act based on the assumption that others also use the rating agencies as benchmarks, unless they know this definitely not to be the case.

What is missing in Lincoln's argument about authority is an understanding of the criteria that determine when the elements he identifies as the "right ones" actually become right. What generates authority is, as he suggests, a reflection of circumstances encountered and is therefore highly individuated. But the basic relationship between those with authority and those who acknowledge authority can be discerned. This relationship centers on the social efficacy of the ideas those claiming authority hold. In terms of foreign policy, it has been suggested, ideas "provide road maps that increase actors' clarity about goals or ends-means relationships."[60] This road map analogy establishes a concrete mechanism controlling the relationship between the authoritative and the nonauthoritative, which might otherwise seem nebulous.

Creditworthiness is a road map providing a mechanism for the relation between authority and nonauthority. Creditworthiness is both a causal belief—being creditworthy means that debt issuers are likely to repay their debts—and a principled

59. Sushil Bikchandani, David Hirshleifer, and Ivo Welch, "A Theory of Fads, Fashion, Custom, and Cultural Change as Informational Cascades," *Journal of Political Economy* 100, no. 5 (1992): 1016.

60. Judith Goldstein and Robert O. Keohane, "Ideas and Foreign Policy: An Analytical Framework," in Goldstein and Keohane, eds., *Ideas and Foreign Policy: Beliefs, Institutions, and Political Change* (Ithaca: Cornell University Press, 1993), 3.

belief, in that placing a priority on repaying debt is morally right and obligatory. As a belief, creditworthiness becomes embedded in rules and norms, that is, institutionalized, acting like other beliefs in the manner of "invisible switchmen" to "constrain public policy" by "turning action onto certain tracks," thus obscuring other tracks from view.[61] Katzenstein suggests that institutionalized norms like creditworthiness do not merely influence behavior by prescribing ends but also indirectly organize action.[62] How creditworthiness came to be institutionalized like this is a fascinating question, requiring what Goldstein and Keohane call an "archaeology of ideas."[63] In any case, the mechanism is not monolithic. As Katzenstein warns, norms remain contested and contingent.

In an insightful analysis of financial auditing, Michael Power makes an argument similar to Goldstein and Keohane's about semantic or programmatic effects.[64] The subject cannot be reduced merely to the technocratic and the functional, he argues. Auditing is "implicated in the framing of organizational life," contributing a style of evaluation or self-monitoring that underpins how organizations work. Like rating, auditing involves a "certain obscurity in the professional craft," which contributes to its monopoly privilege. Practitioners defend this obscurity against codification, to preserve their scope for judgment.

Unlike intellectuals, auditors—and raters, too—do not invite public dialog, debate, or democratic deliberation. Audit reports, like ratings, are labels. By virtue of a rhetoric of "neutrality, objectivity, dispassion, expertise," reports and ratings do not communicate passively but tell or as Power says, "give off" an understanding or view premised on trust in experts—authorities. But this understanding is not meant for public deliberation. Like an auditor, a rater has emerged "not just as one who exercises expert judgement but also as one who is in the role of judge."[65]

Two more specific claims about governance and rating agencies are addressed in this discussion: first, nonstate forms of governance increasingly matter in the contemporary world, and second, the forms of governance rating agencies "encourage" contribute to patterns of public and private policymaking.

As we have seen, bond rating agencies are unusual entities to consider politically. They are privately owned and not directly involved in electoral politics. The analysis is different from that for legislatures, regulatory agencies, or political parties, even though the agencies are also subject to constraints relating to their organizational character. No doubt, many of the conceptual tools applied to public bureaucracies could be used to establish a better understanding of them, too (if the same

61. Ibid., 12.
62. Peter J. Katzenstein, "Coping with Terrorism: Norms and Internal Security in Germany and Japan," in Goldstein and Keohane, eds., 1993, 267.
63. Ibid., 21.
64. Michael Power, *The Audit Society: Rituals of Verification* (Oxford: Oxford University Press, 1997). Peter Katzenstein and Dieter Kerwer separately suggested Power's book to me.
65. Ibid., 8, 74, 127, 40.

sort of internal data was available). However, a critical first evaluation of bond rating agencies must get at the governance outputs they produce. What is it about the
type of institution rating agencies represent that is different from those political scientists more usually analyze?

Governance focuses on the processes associated with the exercise of control
rather than on administrative mechanisms considered in abstraction.[66] In the orthodox view, transactions are understood to occur exclusively in the realm of the market, and legal authority is a feature of governments. However, this orthodoxy is less
persuasive in the contemporary world. A more effective conception acknowledges
that nonstate forms of governance have always been important but that financial
globalization has made these institutions and networks more central to capitalism.
Their interactions with each other and with states are essential to an understanding
of contemporary governance.

Ferguson and Mansbach contend that states are less important as a result of "historical sea changes," which have displaced one form of political organization from
"pride of place" in our world.[67] Limitation of authority to the legally binding actions
of governments is no longer persuasive. Instead, they suggest the idea of *"effective
governance"* is more useful today.[68]

Miller and Rose endorse this concern.[69] They add that "technologies of
thought," such as writing, numbering, compiling, and computing, render a realm
knowable, calculable, and thus governable. This notion is clearly applicable to the
world of rating. "Procedures of inscription" make objects like the economy and the
firm amenable to intervention and regulation. Such "humble and mundane mechanisms," combined with interventionary policy goals (what Miller and Rose call
"programs of government"), have over time dissolved the distinction between state
and civil society. What has been most vital are the ways in which these indirect mechanisms of rule have enabled *"government at a distance"* to be maintained. This form
of domination involves "intellectual mastery," based on the possession of critical
information, by those at the center over persons and events distant from them.[70] The
objective of rule at a distance is to create a framework in which social forces are self-
regulating within the norms of the system.

Rating agencies have an impact on the governance undertaken by other institutions. Financial globalization has created an unprecedented degree of volatility in

66. James N. Rosenau, "Governance in the Twenty-First Century," *Global Governance* 1, no. 1
(1995): 13.

67. Yale H. Ferguson and Richard W. Mansbach, "Between Celebration and Despair: Construc-
tive Suggestions for Future International Theory," *International Studies Quarterly* 35, no. 4
(December 1991): 371.

68. Ibid., 376.

69. Peter Miller and Nikolas Rose, "Governing Economic Life," *Economy and Society* 19, no. 1
(February 1990): 2, and "Political Power beyond the State: Problematics of Government," *British
Journal of Sociology* 43, no. 2 (June 1992): 173–205.

70. Ibid., 1990, 5, 8, 9.

socioeconomic circumstances. One response to this has been initiatives to separate central bank monetary policy from legislative intervention and to establish "fiscal responsibility acts," as in the case of New Zealand, which set out principles for "prudent" fiscal policy.[71] Another response has been a shift in emphasis between what have come to be called "fire alarm" and "police patrol"-type surveillance forms.[72] The fire alarm metaphor refers to a problem-focused, episodic approach to governance. Municipal fire departments give problems like fires attention only when they have been identified and called in by nonspecialists. A framework is established—fires are reported by those who see them—that requires only occasional enforcement. Inspections are infrequent (perhaps annually), and the emphasis is on self-regulation in self-interest. In the case of police patrols, a much more aggressive process of looking for law-breaking is characteristic. The idea is that many problems never mature into crises because of surveillance and early intervention.

Although fire alarm approaches may be cheaper in cost-benefit terms, police patrol surveillance is attractive when the immediate costs of disgovernance are very high and losses are "lumpy"—what Hubert calls low-probability, high-consequence risk. An example of the latter is when a major bond issuer unexpectedly defaults and a crisis of confidence arises in financial markets as a whole.[73]

Public institutions seem to be increasingly moving from the police patrol to the fire alarm approach, under fiscal and competitive deregulation pressures from financial globalization. Paradoxically, a tightening of governance is developing in the private realm, as institutions with the capacity for governance seek to compensate for the risks and opportunities change creates. Rating agencies are part of this tightening.

Rating agencies adjust the "ground rules" inside international capital markets and thereby shape the organization and behavior of institutions seeking funds. This anticipation effect is reflected in capital market participants' understandings of the agencies' expectations. In turn, from this point of origin, business and policy initiatives are developed. This coordination, or government-at-a-distance effect, narrows the expectations of creditors and debtors to a shared set of norms derived from the prevailing orthodoxy about corporate governance and public policy structures. Thus, the agencies do not just constrain the broad capital markets, but they actually

71. "The Great Escape?" *Economist*, April 1, 1995, 60.

72. Mathew D. McCubbins and Thomas Schwartz, "Congressional Oversight Overlooked: Police Patrols versus Fire Alarms," in McCubbins and Sullivan, eds., *Congress: Structure and Policy* (Cambridge: Cambridge University Press, 1987), 427.

73. Don Hubert, "Popular Responses to Global Insecurity: Public Encounters with Low-Probability High-Consequence Risk," paper presented to the annual meeting of the International Studies Association, Chicago, February 1995; also see Virginia Haufler, "Learning to Cope: International Risk Management in History," paper presented to the annual meeting of the International Studies Association, Chicago, February 1995; Ulrich Beck, *Risk Society: Towards a New Modernity*, trans. Mark Ritter (Newbury Park, Calif.: Sage, 1992); and Anthony Giddens, *Modernity and Self-Identity: Self and Society in the Late Modern Age* (Cambridge, UK: Polity, 1991).

exert significant pressures on market participants, contributing to their internal constitution or identity as market agents.

Mental Framework of Rating Orthodoxy

The purpose of a mental framework of rating orthodoxy, presented in table 5, is to clarify the fundamental assumptions underlying rating, set out here in ideal-typical form. Fundamental principles central to the agencies—orthodox, synchronic principles—are contrasted with a heterodox, diachronic set. Like the first set, the second is not exhaustive but merely indicates the diversity of conceivable thinking.

The framework is a codified version of the "rating myth." Myth, as Meyer and Rowan and Power have noted, is a key to understanding why institutions are organized as they are and operate as they do. The components of the rating myth within the mental framework of rating orthodoxy should be seen as a set of norms for the agencies' work.

Conclusions

What is rating? In a narrow sense, rating is simply a technical support system for the new global capital markets. In a broader view, bond rating is much more than a technical support system. It is the archetype of a new form of institutional coordination developing in conditions of financial globalization. Based in markets rather than formal governmental structures, bond rating is at odds with the consensus that underpinned the post–World War II political economy of embedded liberalism. That postwar world order was built on a compromise between producer and consumer, owner and worker, investor and employee.[74] The work of bond rating agencies, as the mental framework of rating orthodoxy suggests, implicitly attacks these compromises and promotes the interests of investors, as interpreted and constructed by the rating agencies.[75]

Rating agencies should be understood therefore as a crucial nerve center in the world order, as a nexus of neoliberal control.[76] Like an operating system in a personal

74. John Gerrard Ruggie, "Embedded Liberalism and the Postwar Economic Regimes," in Ruggie, *Constructing the World Polity: Essays on International Institutionalization* (New York: Routledge, 1998); also see Mark Rupert, *Producing Hegemony: The Politics of Mass Production and American Global Power* (Cambridge: Cambridge University Press, 1995); and Robert W. Cox, *Production, Power, and World Order: Social Forces in the Making of History* (New York: Columbia University Press, 1987).

75. On the interests of investors, see Adam Harmes, "Institutional Investors and the Reproduction of Neoliberalism," *Review of International Political Economy* 5, no. 1 (Spring 1998): 92–121.

76. Kees van der Pijl, *Transnational Classes and International Relations* (New York: Routledge, 1998), 5.

Table 5. The mental framework of rating orthodoxy

		Synchronic-rationalist principles (orthodoxy)	Diachronic-constructivist principles (heterodoxy)
Investment	•	Ratings are the result of rational professional processes.	• Ratings are the result of judgments.
	•	Emphasis on short-terms returns and the specification of liabilities.	• Emphasis on sustainable growth in environment of collective absorption of risk.
	•	Valuation of profit-making as means of repayment. May take place in production or financial markets.	• Valuation of profit-making and taxation as means of repayment, based on investment in productive capabilities and social infrastructure.
Knowledge	•	Knowledge is objective, cross-cultural and instrumental.	• Social dynamics are central to the creation, content and eminence granted to different knowledges.
	•	Markets are natural and sponta-neous, not social phenomena.	• Markets are social phenomena
	•	Technical expertise is essential to creation of knowledge. All knowl-edge producers are equal and are only as good as their last output. Competition between sources of knowledge negates any perverse social dynamic to falsely accord eminence to knowledge producers.	• Reputation, based on experience, underpins epistemic authority (e.g. embedded knowledge net-works). All knowledge producers are not equal—the intersubjective identity of a knowledge producer as an epistemic authority gives authority to this knowledge pro-ducer's subsequent output (good or bad).
Governance	•	Rating is not political.	• Rating is political.
	•	Rating challenges historically-derived norms and practices assumed to inhibit efficient resource allocation.	• Emphasis on valid role of multiple stakeholders and the social distri-bution of costs and benefits.
	•	Emphasis on self-regulatory "police patrol"-type systems. Priva-tization may result. This is seen as politically neutral.	• Influence of rating establishes potential for government-at-a-distance.

computer, rating agencies, although usually unseen, monitor global life at the high-est levels, with important social and political effects. In conditions of financial glob-alization, rating agencies serve as intelligence-gathering, data-analyzing mechanisms.

The mid-range arguments made in chapter 1 were developed here conceptually and empirically. The ideas presented here, as captured by the rating orthodoxy framework, provide the analytical core for the following substantive chapters. Rat-ing incorporates both quantitative and qualitative variables. It is crucial to acknowl-edge this, for much of the commentary in the financial media passes over the inherent indeterminacy of bond rating. What follows from this observation that ratings are judgments is that rating is more contestable than it at first appears.

Particular solutions to problems, such as how to fund the construction and maintenance of a bridge, can have very different answers. Some answers, such as funding from general revenue, bias the distribution of resources toward certain groups (such as drivers) and away from others (e.g., taxpayers). Other solutions, such as the imposition of tolls, target all who drive over a bridge but negatively affect low-income people, whose mobility is reduced accordingly. These distributional effects are key political consequences of rating, but they rarely receive acknowledgment.

What are some consequences of this new form of power? Rating agencies and the rating process provide a means for transmitting policy and managerial orthodoxy to widely scattered governments and corporations. In this sense, the agencies are nominally private makers of a global public policy. They are agents of convergence who, along with other institutions, try to enforce "best practice" or "transparency" around the globe. The rating agencies are promoters of an American-derived, synchronic mental framework. The most significant effect of rating agencies is not, therefore, their view of budget deficits or some other specific policy but their influence on how issuers assess problems in general. This adjustment of mental schemata is the most consequential impact of their work.

CHAPTER FOUR

Rating Corporations

> Swiss bankers are trained to believe that there is a higher goal than
> making profits. Their priority has been to retain "triple A" credit
> ratings, the *badge of good banking.*
>
> ROBERT PRESTON, *Financial Times,* 1992

T he three supporting arguments about debt rating are germane to the
rating of corporations. What are the implications of investment judgment centralization
in the corporate world? In what ways does the rating of corporate bonds demonstrate
the subjectivity of the rating process and the dominance of instrumental knowledge?
How significant is rating to the activities and organization of market institutions? What
ideas are articulated in corporate rating, and how best should these be interpreted?

In pursuing these questions, the counterfactual method introduced in chapter 1 is
used to contrast rationalist and constructivist accounts. In counterfactual analysis, the
factor thought most likely to be causal in the phenomena under consideration is
excluded from a second, alternative scenario. In these changed causal conditions, if a
different result seems likely, it is probable that the correct causal element was identified
in the initial analysis. In developing these scenarios, principles derived from the opposing
dimension of the mental framework of rating orthodoxy (table 5 in chapter 3) are
deployed. So, if a synchronic-rationalist argument is developed as the primary analysis,
diachronic-constructivist principles inform the second, counterfactual scenario.

Investment

> The kind of bonds which I want to be connected with are those which can be recommended
> without a shadow of a doubt, and without the least subsequent anxiety, as to
> payment of interest, as it matures.[1]

1. J. P. Morgan, quoted in Ron Chernow, *The House of Morgan: An American Banking Dynasty
and the Rise of Modern Finance* (New York: Simon and Schuster, 1991), 37.

The following analysis of investment in relation to corporate rating has three elements: the relationship between rating levels and the typical cost of debt, the nature of the agencies' power, and the agencies' scrutiny of the automobile industry.

Rating and the Cost of Debt

Ratings affect the cost of issuing debt. Other things being equal, shifts in prevailing interest rates determine the price that issuers must offer to attract funds into their market away from other investment opportunities, such as Treasury bonds, the stock market, and real estate. The particular characteristics of the debt instrument itself also influence its cost; for example, whether a bond is backed by a sinking fund, in which the issuing company sets aside revenue for debt repayment.[2] However, apart from interest rates and these other issues, the primary factor that distinguishes between different bonds is the creditworthiness of the issuer.

The effect of rating can be understood by comparing the cost of rated and unrated debt, and the difference in yield spread in basis points between highly rated and lower-rated issues. One study indicated that getting a rating can create savings of $0.66 million on a $200 million bond issue, over a twenty-year term.[3] Although there is little disagreement about this effect, there is controversy about the impact of subsequent downgrades on yield spreads. It is often unclear whether the market has already anticipated the rating agency's actions and discounted the issuers' creditworthiness by the time the agency makes an announcement.[4] In any case, it is clear that rating has a major influence on the cost of capital to corporations that issue debt.

Rating Power in the Corporate World

The rating constraint and the relatively high interest rates banks charge on loans led to the re-emergence of a high-yield (or junk bond) market in the late 1970s. That market was based in part on the work of Michael Milken, formerly of the investment firm Drexel Burnham Lambert. Milken's arguments about capital access and the credit rating system and his activities as the "junk bond king" during the "junk bond decade" (1977–87) remain the subject of considerable dispute.[5]

During his graduate education at the University of Pennsylvania's Wharton School in Philadelphia, Milken read W. Braddock Hickman's work on returns in the bond market.[6] Hickman claimed that low-grade or junk bonds promised high

2. Staff of the New York Institute of Finance, *How the Bond Market Works*, 1988, 175–76.
3. Study by Stephen Dafoe, analyst, Canadian Bond Rating Service, Montreal, June 1992.
4. Interview with Brian I. Neysmith, president, Canadian Bond Rating Service, Montréal, June 16, 1992.
5. See, e.g., Benjamin J. Stein, *A License to Steal: The Untold Story of Michael Milken and the Conspiracy to Bilk the Nation* (New York: Simon & Schuster, 1992).
6. W. Braddock Hickman, *Corporate Bond Quality and Investor Experience* (Princeton: Princeton University Press, 1958).

yields when held in large numbers in a diversified portfolio by "large permanent investors." He suggested that these returns more than compensated for the additional default risk of the lower-rated debt.[7] A recent study, which incorporates data from the junk decade, has drawn the stronger conclusion that in the context of a well-diversified portfolio, the risk of lower-grade bonds was actually "no greater" than that of investment grade bonds.[8]

According to Bailey, Milken formed the view that ratings had, over time, "become moral absolutes" among investors.[9] The view that ratings are really judgments, as in the diachronic-constructivist account, had been firmly displaced by the orthodox notion, derived from the synchronic-rationalist account, that ratings are the result of rational professional processes. Following some of Hickman's conclusions, Milken observed that downgraded bonds "were held in more contempt by investors than they deserved to be." Like some of the investment trade journal writers of the time, Bailey claims Milken saw that the primary problem with the ratings process was that it was too much based on past performance. However, bonds were obligations for future payment, and even an AAA rating was "no guarantee" against a subsequent default. According to Bailey, Milken frequently observed that of the twenty-three thousand U.S. companies with sales of more than $3 million, only 5 percent could secure investment grade ratings. The rest had to turn to bank or insurance company loans, with their higher interest rates, short-term maturities, and restrictive covenants, or to equity, which was yet more expensive and meant diluting corporate control.[10]

Milken saw two major problems with the historical approach the agencies used. First, their focus was on assets and liabilities, or debt/equity ratio analysis, when in his view cash flow really determined a company's ability to service its debt, given that holdings of current debt were always refinanced. Second, he believed the agencies were not really interested in the "intangibles" of corporate performance he thought so important: management skill, strategic thinking, and innovation.[11] This rationale underpinned Milken's promotion of junk bonds to clients. He endeavored to show there was more value in these bonds than the agencies, other investors, or even their issuers had believed.

7. Ibid., 26.

8. Marshall E. Blume and Donald B. Keim, "Risk and Return Characteristics of Lower-Grade Bonds, 1977–1987," in Edward I. Altman, ed., *The High-Yield Debt Market: Investment Performance and Economic Impact* (Homewood, Ill.: Dow Jones-Irwin, 1990), 15.

9. Fenton Bailey, *The Junk Bond Revolution: Michael Milken, Wall Street and the Roaring Eighties* (London: Fourth Estate, 1991), 25.

10. Ibid., 25, 26, 29.

11. Jesse Kornbluth, *Highly Confident: The Crime and Punishment of Michael Milken* (New York: William Morrow, 1992), 41; also see Bailey, 1991, 29, and Robert Sobel, *Dangerous Dreamers: The Financial Innovators from Charles Merrill to Michael Milken* (New York: John Wiley, 1993), 70.

Milken's career as a bond underwriter and trader came to a close in late 1988, when he was charged and later convicted of a series of SEC disclosure violations, spending two years in a U.S. federal penitentiary.[12]

According to Toffler, Milken attempted to establish a new order in the financial industry. As Toffler saw it, the industry was "hidebound and protected" and a "major barrier to change." Only smokestack, blue-chip industrial "dinosaurs" could get long-term investment capital, because the two rating services "guarded the gates of capital."[13] Toffler observed that conflict between those (like J. P. Morgan) who wanted to "restrict access to capital so that they themselves could control it," and those like Milken, who supposedly sought a "democratization of capital," has a long history in the United States and elsewhere.[14] Whatever Milken's motivations, the result of the initiative of Milken and others, as Grant has noted, was that "marginal" borrowers "received the benefit of the doubt" in the 1980s.[15] This tendency threatened to foster an "emerging power structure" that would change the "game," as Grant put it.[16] According to Bruck, "Milken had long professed contempt for the corporate establishment . . . whose investment grade bonds, as he loved to say, could move in only one direction—down."[17]

The broader movement to change credit standards posed a challenge to established relationships on Wall Street and in corporate America. In ten years at Drexel, Milken had raised $93 billion, and the junk bond market had grown to $200 billion, serving more than one-thousand, five hundred companies.[18]

Milken was no revolutionary. He was a critic of prevailing assumptions about securities and their creditworthiness, applying his own understanding of the diachronic-constructivist principles elaborated in table 5. Although never spelled out in a systematic way, his analysis, following Hickman, was actually a social one. That is, he saw the judgmental and interpretive content in the agencies' rating processes.

During the 1980s, lobbying efforts to review high-yield financing were launched, organized by the Business Roundtable (representing the Fortune top 200 corporations), the American Petroleum Institute, and others. Thirty-seven U.S. states subsequently passed restrictive legislation to control leveraged buyouts. Congressional testimony into junk financing suggested that Milken's indictment sealed the fate of

12. Sobel, 1993, 215.

13. Alvin Toffler, *Powershift: Knowledge, Wealth, and Violence at the Edge of the Twenty-First Century* (New York: Bantam, 1990), 44–47. (Stephen Gill suggested the relevance of Toffler's work.)

14. Ibid., 49–50.

15. James Grant, *Money of the Mind: Borrowing and Lending in America from the Civil War to Michael Milken* (New York: Farrar Straus Giroux, 1992), 437.

16. Ibid., 393, quoting a *Business Week* article, "Power of Wall Street," July 1986.

17. Connie Bruck, *The Predators' Ball: The Inside Story of Drexel Burnham and the Rise of the Junk Bond Traders* (New York: Penguin, 1989), 12.

18. Glenn Yago, *Junk Bonds: How High Yield Securities Restructured Corporate America* (New York: Oxford University Press, 1991), 25.

Drexel's high-yield operations and the use of junk bonds to finance LBOs.[19] Wyss observed that the tax deductibility of interest paid on debt and the nondeductibility of dividend payments (on equity) established an incentive structure that favored debt growth in corporate America. Milken's operation was built on these incentives and was evolving into a relationship finance system similar to what Zysman observed in Germany. This would be "inconceivable" in the United States, and "possibly illegal." Milken's indictment put a stop to this development. Wyss suggested that the "indictment said to the market, you cannot shift in this direction."[20]

The testimony of rating agency officials revealed their opposition to what they called the "extreme financial leverage" attributable to the junk bond financing of LBOs in the late 1980s.[21] Bachmann emphasized probable constraints on innovation, as well as the tendency of managers to sell assets and skimp on strategic planning under such heavy debt loads.[22] Grant, a noted Wall Street newsletter publisher and writer, cast the net wider in his testimony. As he saw things, in the 1980s, "Every American with a mailbox was invited to borrow."[23] He blamed this "explosion of the credit supply" on "the long-standing tendency toward the socialization of credit risk that had its roots in the reforms of the early 1930s." Milken had to be understood, Grant implied, in terms of a profligate US government whose net worth in 1988 was negative $2.5 trillion.[24] As Wyss noted in response to questions, the government had subsidized junk-financed LBOs as well. First, it had allowed deductibility of interest payments.[25] Second, it had required pension funds' equity assets (but not fixed-income or debt assets) to be marked down to current market value rather than nominal or book value.[26]

Milken applied heterodox principles to rating, based on an implicit diachronic-constructivist understanding of the rating agencies and their work in the 1970s and 1980s. The effect was to contribute to the disintermediation of U.S. finance, a

19. Testimony of David A. Wyss, senior vice president, DRI/McGraw Hill, "High Yield Debt Market/Junk Bonds," hearing before the Subcommittee on Telecommunications and Finance of the Committee on Energy and Commerce, House of Representatives, 101st Cong., 2nd sess., March 8, 1990 (Washington, D.C.: U.S. Government Printing Office, 1990), 3–4.

20. Ibid., 7, 8, 3–4, 42.

21. Testimony of Mark Bachmann, senior vice president, Corporate Finance Department, Standard & Poor's Ratings Group, "High Yield Debt Market/Junk Bonds," hearing before the Subcommittee on Telecommunications and Finance of the Committee on Energy and Commerce, House of Representatives, 101st Cong., 2nd sess., March 8, 1990 (Washington, D.C.: U.S. Government Printing Office, 1990), 12.

22. Ibid., 13.

23. Testimony of James Grant, *Grant's Interest Rate Observer,* "High Yield Debt Market/Junk Bonds," hearing before the Subcommittee on Telecommunications and Finance of the Committee on Energy and Commerce, House of Representatives, 101st Cong., 2nd sess., March 8, 1990 (Washington, D.C.: U.S. Government Printing Office, 1990), 18.

24. Ibid., 22.

25. Wyss, March 8, 1990, 34.

26. Ibid., 46–47.

process that actually expanded the agencies' potential scope of operations. Ironically, if Milken's purpose was to break out of an orthodoxy, the longer-term implication of what he did was to hasten the centralization of finance around debt issuance, for a wider range of companies. Although an immediate problem for the agencies, this challenge had much the same effect as the Asian financial crisis: the rating system did not displace centralization but instead increased its reach.

In a counterfactual scenario, the absence of Milken's alternative intellectual road map about rating and its efficacy would have retarded efforts to build a junk bond market. Disintermediation would have advanced less rapidly because lower-grade companies would have had to finance their operations through bank loans. Rating agencies would be important for a smaller group of companies, the investment centralization process would be less advanced, and the agencies would be less powerful than they otherwise became.

Rating and the Automobile Industry

Rating agencies can at times be understood to "directly intervene in the affairs of a corporation."[27] A useful example of this power is the effect of rating downgrades on U.S. automakers, including General Motors (GM) and the Ford Motor Company. These cases do not support an argument that the ratings made were "wrong" or otherwise deficient. Instead, by showing the impact of the agencies through ratings, these cases support the claims about investment centralization identified as the first mid-range argument. As argued in the preceding chapters, power and politics are not synonymous with institutionalized politics but pervade social and economic life. In a diachronic-constructivist view of the agencies, ratings are an exercise of power prior to considering the consequences of specific ratings.

At the end of 1991, GM announced a "disastrous $4.5 billion loss" on operations.[28] Subsequently, the corporation declared that it would close twenty-one plants and cut seventy-four thousand jobs.[29] According to Cox, this action "was intended, by appearing as a token of the corporation's intention to increase competitiveness, to deter a downgrading of its bond rating which would have increased the corporation's cost of borrowing."[30] The perceived threat of a downgrade was reinforced by the *Wall Street Journal*, which noted that the potential rating reduction had "hung

27. Beth Mintz and Michael Schwartz, "Sources of Intercorporate Unity," in Schwartz, ed., *The Structure of Power in America: The Corporate Elite as a Ruling Class* (New York: Holmes & Meier, 1987), 30.

28. Kathleen Kerwin, James B. Treece, and Zachary Schiller, "GM Is Meaner, But Hardly Leaner," *Business Week,* October 19, 1992, 30.

29. Joseph B. White and Bradley A. Stertz, "GM's Debt is Downgraded by Moody's," *Wall Street Journal,* January 8, 1992, A2.

30. Robert W. Cox, "Global Restructuring: Making Sense of the Changing International Political Economy," in Richard Stubbs and Geoffrey R.D. Underhill, eds., *Political Economy and the Changing Global Order* (Toronto: McClelland & Stewart, 1994), 48.

heavily" over Robert C. Stempel, GM's chairman, and had "pushed" him to speed restructuring plans.[31] However, Stempel's strategy did not work. The corporation was downgraded by Moody's in January 1992, and by Standard & Poor's in March of that year.[32] In explaining their action, Moody's officials said the automaker's restructuring plans were unlikely to solve its competitive problems.[33]

Pressure on GM from the agencies did not end with these downgradings. According to Judith H. Dobrzynski of *Business Week,* "The prospect of sinking credit ratings that would deny it access to equity and commercial paper, eventually prompted independent directors" to pressure GM's "old guard," as personified by Chairman Stempel, to quit in late October 1992.[34] Subsequently, the agencies issued further warnings of downgrades, including the possibility that GM's debt might be relegated to junk bond status.[35] The agencies subsequently acknowledged improvement in GM's operating performance. But what seems to have led the agencies to further downgrades in late November 1992 and February 1993 were unfunded pension and medical benefit liabilities. These liabilities threatened to seriously compromise GM's balance sheet.[36] As S&P observed,

> Servicing its massive benefits obligations will be a substantial drain on the company's financial resources—and a significant competitive disadvantage—for the foreseeable future. . . . GM's unfunded pension liability increased to $14.0 billion at year-end 1992, from $8.4 billion one year earlier. . . . The company has reported a retiree medical liability of $24 billion. . . . Adjusting for these liabilities effectively eliminates GM's consolidated net worth.[37]

Fearing this sort of judgment, which hampered General Motors Acceptance Corporation (GM's finance company subsidiary) by raising the cost of commercial

31. White and Stertz, 1992.
32. Joseph B. White, "General Motors Debt Ratings Are Cut by S&P," *Wall Street Journal,* March 16, 1992, A2.
33. White and Stertz, 1992.
34. Judith H. Dobrzynski, "A GM Postmortem: Lessons for Corporate America," *Business Week,* November 9, 1992, 87; Kathleen Kerwin, James B. Treece and Zachary Schiller, "Crisis at GM: Turmoil at the Top Reflects the Depth of it Troubles," *Business Week,* November 9, 1992, 84.
35. Joseph B. White, "S&P Issues New Warning on GM Stock," *Wall Street Journal,* November 12, 1992, A3.
36. Ibib., Joseph B. White and Neal Templin, "GM to Disclose More Details on Pension Gap," *Wall Street Journal,* November 16, 1992, A3; Joseph B. White, "GM's Ratings on Debt, Paper Cut by Moody's," *Wall Street Journal,* November 25, 1992, A3; Kathleen Kerwin, "GM Isn't Running on Fumes—Yet," *Business Week,* November 30, 1992, 35–36; and Joseph B. White, "GM Ratings Are Downgraded by S&P, But Stock Jumps on Car Sales Data," *Wall Street Journal,* February 4, 1993, A4. Pension deficits became a systemic issue ten years later: Alexander Jolliffe and Tony Tassell, "Deficits on Pension Funds May Hit Credit Ratings," *Financial Times,* August 7, 2002, 2; Silvia Ascarelli, "Pension Deficits Threaten Ratings of Twelve Companies," *Wall Street Journal Europe,* February 10, 2003, M1.
37. Standard & Poor's, "General Motors Corp. and Related Entities," *Standard & Poor's Creditweek,* February 22, 1993, 44, 46.

paper sales, GM was forced to raise bank loans instead of selling bonds. The agency "complet[ed] the largest bank credit package ever," with the attendant extra burden of intermediation.[38] GM also sought funds by issuing relatively high-cost equity capital in response to reduced credit ratings on its debt financing.[39]

Counterfactually, if we exclude the 1992 and 1993 downgrades, it is unlikely, given the relative cost of bank versus debt finance and the dilution of governance inherent in further issuance of equities, that GM would have sought these alternative forms of financing willingly. The probability is that in the absence of the downgrades GM would have continued to issue debt securities.

The power rating agencies exercise—reflecting investment centralization—was more recently experienced by Ford. Long considered the best managed of the Big Three automobile manufacturers, Ford had embarked on an ambitious strategy in the late 1990s to reinvent the corporation as a consumer company. In the words of its former chief executive officer, Jacques Nasser, Ford "happens to provide automotive products and services."[40] Nasser planned to use the Internet to transform how the company did business by cutting out dealers, thereby reducing the cost of selling cars. Unfortunately for Nasser, those plans began to come unstuck after 1999, with the dot-com bust and the onset of recession in the United States in 2000. Ford's usual rate of return on total capital of about 10 percent slipped to 9 percent in 1999, and then to 6 percent in 2000.[41] Prior to the September 11, 2001 terrorist attacks, Ford sales had slumped 12.7 percent during July. The market itself slipped 5 percent.[42]

It was a bad year for the Big Three in 2001. Recession made consumers hungry for deals in the summer and fall, including zero percent financing of new cars and trucks, especially after the terrorist attacks. Each deal of this sort cost around $3,000 per vehicle to the automakers.[43] This financing expanded sales and overall sales numbers were not much lower than in 2000, a boom year.[44] According to S&P, "Sales for full-year 2001 will likely total in the range of 16.2 million to 16.4 million units, making this year the third-best sales year ever. (The best year was 2000, with 17.3 million units; 1999 was the second-best, with 16.9 million units)."[45] The problem was, sales also grew at Honda, Toyota, and premium European brands, even though

38. "GM Secures $20.6 Billion in Credit Lines with Banks," *Wall Street Journal*, May 20, 1993, A3.

39. Kerwin, November 30, 1992; White, November 12, 1992.

40. James Flannigan, "Basics, Not Free Loans, Will Help Auto Firms," *Los Angeles Times*, November 4, 2001, pt. 3, p. 1.

41. Ibid.

42. Keith Bradsher, "Ford Weighs Plans to Cut White-Collar Work Force," *New York Times*, August 17, 2001, sec. C, 1.

43. Terril Yue Jones, "S&P Drops Boom on Ford, GM," *Los Angeles Times*, October 16, 2001, pt. 3, p. 1.

44. Standard & Poor's, "Big 3 Automakers' Credit Quality Deteriorates," October 16, 2001, available at www.standardandpoors.com, accessed February 5, 2001.

45. Ibid.

these companies did not offer free financing. Even though the Big Three sold a lot of cars in the last quarter of 2001, little profit was actually made on these vehicles. Tastes were changing, and the imports were tough competition. Foreign makers were producing better SUVs (sport utility vehicles) than the U.S. makers, who had introduced the concept and made most of their profit on these vehicles in the 1990s.

In addition to the market problems that afflicted all the Big Three, Ford had specific problems of its own. Ford incurred liabilities of around $3 billion to replace thirteen million Firestone tires it blamed for accidents on its SUVs and light trucks.[46] The company faces a series of lawsuits related to these accidents. An S&P analyst observed that the Firestone affair "at least has been a major distraction and affected productivity and quality. . . ."[47] These quality problems have been significant. An auto dealer observed that "Ford went from the penthouse to the outhouse on quality," as CEO Nasser pushed component manufacturers to produce at lower price points.[48]

S&P and Moody's began to suggest that a crisis was developing at Ford in the spring of 2001. S&P had put a "negative outlook" on Ford in February. According to Scott Sprinzen, S&P's automotive industry managing director, the agency had been "warning actively" that Ford's rating "could possibly be lowered within a few quarters."[49] On May 22, Moody's changed the outlook for Ford from stable to negative, anticipating possible future downgrades.[50] Ford responded toward the end of the summer with the announcement of five thousand white-collar layoffs, mainly in the Detroit area, at a cost of $700 million. Ongoing savings were projected at $300 million annually in salaries and other costs.[51] According to Bradsher, S&P was not impressed and said Ford's "efforts to reduce costs have been inadequate."

Immediately, S&P put Ford (and General Motors) on credit watch, with a view to possible downgrade. According to Tait, S&P's move reflected "growing misgivings" about profit prospects.[52] Ford stock sank 8 percent (and GM's lost 5 percent) in reaction.[53] Moody's began to review Ford "for possible downgrade."[54] Bonds of

46. Jack Sirard, Jack Sirard Column, *The Sacramento Bee,* August 21, 2001, 8, Lexis-Nexis, accessed February 5, 2002.

47. Terril Yue Jones, "S&P Drops Boom on Ford, GM," *Los Angeles Times,* October 16, 2001, Part 3, 1.

48. James Flannigan, "Basics, Not Free Loans, Will Help Auto Firms," *Los Angeles Times,* November 4, 2001, part 3, 1.

49. Keith Bradsher, "Ford Weighs Plans to Cut White-Collar Work Force," *The New York Times,* August 17, 2001, C1.

50. www.moodys.com, accessed February 5, 2002.

51. Keith Bradsher, "Ford to Curtail Auto Production and Cut 5,000 Jobs," *The New York Times,* August 18, 2001, A1.

52. Nikki Tait, "Ford Cuts 5,000 Jobs in North America; Automobiles Fierce Competition Forces Carmaker into Restructuring," *Financial Times,* August 18, 2001, 15.

53. Ibid.

54. List of rating actions for Ford Motor Company at www.moodys.com, accessed February 5, 2002.

both companies traded "lower in the secondary market since the agencies' statements."[55] As often occurs in these situations, the markets anticipated the likely future downgrades following these announcements, considering it, in the words of Morley, a "fait accompli."[56]

S&P acted on October 15 by downgrading outstanding long-term debt from A to BBB+, while Moody's downgraded from A2 to A3 on October 18.[57] S&P was more bearish than Moody's, signaling that a future rating downgrade, if any, might push the credit into the noninvestment grade or junk bond area. S&P noted, however, that a "further rating change within the next few years was unlikely. Present ratings reflect the expectation that financial performance could be relatively weak for a sustained period."[58] The severity of the S&P move was unexpected and led to a 10 basis point increase in Ford's bond spread.[59]

How did Ford react to the downgrade? Like GM, Ford said in one breath that it was unfortunate and not necessary and, in the next, that "plans" were being developed to take action.[60] A few days after the rating announcements, Ford said the corporation planned to go into the capital market to sell $3 billion in bonds in a market that, since the downgrades of a few days earlier, had widened by between 15 and 20 basis points.[61] Subsequently, Ford changed this plan and decided to sell $7.5 billion worth of securities, just after announcing a $692 million third-quarter loss.[62] According to Wiggins of the *Financial Times*, the "positive ruling" by Moody's on Ford Credit, the Ford consumer credit company, encouraged Ford to increase the size of the deal. Moody's, noted Wiggins, saw Ford Credit as a better risk than the automaker itself.[63]

Although it might seem that Ford was not affected by the ratings actions in 2001, the opposite was actually the case. Ford lost access to the short-term market because its rating fell below the crucial A1/P1 benchmark, required by most money market funds. Ford then had the problem of how to finance its existing short-term

55. Rebecca Bream, "Ford and GM Ratings in Focus," *Financial Times*, August 21, 2001, p. 27.

56. Kevin Morley, co-head of investment grade research at Credit Suisse First Boston, quoted in Jenny Wiggins, "Further Rating Fall for Ford Expected," *Financial Times*, August 24, 2001, p. 25.

57. As detailed in the respective web sites.

58. Standard & Poor's, "Ford Motor Company," www.standardandpoors.com, accessed February 5, 2002.

59. Rebecca Bream, "Motor Vehicle Spreads Widen," *Financial Times*, October 16, 2001, 37.

60. On GM, see Nikki Tait, "S&P Lowers Debt Ratings on GM and Ford," *Financial Times*, October 16, 2001, 32; on Ford, see Jamie Butters, "Ford, GM Get Lowered Credit Ratings," *Detroit Free Press*, October 15, 2001, 7, Lexis-Nexis, accessed February 5, 2002.

61. Rebecca Bream and Jenny Wiggins, "Ford Plans $3 Billion Bond Issue," *Financial Times*, October 19, 2001, 35.

62. Reuters, "Automaker Plans to Sell $7.5 Billion in Bonds," *New York Times*, October 20, 2001, sec. C, 4.

63. Jenny Wiggins, "Ford Doubles Its Bond Issue Size to $7.5 bn," *Financial Times*, October 20, 2001, 18.

borrowings, pushing it into the long-term debt market.[64] The worsening credit conditions for big issuers like Ford shrank the proportion of short-term assets in money market funds from 36.7 percent in early 2001 to 34.5 percent, as of October 2001.[65]

Nasser, Ford's CEO, Internet visionary, and cost-cutter, was removed from his position at the head of the company on October 30, 2001. Chairman William Clay Ford Jr., who took over Nasser's CEO duties, said Ford would return to its "core business" of building cars and trucks.[66] The financing program continued, especially in the asset-backed market, where Ford sold $5 billion worth of securities in January.[67] Soon after, on January 11, Ford announced its Ford Revitalization Plan. The plan included new products, plant capacity reduction, asset sales, reduced dividends, and about thirty-five thousand job losses for salaried and hourly workers. These actions were projected to improve results by $7 billion annually and by as much as $9 billion by the mid-2000s.[68]

The plan was "not well received" by the agencies. Fitch downgraded, and both Moody's and S&P announced their ratings might be downgraded, too.[69] S&P affirmed its BBB+, but it changed the outlook for Ford to negative from stable. On January 16, Moody's downgraded Ford from A3 to Baa1. In addition to the automaker, this time Moody's also downgraded Ford Credit and Hertz, Ford's rental car subsidiary. The bad news at Ford continued into 2002 and 2003, despite the turnaround efforts.[70]

Ford's experience with bond rating reflected a more assertive rating industry, underpinned by the growth of capital market financing and its corollary, the centralization of investment judgment. At first glance, the rationalist view of rating appears most viable in this case. Counterfactually, had rating agencies not closed off Ford's access to the short-term money market in 2001, the policy and personnel shifts at the company in early 2002 may have been delayed. However, the rationalist account does not capture the whole picture. In addition to the closing off of market access, Moody's and S&P's rating actions, warnings, and commentary gave the markets a

64. Lex Column, "Corporate Bonds," *Financial Times*, October 25, 2001, 24.

65. Jenny Wiggins, "Funding Dries Up for Commercial Short-Term Paper," *Financial Times*, October 30, 2001, 32.

66. Ford quoted in Flannigan, November 4, 2001.

67. Adam Tempkin, "Plain Vanilla Tastes Good: Ford's $5 billion ABS Deal Sets the Pace in a Strong Market," *Investment Dealers Digest*, January 7, 2002, Lexis-Nexis, accessed February 5, 2002.

68. PR Newswire, "Ford Motor Company Announces Revitalization Plan," January 11, 2002, Lexis-Nexis, accessed February 5, 2002.

69. The Associated Press State and Local Wire, "Ford Credit Rating Lowered by One Company, on Notice from Two Others," Lexis-Nexis, accessed February 5, 2002.

70. Norihiko Shirouzu, "Ford's Turnaround Stalls on Downgrade," *Wall Street Journal Europe*, October 17, 2002, A1; "Junkyard Blues; Ford Motor Company; Fresh Talk That Ford Might Go Bust," *Economist*, March 15, 2003, 77.

developing view of Ford. This view or intersubjective understanding helped to define the context in which the market audience interpreted Ford's operations. Moody's and S&P's actions fell short of being a crisis of fact, but they managed to create an atmosphere of crisis at Ford, this crisis being a social fact. Ford's experience with the agencies can, therefore, in part be understood in constructivist terms.

Knowledge

Rating agencies reproduce an instrumental form of knowledge through their work. This knowledge form reduces the scope for social conflict over ideas to those that fit within narrow purposive assumptions. How knowledge definition occurs is a vital political battle, which takes place before issuers can even begin to debate appropriate policy choices and strategies for internal change.

The rise of a ratings "advisory" industry is evidence that instrumental knowledge dominates within the rating agencies. Traditionally, investment banks advised their clients on how to present themselves to raters. With the rise of the high-yield market, greater interest on the part of global issuers in selling bonds in the Yankee market, more innovative financing by U.S. and foreign municipalities, and the expansion of domestic bond markets, former rating officials started to establish businesses to take advantage of their knowledge of the rating process. On the whole, these are small enterprises with, at most, a handful of staff. Two of the most prominent are Cantwell & Company in the New York metropolitan area and Everling Advisory Services in Frankfurt, Germany.[71] Cantwell publishes an annual survey of attitudes to credit rating.

The advisory services are useful in a context in which rating agencies may meet with a rich multinational on a Tuesday and a mid-size tool-and-die maker the following day. Often former raters themselves, the advisers are more likely to understand the culture of the rating agencies than investment bankers, immersed as they are in a different environment. The existence of these services underlies the perception that presentation is key to better ratings, judgment is a fundamental part of the rating business, knowledge can be organized in different ways, and the rating process requires knowledge to be presented in ways that meet raters' expectations. More substantially, the existence of advisory firms highlights the increasing pervasiveness of a culture of monitoring.

For rating advisory firms, the cause of their existence is the role of perception and intersubjective understanding in the rating process. If, in an alternative scenario, we remove perception and intersubjectivity, the need for issuers to focus on presentation is eliminated (along with these firms). Confirming the initial causal claim

71. Cantwell's web address is www.askcantwell.com. Everling Advisory Services can be found at www.everling.de.

about these firms supports the diachronic-constructivist views of knowledge (the right side of table 5) in the mental framework of rating orthodoxy. These heterodox claims focus on the social dynamics of knowledge, as opposed to the idea that knowledge is objective and cross-cultural.

How does the agencies' rating of corporate debt securities promote instrumental knowledge? The agencies make it appear their decisions are the product of a scientific process impartial toward all involved parties. As was noted in chapter 2, rating agencies acknowledge in their publications that ratings reflect both qualitative and quantitative information and analysis; the final product is therefore inherently subjective. However, the agencies do not make an issue of this subjectivity in their press releases. By not making it clear that their decisions are judgments, they foster the popular myth that rating actions reflect simply the facts revealed by economic and financial analysis. Consequently, they make it seem that any clear-thinking person, possessed of the right sort of knowledge, would come to the same view.

Issuers are also involved in this process. They are not above using rating agencies to justify rapid changes in corporate structure, which may have dire consequences for employees.[72] This process of "referring back to the agencies" reinforces the notion that their judgments are somehow different and that they have the secret to the "right" way of thinking. Ratings emerge as a valid framework for thinking about corporate decision-making.

The instrumental form of knowledge is at the center of rating analysis, and its logic helps reinforce the synchronic organization of capitalist enterprises. This synchronic organization influences everyday life, shaping the experience of work and the expectations of employers and of government. It is as if there is a tension in capitalism, between private property on the one hand and growth on the other. The rating process normalizes capitalism by regulating it, just as computers do the engines of modern cars. In normalization, the historically diachronic character of capitalism—its boom and bust, its inherent tendency to hubris followed by crisis—is demonized in an effort to regularize or tame it.[73] The rating experiences of the major telecommunications corporations during 2000 and 2001 demonstrate this tension.

72. An example of this tendency to use the rating agencies to justify or explain change were public comments the Chrysler Corporation made in connection with Standard & Poor's 1993 upgrade. The upgrade, to the bottom rungs of investment grade, was an "endorsement" of Chrysler's "strategic direction" and an "acknowledgement of Chrysler's ongoing efforts to improve its cost structure, increase liquidity and reduce leverage"; see "Chrysler Sheds Junk Status at Second Credit Rating Firm," *Toronto Star,* October 5, 1993, D16.

73. On these themes, see Joseph A. Schumpeter, *Capitalism, Socialism and Democracy* (New York: Harper Torchbooks, 1976 [1942]); also see, among other entries, Alexander Ebner, "Schumpeter, Joseph Alois (1883–1950)," in R. J. Barry Jones, ed., *Routledge Encyclopedia of International Political Economy* (New York: Routledge, 2001), 1368–73.

Rating and Telecommunications

The 1990s were one of the most prosperous periods in recent history—at least for citizens of the rich countries—even though the decade began with a recession. The United States, Britain, and to a lesser extent Europe, enjoyed relatively high growth and a return to the optimism of the mid-1980s and, before that, of the mid-1950s to mid-1960s. Only Japan failed to return to the growth path. Before the Asian financial crisis of 1997–98, there was much talk about Asian "tigers." The notion of "emerging markets" replaced that of "developing countries," for states like Taiwan, Malaysia, Thailand, and Korea.

The computer made enormous inroads into commerce and education in the 1980s. But the commercialization of the Internet in the mid-1990s brought a huge growth in expectations about the role computers would have in the lives of Western consumers. No longer would the computer be a glorified typewriter. It was networked and could talk to other computers. It is hard to exaggerate the enthusiasm that supported the digital revolution, especially in the rich countries, where cheap labor was not a competitive advantage.

Before the Internet revolution, telecommunications companies outside the United States were fairly staid institutions with conservative business strategies. Typically, they had the advantage of a government-protected monopoly and could pick and choose how and when to invest in new technology, at a rate that kept their finances in excellent condition. Once deregulation and liberalization of these markets began in the late 1980s, all of this changed. Competition replaced the old regime of comfortable monopolies, jobs for life, and a three-month wait for a phone line. Suddenly, with the Internet revolution and the explosion of cellular phone use, technology investment looked like a good way to beat the competition. But technology, especially new technology, is expensive, and the investments the phone companies contemplated in the late 1990s were huge.

Moody's estimated the total cost of introducing third-generation cellular phones, which deliver Internet-like services to customers, at around $270 billion. About half of this figure would pay for the technology, and the rest would go for the government licenses.[74] The subsequent cost of failure was high, too. S&Ps downgrading of France Telecom in July 2002 was estimated to add €110 million to the firm's existing €3.85 billion interest bill for 2002, and €230 million in 2003.[75]

The ratings story starts with Deutsche Telekom's (DT) giant bond issue of June 2000. What was important about DT's $8–15 billion offering is that it was made with a guarantee: the coupon or interest rate paid would rise by 50 basis points (0.5 percent) if Deutsche Telekom's rating fell below single A into the BBB territory. Many

---

74. Aline Van Duyn, "DT to Offer Protection for Downgrading," *Financial Times*, June 16, 2000, page 36.
75. Vincent Collen and Jamal Henni, "Rerating May Cost France Telecom €2bn," *Financial Times*, July 3, 2002, 21.

fund managers avoid that rating as a matter of policy and, in some localities, as a matter of law. Things became bleaker for DT when Moody's downgraded to Baa3— the lowest investment grade.[76] DT was following a trend Vodafone started during the $5 billion financing of its takeover of Mannesmann in early 2000. As Van Duyn explains, mergers or big technology investments can be interpreted as pitting the interests of shareholders and bondholders against each other. The benefits to shareholders from beating the competition—growth and increasing profits—are captured (at least in part) by stock price. But bondholders can only ever hope to get back their principal plus the agreed interest payments. Even if a company hits the proverbial growth jackpot, the debtholders share in none of it.[77] Their only risk is "downside,"—that the creditworthiness of the issuer will deteriorate—risking default and the loss of their investment.

Pressure from the rating agencies became evident in August 2000, when British Telecom (BT), DT, and the other major telecom players were put under review by both Moody's and S&P.[78] Fears of a BBB rating delayed BT's $10 billion bond issue.[79] Moody's downgraded BT, an AAA company until early 1997, from Aa1 to A2 (but not as low as BBB) on September 6, 2000. This was good news in the sense that a high BBB would have cost BT at least 50 basis points. On $10 billion, 50 basis points equals $50 million a year—a considerable sum for any institution.[80] Because the bond markets were so nervous about these issues, the telecom companies began to push their investment bankers to come up with bank loans instead.[81] Subsequently, Moody's did downgrade BT again, on May 10, 2001, to Baa1. Marconi, the telecom equipment manufacturer, had a worse time as the telecom companies held back on other expenditures. Its rating collapsed from investment grade down to B2 junk, in four downgrading events between August 8, 2001 and January 18, 2002.

In 2000 and 2001, the relative newness of the corporate bond market might have contributed to the anxiety in Europe about telecom debt. Moreover, speculative bond issues were new and the volume of debt unprecedented. Before 1990, corporate bond issues were rare. Those that did occur were typically undertaken by conservative

76. Stephanie Kirchgaessner and Aline van Duyn, "Moody's Deals Debt Blow to Deutsche Telekom," *Financial Times*, January 11–12, 2003, 15; Bertrand Benoit, "Investors Unswayed by DT Downgrade," *Financial Times*, January 14, 2003, 26.

77. Aline Van Duyn, "Survey—International Mergers and Acquisitions," *Financial Times*, June 30, 2000, 9.

78. Rebecca Bream, "Telecoms Get a Wake-up Call from Worried Bond Markets," *Financial Times*, August 22, 2000, 1.

79. Chris Ayres, "Delay for BT Bond over Credit Worries," *Times* (London), August 23, 2000. Also see Aline Van Duyn and Rebecca Bream, "Credit Rating Agencies Show Their Teeth," *Financial Times*, February 27, 2001, 34.

80. "Rising Debt, Sliding Credibility," *Economic Times of India*, Lexis-Nexis, accessed February 3, 2002.

81. Charles Pretzlik and Aline Van Duyn, "Indebted Telecoms Face Tough Times Finding New Lenders," *Financial Times*, October 6, 2000, 28.

companies in a conservative atmosphere. The telecom issues of 2000–2001 really mark the beginnings of creditworthiness disaggregation in Europe, thus creating the basis for further work for the rating agencies. In America, the disaggregation had gone much further. According to Merrill Lynch, telecommunications bonds comprised a full 18.6 percent of the U.S. high-yield bond market in the year to September 30, 2000, ahead of the next-largest industry, cable TV at 8.63 percent.[82]

A contradiction is evident here. On one side is a fundamentally diachronic capitalism of dramatically increased competition, technical innovation, and colossal investment of resources. On the other is the instrumental knowledge arising from the synchronic rationalist approach, which above all defends property rights. This contradiction has been noticed by market participants. Beyond obvious comparisons with the Milken era, Ravi Suria, formerly of the investment bank Lehman Brothers, suggested that telecom investment can best be compared to other big infrastructure programs in modern history: electricity generation, railroads, highways, airports, ports. These investments were typically undertaken in a closely regulated environment or where monopolies ensured ready guaranteed income (as in the case of the railroads).[83]

Trying to finance such activities in conditions of globalization, with monitoring institutions like rating agencies—whose way of thinking is grounded in an entirely different logic, indeed a different form of knowledge—signals a profound shift. The hegemony of a social interest linked to growth and expansion gives way to an interest more narrowly concerned with the reproduction and safeguarding of its wealth.

The claim here is that the rating agencies produce knowledge actually at odds with the real life of modern capitalism. That world is one of change, typified by growth and decay. The form of knowledge at the heart of rating belongs, in a sense, to a utopia of static social relations. Counterfactually, if we were to remove synchronic-rationalist knowledge from rating determinations, actual rating decisions might take into account the circumstances Suria described, and the outcomes would be different. But if the risks of growth are not socialized away from investors, other mechanisms might be sought out by investors to compensate for the lack of instrumental knowledge in the rating process. This counterfactual scenario supports the synchronic-rationalist account of knowledge. It suggests that before the advent of rating agencies, investors were, as the agencies like to suggest, poorly served.

Governance

The end of the postwar boom and the dynamic of mass production and consumption have corroded the economic and political hegemony of OECD institutions in

---

82. Gretchen Morgenson, "Bond Believers See Prelude to a Fall," *New York Times*, November 19, 2000, sec. 3, p. 1.
83. Ibid.

the postwar era. Once-masterful institutions within civil society, such as commercial banks, have had their capacity for exercising authority substantially reduced by the way financial resources have been routed to borrowers. These transformations have made the global economy a "risk culture."[84] In this era, "The concept of risk becomes fundamental to the way both lay actors and technical specialists organize the social world."[85] Risk monitoring becomes a central activity of elite reflection. More resources are devoted to *"risk profiling*—analyzing what, in the current state of knowledge and in current conditions, is the distribution of risks in given milieux of action."[86] Among the types of risk evaluated are market risk (price fluctuations), liquidity risk (asset sale difficulties), operational risk (such as fraud, computer error), exchange rate risk, and event risk (especially takeover threats and opportunities).[87]

In reacting to risk, the rating agencies foster models of corporate organization that challenge established governance structures. The global oligopoly, Moody's and S&P, advocates the capital market-centered system of control, corresponding to Zysman's model.[88] Their approach emphasizes the voting mechanism or "approval rating" available in liquid markets. When those with a financial stake in a corporation do the " 'Wall Street walk': sell . . . wise bosses get the message."[89] As Woodward noted of the bond market and the Clinton White House, rating provides a "barometer" with which corporate performance is checked regularly.[90] This form of governance is different from the German and Japanese systems, where trusted intermediaries—banks—traditionally have undertaken the monitoring. Rating agencies constitute a new clearinghouse in which an "approval rating" is constructed and articulated to market agents.

Key ideas of this view of corporate governance can be gleaned from rating publications. S&P includes a series of "organizational considerations" in its corporate criteria.[91] The criteria emphasize that priority should be placed on the "finance function" and that concentration in ownership potentially compromises management.

84. Giddens, 1991, 3; also see Ulrich Beck, *Risk Society: Towards a New Modernity*, trans. Mark Ritter (Newbury Park, Calif.: Sage, 1992); John Adams, *Risk* (London: University College London Press, 1995); and Stephen Gill, "The Global Panopticon? The Neoliberal State, Economic Life, and Democratic Surveillance" *Alternatives* 20, no. 1 (Jan–Mar 1995): 1–49, 28–29.

85. Giddens, 1991, 3.

86. Ibid., 114, 119.

87. See John Plender, "Through a Market, Darkly: Is the Fear That Derivatives Are a Multi-Billion Accident Waiting to Happen Justified?" *Financial Times*, May 27, 1994, 17, as cited in Gill, 1995, 28–29.

88. John Zysman, *Governments, Markets, and Growth: Financial Systems and the Politics of Industrial Change*, (Ithaca, NY: Cornell University Press, 1983) 18.

89. "Watching the Boss: A Survey of Corporate Governance," *Economist*, January 29, 1994, 4.

90. Bob Woodward, *The Agenda: Inside the Clinton White House* (New York: Simon and Schuster, 1994), 224.

91. Standard & Poor's, *S&P's Corporate Finance Criteria* (New York: Standard & Poor's, 1992), 19.

The agency also emphasizes the transition from "entrepreneurial or family-bound" to "professional and organizational" corporate control, although it does not define the latter.[92] S&P's "organizational considerations" correspond to the neoliberal emphasis on "contestability," whereby control is contingent on performance as judged by owners, rather than other nonmaximizing criteria.[93]

Rating Japanese Banks

Japanese banks are no strangers to the rating agencies. The efforts of Moody's and Standard & Poor's to foster change in the Japanese financial industry go back a decade. Their activities parallel those of the U.S. government. U.S. agitation over Japanese regulation and market practices were evident in the yen-dollar negotiations of the mid-1980s and, more recently, during former Treasury Secretary Paul O'Neill's January 2002 visit to Tokyo, for discussions about the Japanese economic malaise.[94] As Zysman has observed, the postwar role of banks in Japan was quite different from the American model. Banks in Japan have traditionally been much more leveraged than Western institutions, because they support the industrial companies with which they are affiliated. Banks usually have much of their capital in corporate stock and, until recently, did not list this stock at current market value (or mark to market) on their books. Moreover, a history of cooperation between strong and weak banks prevented weaker institutions from going out of business. Subsequent changes in the regulatory system and the collapse of asset prices pose considerable challenges to this pattern.

It is a mistake to imagine that in Japan the rating agencies are able to exercise great power. Despite the poor record of Japanese finance in the past decade, Japan remains a rich country, with great resources and a strong desire to avoid change that generates stark winners and losers. Current bank ratings reflect this approach by anticipating some sort of government intervention to prop up ailing institutions. That occurred in early 1999, when the Japanese government infused 10 trillion yen into the banking system.[95]

From the beginning of the late-1990s banking crisis, the rating agencies were pushing Japanese banks to change how they did business. A series of downgrades began in 1997, prior to the failure of Yamaichi Securities in November—the biggest corporate collapse since World War II.[96] These events spurred Japanese banks to use

92. Ibid., 19.
93. "Watching the Boss," January 29, 1994, 5.
94. Tony Barrett, "U.S. Takes Hard Line on Japan's Bank Crisis," *Sunday Business*, January 27, 2002, 16.
95. Standard & Poor's, "Japan Credit Trends 2002: The Downside Deepens," available at www.standardandpoors.com, accessed February 9, 2002, 6.
96. Moody's began a review of Japanese banks in February of that year; see Gwen Robinson, "Moody's Reviews Japan Credit Banks," *Financial Times*, February 19, 1997, 33; on Yamaichi Securities, see "Bailout Pressure Rises in Japan," *Boston Globe*, November 26, 1997, C6.

financial innovation rather than balance-sheet improvement to get themselves out of trouble. In one case, S&P refused to rate a deal, leading to poor investor response and abandonment of the project.[97] A Japanese regulatory agency found that banks had miscalculated their bad loans by about 10 percent in 1998.[98]

Many aspects of this story only get worse after the government bailout in early 1999. On March 14, 2001, the banking sector lost 5 percent of its stock market value after Fitch announced it was reviewing nineteen Japanese banks for downgrade. Banks were still heavily exposed to the stock market at 150 percent of capital, compared to 10–20 percent in Western banks.[99] Fitch observed in the fall of 2001 that bad loan statistics "grossly underestimate" the real level of nonperforming assets. Fitch suggested two things seem to constrain the banks from changing their business practices. One is a reluctance to get ahead of government and public sentiment toward restructuring and redundancy. The second is the "main bank" system, in which corporations buy bank equity in exchange for better credit terms, reciprocal equity purchases, and promises of support from the bank in bad times.[100]

As the fragility of the Japanese system became more apparent, even change seemed dangerous. Moody's signaled in January 2002 that an end to deposit insurance in April 2002 might be destabilizing, given the system's "grossly inadequate financial shape." Moody's pushed for a sharing of the burdens of adjustment.[101] With the impending changes, forty-six credit unions collapsed in 2001, plus Ishikawa Bank, a larger regional lender.[102] Moody's said subsequently it was losing confidence in the ability of the "Japanese system" to deal with the crisis.[103] S&P followed Moody's announcements with further downgrades of its own.[104] In a report on these actions, S&P made it clear that only government intervention could support the existing level of ratings. The agency expected this intervention to continue after deposit protection ended, via the government's crisis management account.[105]

97. "Japan Banks Resist Disclosure," *Asset Sales Report International*, March 23, 1998, 1.

98. Naoko Nakamae, "Japan's Banks Understated Risky Loans, Audit Shows," *Financial Times*, December 28, 1998, 4.

99. Doug Cameron and Emiko Terazono, "Japan Banks Face Possible Downgrade," *Financial Times*, March 15, 2001, 34.

100. Fitch Inc., "Running Out of Borrowed Times," *Banker*, October 1, 2001, n.p., accessed via Lexis-Nexis January 20, 2002.

101. "Moody's Revises Major Japan Banks' Outlook to Negative," *Jiji Press Ticker Service*, January 21, 2002, n.p., accessed via Lexis-Nexis March 10, 2002.

102. Ken Belson, "Jitters in Japan for Savers and Banks," *New York Times*, January 23, 2002, sec. W, 1.

103. "Moody's Cuts Japan Banks' Ratings Outlook," *Star* (Malaysia), January 25, 2002, n.p., accessed via Lexis-Nexis.

104. "S&P Cuts Ratings on 7 Major Japan Banks, Affirms 4," *Jiji Ticker Service*, February 5, 2002, n.p., accessed via Lexis-Nexis.

105. Standard & Poor's, "Ratings on Seven Major Japanese Banks Lowered, Four Affirmed," available at www.standardandpoors.com, accessed February 9, 2002.

In a wide-ranging report on credit conditions in Japan, S&P cautioned that things would get much worse before they got better and commented on the awareness among Japanese officials and market actors that meaningful credit risk was increasingly a fact of life. The report suggested a basic mismatch between assets and returns, and that Japanese banks have been "battling the incessant emergence of new bad loans since the collapse of the bubble economy in 1991."[106] Elsewhere, S&P observed that simply giving more money to the banks does not solve their problems. Banks had to "reform their lending practices, strengthen their corporate governance and improve their profitability."[107] Moody's made further downgrades in July 2002.[108]

The case of Japanese banks is interesting because it is an example of confrontation between the rating agencies and historically entrenched norms and practices. Unfortunately, the problems have not been resolved even after a decade or more of problems. From a counterfactual perspective, if the agencies had not been willing to confront these historically derived norms in the Japanese banking industry, the Japanese government might have been less willing to socialize risk and (partly or temporarily) stabilize the system. This alternative scenario suggests that synchronic-rationalist considerations drove these rating actions but that politics had a role, too, in getting government to take responsibility. The diachronic-constructivist view of rating and how it works therefore contributes an important element to understanding the Japanese case.

Conclusions

In this chapter the three mid-range arguments were applied to the rating of corporations. The emphasis of the section on investment was that rating makes a considerable difference to the cost of financing. The centralization of investment judgments was demonstrated by the struggle over junk bond financing and the LBO movement. The cases of General Motors and Ford also show the disciplinary effect of these processes in both more narrow rationalist terms and in a wider constructed sense.

In the section on knowledge, it was argued that rating advisory services are evidence that the rating process is judgment-filled. The agencies contribute to the construction of a synchronic, instrumental form of knowledge, by at all times seeking to appear as if their judgments, like those of auditors, are scientific and impartial.

106. Standard & Poor's, "Japan Credit Trends 2002: The Downside Deepens," available at www.standardandpoors.com, accessed February 9, 2002, 6.

107. "S&P Cuts Ratings," February 5, 2002, n.p.

108. Bayan Rahman, "Moody's Downgrades Japanese Banks," *Financial Times*, July 3, 2002, 30. In September 2003, the Japanese government-backed bank recovery agency determined that many banks were overvaluing the collateral of borrowers, suggesting that many institutions could be underprovisioning for their bad loans (David Pilling, "Some Japanese Banks Found To Be Overvaluing Borrowers' Collateral," *Financial Times*, September 30, 2003, 14).

There is a tension between the impulse to normalize capitalism around synchronic expert knowledge and the reality that major social investment in infrastructure, like telecommunications, has traditionally taken place in a broader diachronic context.

In the final section, on governance, it was shown that the agencies are key institutions in which responses to risk are developed. The crisis-prone Japanese banks provide an example of how the agencies apply specific views of corporate governance. Next, we examine how the agencies rate municipal governments.

CHAPTER FIVE

Rating State and Local Governments

No complaint is more frequently voiced than the lack of clarity about what the ratings actually measure. While ratings are intended by the agencies to gauge the relative degrees of credit quality . . . how such factors are weighted—and why—in making the final rating decision remains unclear.

JOHN E. PETERSEN, *The Rating Game,* 1974

State and local governments, like corporations, are subject to the scrutiny of rating agencies. This analysis of the rating of municipal or subnational governments also concerns the impact of the rating process on policy and democratic accountability at the local level. Municipal governments include those of states and provinces, regions and counties, cities and towns, and utilities and services. Governments at the local level are a major influence on social life, and they, too, are subject to the pressures of financial globalization. The mid-range arguments about investment, knowledge, and governance structure the following analysis.

Municipal finance is a big business. Moody's estimated the U.S. nonprofit health-care sector to have around $50 billion in debt outstanding in February 2000.[1] Universities in the U.S. and increasingly elsewhere now have credit ratings.[2] In the water and sewerage sector alone, Moody's maintains nearly one thousand, five hundred ratings. Based on U.S. Environmental Protection Agency figures, Moody's projects that at least $280 billion in investment in these systems will have to be made over the next twenty years just to satisfy current regulation.[3]

---

1. Moody's Investors Service, *2000 Not-For-Profit Healthcare Sector* (New York: Moody's Investors Service, February 2000), 5.

2. David Jobbins, "The Rating Game," *Times Higher Education Supplement,* September 20, 2002, 23.

3. Moody's Investors Service, *Water and Sewer Sector Outlook* (New York: Moody's Investors Service, February 2000), 1, 3.

Municipal bonds can be attractive to investors and compete with corporate bonds, even when the issuing institution itself does not make enormous profits, because the interest payments investors receive are tax free in the United States.[4]

The municipal or public finance sector was one of the mainstays of the rating agencies during the era of rating conservatism. It is a stuffy business no more. In recent years three trends have dominated. The first is fiscal volatility. As Western governments experienced fiscal problems from the early 1970s onward, and, more recently, during the recession of the early 1990s, they have responded by trying to shed many activities and liabilities, often making local and regional governments assume these tasks. Not only have municipal governments had extra responsibility, but they have faced more uncertainty about where resources were going to come from. The second trend—more complex deal making—is partly the result of this uncertainty, as city governments and other public bodies have taken advantage of financial innovation.[5] The third is internationalization. Increasingly, non-U.S. municipalities are issuing bonds and seeking ratings instead of relying on their central government and banks, and some U.S. cities are looking for funds outside the U.S. market.[6] Standard & Poor's now rates the Lisbon, Portugal mass transit authority, industrial towns in Russia, and small cities in rural Mexico.[7]

As in the analysis of corporate rating, the mid-range arguments about investment, knowledge and governance, applied to the rating of state and local governments, are framed in terms of the counterfactual method, as a means of contrasting rationalist and constructivist interpretations. So, in situations where a synchronic-rationalist argument is the primary means of analysis, diachronic-constructivist principles inform the counterfactual scenario. The objective in offering counterfactual scenarios is not to contrast a bad effect with one somehow thought "better." Counterfactuals are deployed to highlight the causal process and the politics at stake.

Investment

Gatekeeping is nothing new in the world of municipal finance. Rating is well established in this arena, having been standard requirements for U.S. municipal bonds

4. Edward V. Regan, "End the Municipal Bond Subsidy," *Wall Street Journal*, March 21, 1996, A20.

5. Abby Schultz, "Some Municipal Bonds Leave a Corporate Taste," *New York Times*, February 10, 2002, 9.

6. On non-U.S. municipals seeking ratings, see Khozem Merchant, "Cities Broaden Their Money-Raising Horizons," *Financial Times*, May 3, 1999, 23; on U.S. municipals going outside the United States for financing, see Yasmin Hassany, "U.S. Cities May Begin to Seek Global Financing," *Wall Street Journal Europe*, November 3, 1997, 14.

7. See Standard & Poor's, "Issuer Credit Rating Affirmed at 'AA' on Lisbon Subway, Metropolitano de Lisboa; Outlook Stable," February 6, 2002, "Russian City of Cherepovets Assigned National Scale 'ruBB' Rating," January 28, 2002, and "City of Atlixco, Puebla, Mexico Rated 'MxBBB+,'" February 12, 2002, available at www.standardandpoors.com, accessed February 13, 2002.

since the 1930s. The effect of centralized investment judgment is perhaps more pronounced here than in any other type of rating. Two dimensions of municipal rating are considered in this context.

One is the influence rating agencies exercise over public investment—the form and extent of this power. And the other is the nature of rating determinations. What assumptions are at work in these decisions, and what are their implications?

In the major U.S. agencies, government rating analysis is typically undertaken in two areas. North American subnational governments and government agencies are covered as municipal credits, while sovereign governments *and* foreign subnational governments are usually handled in the international ratings department, which also deals with foreign corporations. This separation reflects the history of the agencies as U.S. institutions. During the 1990s, Moody's, which originated municipal rating in 1918, maintained around forty thousand ratings on 20,000 municipal issuers.[8] Total accumulated municipal debt levels were around $1.2 trillion in 1994, up from $365 billion in 1980. In 1993, municipalities borrowed some $289 billion, compared to $154 billion in 1991.[9] By 2003, Moody's was maintaining ninety thousand ratings on 22,500 municipal issuers.[10] An outline of the municipal rating process at Moody's is provided in table 6.

Debt issuance has become a relatively more important means of financing the activities of foreign and domestic municipalities. In North America, taxpayers' resistance to higher tax levels has precipitated this trend. This phenomenon is most notable in California, where Proposition 13, a voter-mandated 1978 law, makes raising local taxes very difficult. Resistance to tax increases is also behind the increasing use of innovative financing instruments like derivatives, which offer higher returns.[11] Officials have also turned to bond issues supported by revenue from sources such as bridge tolls. Two thirds of new debt is of this kind.[12]

In Europe, growth of interest in municipal debt issuance reflects an environment of financial liberalization, the empowerment of local governments relative to national governments, and the disintermediation of finance.[13] As Dyer notes, "Devolved power means that local authorities need to borrow more to finance spending and investment."[14] Indeed, in France since 1982, Ministry of Finance records show that

---

8. Moody's Investors Service, *Moody's on Municipals* (New York, 1991), 40.

9. Timothy Appelby, "Orange County Files for Bankruptcy Protection," *Globe and Mail* (Toronto), December 8, 1994, B4; also see Floyd Norris, "Orange County's Bankruptcy: The Overview," *New York Times*, December 8, 1994, D1.

10. www.moodys.com, accessed July 18, 2003.

11. Norris, December 8, 1994; Leslie Wayne, "Local Governments Lose Millions in Complex and Risky Securities," *New York Times*, September 25, 1994, 1.

12. David Stimpson, ed., *Global Credit Analysis* (London: Moody's Investors Service/IFR Publishing, 1991), 517.

13. Geoff Dyer, "Turning to the Capital Markets," *Euromoney*, (June 1993): 101–5.

14. Ibid., 101.

Table 6. Mechanics of Moody's municipal rating process

1.   Application
2.   Municipal calendar entry
3.   Assignment of issue to analyst
4.   Receipt of documentation
5.   Preliminary research
6.   Meeting and/or on-site visit (optional)
7.   Completion of analysis
8.   Analyst's rating recommendation
9.   Sign-off procedure with area manager
10. Presentation to public finance department rating committee
11. Committee decision
12. Rating assignment
13. Rating released to issuer
14. Rating released to public
15. Distribution of municipal credit reports
16. Annual request to issuer for data

Source: Moody's Investors Service, *Moody's on Municipals* (New York, 1991), 42.

"the debt level per inhabitant in the *régions* has increased by 370%."[15] Polish cities began issuing debt in 1996, with the explicit aim of attracting inflows of foreign capital.[16] To meet the Maastricht criteria for entry into the European Union, central governments were required to reduce budget deficits, thereby effectively pushing subnational communities to shoulder greater financial burdens.[17] At the same time, local finance providers like France's Credit Local have withered, given the competition from the capital markets. Banks have too, because shareholders are unwilling to see loans made to municipalities at rates not competitive with the market.

The legal and regulatory environment has also become more permissive of debt issuance by territorial communities. In this new market, the city of Moscow became an important player and Moody's upgraded the city a number of times from mid-2000 onward, despite the Russian sovereign defaults of 1998.[18] Even obscure cities in Siberia and Tartarstan made plans to get ratings in the late 1990s.[19] Moody's and S&P have set targets for 30 percent of their revenues to come from non-U.S. ratings.[20]

15. Ibid.

16. "Gdansk to Issue Municipal Bonds," *Financial Times*, November 15, 1996, 34.

17. Conner Middelmann, "EMU Spurs Trend for States to Tap External Funds," *Financial Times*, December 5, 1996, 38.

18. On Moscow, see Edward Luce and John Thornhill, "City of Moscow to Launch Its First Eurobond," *Financial Times*, May 6, 1997, 24; also see Andrew Balls and John Thornhill, "Curious Hybrid of West and East," survey on Russia, *Financial Times*, April 30, 1999, 6.

19. John Thornhill, "Pitfalls in the Paperchase," *Financial Times*, July 1, 1997, 23.

20. Edward Luce, "Agencies to Target Europe's Burgeoning Bond Market," *Financial Times*, December 17, 1998, 37.

Recently, investors in European issues, including central and east European issuers and cities like Avignon in France, have begun looking for higher yields from low-interest-rate debt.[21] Issuers are using bond insurance to compensate for lower ratings, as are 50 percent of municipal issuers in the United States.[22] U.S. government agencies make use of the new ratings in east and central Europe to identify suitable candidates for federal government aid.[23] German banks have also made use of ratings to broaden coverage of their *pfandbriefe* (collateralized bond) portfolios.[24]

As in corporate rating, the rating agencies exercise both a behavioral power and structural power in rating state and local governments. Quantitative research into the power the rating agencies exert on governments has emphasized the complexity of the process, the many significant variables, and the probable importance of administrative and institutional factors.[25] The difficulty in predicting municipal ratings means that the professional judgment of rating officials is a major component of each decision. In what follows, examples of leverage over public finance and public investment are identified.

Philadelphia's Rating Experience

Philadelphia, in which during the early 1990s, "one of every four [residents], including almost half its homeowners, lives below the poverty line," was subject to the judgments of the major rating agencies in 1990. During the summer and again during the fall, ratings on around $2 billion of its outstanding debt were downgraded.[26] On June 8, Standard & Poor's reduced Philadelphia's rating two steps, to BBB–. At the time, this was S&P's lowest rating for a major city, ahead of the BBB ratings of Detroit and St. Louis.[27] According to S&P, this action reflected the lack of "fiscal stability" or balance in the city's new budget. On June 30, Moody's already had Philadelphia at Baa, the lowest rung of investment grade. In response to what the

21. Tomas Prouza, "Finance: Only for the Best," *Prague Tribune,* December 22, 1999, accessed via Lexis-Nexis, February 20, 2002; on Avignon, see "Avignon's Financial Situation Stabilises," *Les Echos,* February 10, 2000, 6, accessed via Lexis-Nexis, February 20, 2002.

22. Rebecca Bream, "Europe Wakes Up to Credit Enhancement," *Financial Times,* June 29, 2000, 42.

23. "Sofia to Receive U.S. Credits without State Guarantees," *PARI Daily,* November 17, 2000, accessed via Lexis-Nexis, February 20, 2002.

24. "Madrid Euro Debut to Boost Spanish Municipal Bond Market," *Financial News (Daily),* December 12, 2001, accessed via Lexis-Nexis, February 20, 2002.

25. Paul G. Farnham and George S. Cluff, "The Bond Rating Game Revisited," *Journal of Urban Affairs,* b, no. 4 (Fall 1984): 21–37.

26. Michael de Courcy Hinds, "After Renaissance of the Seventies and Eighties, Philadelphia Is Struggling to Survive," *New York Times,* June 21, 1990, A16.

27. Ibid.

agency considered to be an "unrealistic budget," it lowered the rating to Ba, the top category of the speculative grade.[28]

On August 13, just as city officials were preparing to raise additional cash to cover an estimated shortfall of $300 to $500 million in its budget year, from July 1 to June 30, S&P placed the city's outstanding debt on CreditWatch. With access to the municipal market now available only at a premium, city officials tried to arrange financial backing from a major bank. Earlier, that month, virtually no interest had been shown by the market in a regular offering of tax anticipation notes. This new offering—worth $400 million—was to have been secured only by the city's taxing power, as is common practice in municipal finance.[29]

City officials hoped that investors would be assured by the solvency of the lending institution. A lower rate of interest would thus have to be paid to bondholders and hasten the sale of the otherwise risky bonds and commercial paper, which were not available to regulated pension funds. (Such funds may purchase only investment-grade offerings.) In mid-September, it appeared that this strategy was working. Swiss Bank Corporation agreed to back $50 million worth of tax anticipation notes and to issue letters of credit on a further $175 million, with the proviso that other banks back this sum in due course. However, two days later, their offer was withdrawn. Their withdrawal made it "impossible for the city to borrow at an interest rate it could afford."[30]

According to a subsequent report, the financing was withdrawn because of the credit rating downgrade.[31] Domestic banks were joined by other foreign banks in shying away from Philadelphia. Felix Rohatyn, the investment banker who helped resolve New York City's fiscal crisis in the mid-1970s, noted that "when a city has this kind of experience with a bank pulling out it leaves a stain."[32]

This stain became very evident two days later, when Moody's and Fitch further downgraded Philadelphia and related authorities. Their action prompted the mayor to declare, "I don't know how much worse it can get."[33] As a Moody's official commented, "The 'B' rating on the general obligation bonds does not suggest imminent

28. "Philadelphia's Credit Rating Lowered by Second Agency," *New York Times,* July 1, 1990, 17; Michael de Courcy Hinds, "Its Cash and Tempers Short, Philadelphia Seeks Solvency," *New York Times,* September 11, 1990, 1. Moody's notes of this category that "bonds which are rated Ba are judged to have speculative elements; their future cannot be considered as well assured. Often the protection of interest and principal payments may be very moderate, and thereby not well safeguarded during both good and bad times over the future. Uncertainty of position characterizes bonds in this class" (*Moody's on Municipals,* 1991, 48).

29. Hinds, September 11, 1990.

30. Michael de Courcy Hinds, "Without Money or Choices, Philadelphia Plans Big Cuts," *New York Times,* September 14, 1990, A14.

31. Michael de Courcy Hinds, "Philadelphia's Financial Crisis Turns on Mayor," *New York Times,* September 25, 1990, A16.

32. Hinds, September 14, 1990, A14.

33. Quoted in Michael de Courcy Hinds, "Philadelphia Crisis Deepens as Bond Ratings Fall Again," *New York Times,* September 15, 1990, 8.

default, but it suggests that there is little assurance that the city will be able to pay principal and interest on its bonds over an extended period of time." Standard & Poor's also downgraded Philadelphia again, to CCC, which means that the debt "has a currently identifiable vulnerability to default."[34] The impact of these rating shifts was quickly felt in the market, when the city again considered selling tax anticipation notes.[35]

Tax receipts would be paid in during the winter, the city was running a substantial deficit, and expenditures were relatively constant. Shutting the city out of the capital markets was not something the city could live with, in the absence of alternative sources of income. Accordingly, the city finance director was, to use her words, "committed to doing everything necessary to get back into the market successfully to sell the short-term notes."[36] While Philadelphia was shut out of the capital markets, political conflict between the black, urban Democrat mayor and the white, suburban Republican-dominated Commonwealth of Pennsylvania legislature precluded state aid to the beleaguered city.[37]

Philadelphia began to run out of cash. To stave off insolvency, the city finance department set up criteria for bill paying. But some social service programs, such as the city's AIDS Activities Coordinating Office, which provided funds to support terminally ill AIDS patients, suffered as payments from the city were suspended.[38]

The following year, the city was able to raise money from employee pension funds and some asset sales. As a first step, the city had to change the rules prohibiting these funds from investing in speculative grade securities. This tack initially was opposed by unions because the debt's junk bond status implied extra risk for their pensioners.[39] Mayor Goode continued to run afoul of a skeptical state legislature and resisted the imposition of an independent financial control system. Most important, Goode could not resolve the ongoing imbalance between costs and revenues, other than by requesting additional taxes. Anita A. Summers, a professor of public policy at the Wharton School, noted that Goode could not contain or reduce operating

34. Michael de Courcy Hinds, "Philadelphia Getting Credit for Reversing a Fiscal Fall," *New York Times*, May 21, 1992, B14. For S&P's definition of the CCC rating, see Standard & Poor's *Ratings Handbook*, (New York: Standard & Poor's, August 1992), 183.

35. "Before the Swiss Bank withdrew its support and scuttled the deal, investors were asking that the city pay 6 percent interest on the notes backed by the Swiss Bank's credit, and they demanded 9.5 percent interest on the notes backed by the city's credit. When the bank withdrew its support, the city decided not to offer the notes on the ground that it would not be able to afford to pay that interest" (Hinds, September 15, 1990).

36. "Philadelphia Stalls Bankruptcy," *New York Times*, September 22, 1993, 10.

37. Michael de Courcy Hinds, "City Waits for Rescue Amid Cries of Chaos," *New York Times*, November 3, 1990, 8.

38. Ibid., 8.

39. Michael de Courcy Hinds, "Its Money Running Out, Philadelphia Offers Plan," *New York Times*, November 10, 1990, 8. Michael de Courcy Hinds, "Philadelphia Might Get Aid from Its Pension Fund," *New York Times*, November 23, 1990, A24.

costs because he "could not "enforce productivity changes on the unions."[40] In an office-space audit, the city controller found at least $40 million misspent on leases and purchases over the previous decade, and the city was likely to spend another $70 million in similar ways in the next few years. Some of the costs related to property standing idle, some of it to property depreciating because of lack of repair, and some to premium rentals on city office space.[41]

In November 1991, Edward Rendell was elected the new mayor. (Term-limits law did not permit Goode to run again, should he have wished to.) Almost immediately, perceptions of the new executive were positive in the local political apparatus. The bond rating agencies also observed "some progress" in moving the city out of fiscal paralysis.[42] Subsequently, the *New York Times* reported progress in getting the city back on track—a credit rating upgrade.[43]

The new mayor's "draconian" five-year fiscal plan called for $1.1 billion in savings through reduced labor costs, management efficiencies, and stricter tax collection. A five-year wage freeze for the city's twenty-five thousand employees was a central part of the cost-savings plan.[44] Modified but still tough versions of these plans were subsequently put into practice.[45] In reporting this seal of approval on the city's fiscal plans, the *Times* commented on the downgrades' effects on the city:

> The city's poor credit rating, still the worst of any major city in the nation, essentially barred it from municipal capital markets for two years. Without access to the customary municipal loans [sic] that help cities maintain a stable cash flow between tax deadlines, many of Philadelphia's building and maintenance projects have been disrupted, payments have been delayed to thousands of creditors, and the city has had to pay premium rates on small loans from local lenders and pension funds.[46]

Philadelphia's fiscal circumstances charged quickly. No deficit was generated in 1992–93 (ending June 30, 1993). "The only test for the city is to keep up the momentum," commented a Moody's official.[47] The rapid turnaround in the city's fortunes suggests that much of the reason for the fiscal paralysis was political rather than

40. Quoted in Hinds, November 10, 1990.

41. Michael de Courcy Hinds, "Audit in Philadelphia Finds Millions Spent on Office Space," *New York Times*, December 17, 1990, B10.

42. Michael de Courcy Hinds, "Philadelphia Mayor Proposes Bailout," *New York Times*, February 21, 1992, A12; on the impact of leadership change on municipal financing more generally, see Richard C. Feiock and James C. Clingermayer, "Leadership Turnover, Transaction Costs, and Political Time Horizons: An Examination of Municipal Debt Financing," paper presented at the annual meeting of the Southern Political Science Association, Atlanta, November 1994.

43. Hinds, May 21, 1992, B14.

44. Ibid., B14.

45. "Philadelphia Workers Accept Wage Freeze," *New York Times*, November 8, 1992, 40.

46. Hinds, May 21, 1992. The article's author means bonds, not loans here.

47. Michael de Courcy Hinds, "Philadelphia Climbs out of Fiscal Depths and Builds by Sharing Sacrifices," *New York Times*, April 6, 1993, A19.

technical. As in the State of New York during the same period, the seemingly intractable conflicts between the mayor, city council, and state government prevented any major rethinking of the way the city did business.[48] In the meantime, the city started to accumulate debts through annual operating deficits. Only when the bond rating agencies cut off access to cheap credit through downgrades was the political deadlock shattered and a consensus around the necessity for creating an agreed plan of action generated.

Moody's analyst for Philadelphia lauded the budget acumen of Mayor Rendell, praising the "vastly improved" cooperation with the city council.[49] S&P had been more generous to the city the previous year, at the end of 1993. But when announcing the upgrade, S&P made it clear that the better rating reflected the city's ability to balance its budget (producing a surplus of $3 million), not an improvement in the city's situation. "Economically, nothing has changed." The city remained overburdened with taxes and poor infrastructure.[50]

Privatization was a key part of the mayor's financial strategy. As he explained it, the city "could not have taxed our way out of these troubles, nor could we have dramatically cut city services."[51] Capital mobility and the taxpayers' mobility was the constraint. Philadelphia was "in competition" with other cities and suburbs as a place to live and work, the mayor noted. He saw the situation as one in which, "like a business facing bankruptcy, we were forced to reinvent ourselves." The emphasis in this reinvention was on getting services at the least cost, with fewest ongoing liabilities. A competitive contracting committee was inaugurated to look at trash disposal, maintenance, and cleaning costs. The mayor claimed to have saved $300,000 annually on the cleaning of Philadelphia City Hall alone. By 1994, the program had eliminated about 450 city positions offering job security, health care, and pensions.[52]

In a November 2000 report, S&P focused on basic structural issues that Philadelphia administrations have had to come to grips with since 1990.[53] Although the city has one of the most diversified economies in the nation, its collection of pharmaceutical, aerospace, health-care, education, and transportation producers are growing relatively slowly. High business costs, large numbers of minimally educated

48. Elizabeth Kolbert, "Bond Rating: A Censure of Bickering," *New York Times*, March 28, 1990, B3; on this theme, also see Charles Gasparino, "Moody's Warns Political Impasse May Affect Rating of N.Y. County," *Bond Buyer*, August 18, 1992, 1.

49. Quoted in "Philadelphia Receives a Dose of Good News: Moody's Raises Rating," *Wall Street Journal*, April 26, 1993, C18.

50. Quoted in "S&P Upgrades Rating on Philadelphia Bonds," *Wall Street Journal*, December 27, 1993, accessed from Proquest, January 5, 2000.

51. Edward G. Rendell, "The Philadelphia Competitive Contracting Story," *Business Forum*, Winter–Spring 1994, 13.

52. Ibid., 14.

53. Standard & Poor's, "Pennsylvania's Major MSAs [Metropolitan Statistical Areas]," available at www.standardandpoors.com, accessed February 13, 2002.

workers, and high tax rates are also problems.[54] S&P noted the lack of population growth, the high cost of living (16 percent above the national average), labor costs (25 percent above the national average), and the largest combined federal, state, and local tax burden of the twenty-five largest U.S. metropolitan areas.[55]

Moody's upgraded Philadelphia again in November 1994 and then to investment grade in March 1995, "ending nearly five years in [the] junk-bond doghouse."[56] By 1999, the city had adjusted from an accumulated deficit of more than $200 million in the early 1990s to six consecutive years of surpluses, including $169 million in 1999.[57] Unfortunately, although city finances were put in order, the same could not be said of Philadelphia Gas Works (PGW), the city-owned energy utility. Moody's downgraded the debt of PGW in February 1999, after a management crisis that led to six of PGW's seven top executives leaving the utility.[58] PGW, which the *Philadelphia Inquirer* described as the city's "crazy aunt in the back room" and where one third of all employees were patronage hires, only just avoided becoming speculative grade.[59] Financial support from the city and rate hikes sustained the utility in 2000.[60] In November 2000, a grand jury recommended that criminal charges be filed against four former executives, amid calls for PGW's privatization.[61] Moody's confirmed the utility's barely investment grade ratings on June 12, 2001.[62]

The Philadelphia rating story shows the rating agencies disciplining a city government through their work. On the one hand, this account is synchronic-rationalist, focused on the city's liabilities and concern about its investment-deterring features. On the other, the Philadelphia case demonstrates a rating mentality that at times goes beyond the immediate logic of budgets and steps into the diachronic-constructivist territory of demography and sustainable growth.

The raters did not make their judgments on the basis of short-run finances alone. Counterfactually, if the rating agencies had not taken action on Philadelphia (or they did not exist), pressure for change would still have come from taxpayers, business, and state politicians. But that pressure might well have been less voluble and organized without the rating downgrades. The ratings were an acute judgment about the

54. Ibid., 2.

55. Ibid., 3.

56. Amy S. Rosenberg, "Bond Rating Rises for City's Financial Overseer," *Philadelphia Inquirer,* November 8, 1994, sec. B, 3; quotation is from Amy S. Rosenberg, "The City's Bond Rating Gets a Boost," *Philadelphia Inquirer,* March 16, 1995, sec. A1.

57. Michael Janofsky, "Mayoral Free-for-All in Philadelphia," *New York Times,* January 18, 1999, A11.

58. "PGW Bonds Are Downgraded by Moody's," *Philadelphia Inquirer,* February 2, 1999, C3.

59. Andrew Cassel, column in *Philadelphia Inquirer,* June 9, 1999, n.p., accessed via Lexis-Nexis, February 13, 2002.

60. Wendy Tanaka, "Philadelphia Approves $45 million Loan to Local Gas Company," *Philadelphia Inquirer,* October 18, 2000, n.p., accessed via Lexis-Nexis, February 13, 2002.

61. Wendy Tanaka, "Some Advocate Sale of Philadelphia's Troubled Gas Utility," *Philadelphia Inquirer,* November 5, 2000, n.p., accessed via Lexis-Nexis, February 13, 2002.

62. www.moodys.com, accessed February 18, 2002.

city's financial prospects, providing a strong signal that change was appropriate. Philadelphia's experience became a benchmark or node for other actors to refer to in understanding the problems of cities.

Rating Australian State Governments

In the relationships between the credit rating agencies and Australian state governments, the agencies have played a "prominent role" in Australian politics.[63] Rating downgrades have been costly in Australia. The South Australian Commission of Audit estimated the cumulative additional cost to the South Australian state government from 1991–92 downgrades at A\$21.5 million over eight years.[64]

Hayward and Salvaris argue that rating agencies' analyses are "value laden" and that these "values have a strong political bent." As an example, they point to Moody's downgrading of the State of Victoria just after the October 1992 state election and before the first "very tough" economic statement of October 26. This rating was a rare, two-notch downgrade, which "helped to create an impression of a debt crisis." The newly elected Kennett government was able to use this downgrade to "great political effect." The treasurer of Victoria, Alan Stockdale, insisted "there is no alternative" to fundamental change: "Moody's downgrading of Victoria two rungs on the credit rating ladder graphically illustrated the consequence of excessive debt."[65] Hayward and Salvaris observe that it was easy to see Moody's decision as an overtly political one that helped the new state government get public support for its tough approach to the budget.[66]

Subsequently, in the (Southern Hemisphere) summer of 1993, A\$730 million was cut from Victoria's education, health, and other programs. Just when these cuts could have aroused strong opposition, S&P and Moody's announced rating upgrades. The Victorian premier greeted this as "the single most important endorsement to date of the Government's financial management."[67]

The experience of the Victoria state government demonstrates the power the agencies exercise on civil society. Rating actions gave the state government the means to externalize and objectify its policy agenda, thus vastly reducing the government's democratic accountability over budgets.

The extent to which the investment authority centralized within the rating agencies becomes an explicitly political factor—and the rating agencies become makers of public policy—was acknowledged in the late 1990s. Then, Australia's Northern

63. David Hayward and Mike Salvaris, "Rating the States: Credit Rating Agencies and the Australian State Governments," *Journal of Australian Political Economy*, no. 34 (December 1994): 1–26.

64. Ibid., 6.

65. Ibid., 14; Stockdale quoted in *The Age* (Melbourne), October 28, 1992, 15.

66. Hayward and Salvaris, December 1994, 15.

67. Ibid., Kennett quoted in *Australian Financial Review*, November 15, 1993, 1.

Territory (NT) treasurer, Mike Reed, observed that the first assignment of Aa2 to NT "signaled a vote of confidence in the Territory's economic future."[68] Moody's commented more explicitly on the State of Victoria's ratings in 1997. When asked about the government's potential for taking an activist economic role, their analyst noted a large difference in "policy attitude" between the two major parties.[69] He warned, "We are still in a period in which governments elected are very much under the influence of recollections of the time of the late 1980s and early 1990s."

More recently, following the U.S. trend, an S&P report noted positively in 2001 that Australian states were replacing their "expensive defined-benefit superannuation [pension] schemes," with "cheaper accumulation schemes." Now pensioners, not pension-providers, would bear the bulk of the financial risk.[70]

The Australian state cases reveal the indirect target of rating actions—civil society, rather than government. In these cases, rating downgrades assisted governments to pursue their policy agendas, in an environment in which entrenched interests wished to retain the existing pattern of fiscal distribution. Here, the role of the agencies does not fit the synchronic-rationalist reading described in table 5. That account precludes the political agency the Australian examples imply. Counterfactually, had the agencies not behaved in this strategic way, would Victoria's budget cuts in 1993 have been so extensive?

The Detroit Rating Controversy

Along with this "power over" dimension, the agencies also exercise structural power in municipal affairs.[71] Structural power confers the "power to decide how things shall be done" through control of frameworks of thought and action.[72] Structural power gives rise to the factoring of external expectations into thought, policy, and action, ahead of events where behavioral power might otherwise be exercised.

Detroit is a sad case of economic and political decay.[73] Its experience over the past decade and a half illustrates clearly the structural power rating agencies can exercise

68. As paraphrased in "Moody's Assigns Australia's NT AA2 Credit Rating," *Asia Pulse*, October 6, 1997, accessed via Lexis-Nexis, February 20, 2002.

69. "Scope for Higher Ratings of Victoria, S. Australia: Moody's," *Asia Pulse*, March 4, 1997, accessed via Lexis-Nexis, February 20, 2002.

70. Standard & Poor's, "Australian States' Strong Balance Sheets Underpin Their Ratings," June 4, 2001, available from www.standardandpoors.com, accessed February 20, 2002.

71. Stephen Gill and David Law, *The Global Political Economy: Perspectives, Problems, and Policies* (Baltimore: The Johns Hopkins University Press, 1988), 73.

72. Susan Strange, *States and Markets*, 2nd edition (London: Pinter, 1994), 25; Gill and Law, *The Global Political Economy*, 71–80.

73. Ze'ev Chalets, "The Tragedy of Detroit," *New York Times Magazine*, July 29, 1990, 24; also see James R. Sellars, "Regime Change and Issue Change: Will Detroit's Political Change Affect the Policy Agenda?" paper presented to the annual meeting of the Southern Political Science Association, Atlanta, November 1994.

in municipal finance. Like Philadelphia, the city was subject to white flight to the suburbs. In 1989, Detroit's median household income was $18,742, ranking it 538th out of 555 American towns and cities with a population of more than 50,000. During the 1980s, the city's median household income dropped by 20 percent (in real terms), and the poverty rate leapt upward, from 22 percent to 32 percent.[74] In 1993, the average house in Detroit sold for $25,000 or less; mansions sold for as little as $150,000.[75] The official unemployment rate in 1989 was 15.7 percent—the highest of any American city. Officially, 20 percent of buildings were unoccupied, but unofficially, the rate was probably 40 percent. During the 1980s, demolition permits exceeded construction permits by 41,800.[76] The city had to scramble to keep its official population above one million persons to retain millions of dollars in state and federal funding.[77] Things were so bad that a city official proposed unoccupied or "below code" buildings be razed, then the land fenced and transformed into urban pasture.[78] As it is, 100 million square feet of shoulder-high brush grew where houses once stood in Detroit.[79]

Detroit's fortunes have been directly linked to the car industry. In the past century, the automobile industry "was the principal factor in its population expansion from 285,784 in 1900, to 993,687 in 1920, to 1,568,662 in 1930."[80] The "rust belt" phenomenon hit Detroit hard. Between 1970 and 1983, Michigan lost 210,000 manufacturing jobs—70 percent of them from Detroit. Even though the state gained 331,100 jobs in the same period, Detroit experienced a net loss.[81]

In the 1990s, Detroit city officials responded to rating agency expectations proactively—reflecting an implicit understanding of the agencies' structural power—albeit without success. In July 1992, Moody's downgraded Detroit from the bottom rung of investment grade (Baa) to the top level of speculative grade (Ba1). What is interesting about this downgrade is that city officials were not being punished for incompetence or lack of attention to city finances, as may have been the case in Philadelphia's fiscal and political gridlock. Indeed, the officials maintained that Moody's should have "come to praise, not bury."[82]

74. "Detroit's Mayor: A Job Fit for Heroes," *Economist*, August 28, 1993, 26.

75. Linda Diebel, "Devolution of Detroit," *Toronto Star*, July 11, 1993, F2.

76. Ibid., F3.

77. Isabel Wilkerson, "Detroit Desperately Searches for Its Very Lifeblood: People," *New York Times*, September 6, 1990, 1.

78. Nancy Costello, "Urban Pasture Proposed as Way to Improve Detroit," *Globe and Mail*, May 7, 1993, A17.

79. Isabel Wilkerson, "Detroit Journal: Giving Up the Jewels to Salvage the House," *New York Times*, September 10, 1990, A18.

80. Hyman C. Grossman, managing director, Standard & Poor's Ratings Group, "Ingredients of Municipal Payment Difficulties," unpublished monograph, February 1977, 10.

81. Joe T. Darden, Richard Child Hill, June Thomas, and Richard Thomas, *Detroit: Race and Uneven Development* (Philadelphia: Temple University Press, 1987), 254.

82. Barbara Presley Noble, "A Downgraded Detroit Cries Foul," *New York Times*, November 3, 1992, D4.

The city's financial director in the administration of former mayor Coleman A. Young, noted that Detroit responded to the agency's concerns two years previously by undergoing "fiscal surgery" and that the city was determined "to keep a scalpel in hand." Moody's acknowledged that the city "diligently maximized its immediate resources, attacking budget deficits, cutting wages and employee benefits, channeling money to repay bonds and swelling its debt service reserves." What ultimately cost Detroit its investment grade rating were long-term, "extraordinarily weak credit fundamentals" having to do with the shrinking population.

Nevertheless, the Detroit case reveals some of the fiscal and policy surgery a government goes through to prevent agency gatekeeping and retain an investment grade rating. This thinking was ingrained in the financial department of the city government. The department would assess controllable variables in terms of their positive or negative effects on the city's creditworthiness. In the end, of course, the government's responses to the agencies' structural power did not save Detroit from downgrade. The city became a victim of judgments that had to do with phenomena largely outside the administration's control.

After twenty years as mayor, Young decided not to run for office again at the 1993 elections.[83] Following a heated succession race among Democrats, Dennis Archer, a highly educated black lawyer and public servant, was elected. He faced a tough 1994, with deficit projections of $88.5 million.[84] Young had been a frequent target of newspaper criticism, often lampooned in cartoons and faulted in investigative journalism. Archer, by contrast, was diplomatic and determined to present the best "report card" on Detroit's progress.[85]

Archer hired a Merrill Lynch staffer, Valerie Johnson, as his finance director. A leading figure among black professionals on Wall Street, Johnson focused on "strategies for dealing with the rating agencies" from Archer's 1993 campaign onward.[86] A "really important focus" for her was reacquiring an investment grade rating from Moody's after the city was reduced to speculative grade in late 1992.[87] According to Joe O'Keefe, a managing director at Standard & Poor's,

> He [Mayor Archer] came right after the election, and he wanted to understand our concerns and he wanted to incorporate them into his strategic plan. . . . He was very open

83. Doron P. Levin, "Tired After Two Decades at City Hall, Young Will Retire as Detroit Mayor," *New York Times*, June 23, 1993, A7. Coleman Young died in 1997.

84. Karen Pierog, "Detroit Hits the Road to Make the Case for a Fiscal Rebirth," *Bond Buyer*, December 16, 1994, 4.

85. On Young, see Levin, June 23, 1993; for a more sympathetic view, see a collection of articles and commentaries put together by the Detroit Free Press at the time of his death in 1997, available at www.freep.com/news/young/, last accessed February 24, 2002. On Archer, see Pierog, December 16, 1994; also see Patricia Montemurri, "Archer Struggled, Didn't Give Up on City," *Detroit Free Press*, December 20, 2001, n.p., available at www.freep.com, accessed February 24, 2002.

86. Karen Pierog, "Trends in the Region: Detroit's Outsider and Insider," *Bond Buyer*, December 20, 1995, 33. The author interviewed Johnson at Detroit City Hall in April 1996.

87. Johnson quoted in ibid.

to our comments, and he was very concerned about what our feelings were. I remember him taking a lot of notes.[88]

In 1995, according to Pierog, the agencies were "listening," although a Moody's representative claimed that the jury was "still out" on Detroit's improved credit quality.[89] In early 1996, Moody's affirmed Detroit's rating at Ba1—still speculative grade—but said the agency was "cautiously optimistic" about the city.[90] The change to investment grade finally happened in the fall, along with a revised outlook from S&P.[91] S&P and Moody's praised the city's economic recovery and fiscal discipline.

This recognition from the agencies "renewed investor faith in the city," according to the *Bond Buyer.*[92] Between 1994 and 1997, $5.5 billion in new investment flowed into the city, more than 1 million potholes were filled, crime fell three years in a row, and the murder rate in 1996 was the lowest in twenty-one years.[93] In December 1997, Moody's upgraded the city again, citing investment flows as positive signals of recovery.[94] S&P followed a few days later, praising city managers as "top notch," especially Archer, Johnson, and the budget director, J. Edward Hannan.[95]

Moody's upgraded again in October 1998, capping two years in which the city was upgraded five times by Moody's, S&P, and Fitch.[96] On leaving the administration at the end of Mayor Archer's second term in late 2001, Hannan, the finance director after Johnson's departure from June 1999, noted that council members did not understand ratings. They could see that if you spent more money on garbage trucks, you bought better trucks. Ratings were more intangible, he suggested, but they did secure lower interest rates and savings. "That's real money," he explained.[97]

What is interesting about Detroit's case, apart from the exercise of power taking place within it, is the emphasis on presentation and communication between the agencies and the new administration, in contrast to the previous regime. The emphasis on

88. Aaron Baar, "With the Gloom Lifting, Dennis Archer Positions Detroit for the 21st Century," *Bond Buyer,* July 16, 1997, 1.

89. Angela Connelly, an assistant vice president and senior credit officer at Moody's, quoted in Pierog, December 20, 1995.

90. Jeanne Wilson, assistant vice president at Moody's, quoted in Karen Pierog, "Moody's Maintains Detroit's Rating, But Notes Progress," *Bond Buyer,* February 23, 1996, 1.

91. O'Keefe quoted in Aaron Baar, "Standard & Poor's Revises Its Detroit Outlook to Positive," *Bond Buyer,* October 24, 1996, 2.

92. Christine Pagan, "What's Selling: Brokers Tell Investors the News about Detroit's Turnaround," *Bond Buyer,* November 13, 1996, 8.

93. "Exorcising Devils," *Economist,* November 8, 1997, 64, 67.

94. Tammy Williamson, "In the Midst of Motor City Resurrection, Moody's Upgrades the Outlook on Detroit," *Bond Buyer,* December 9, 1997, 5.

95. Quoted in Tammy Williamson, "As Agencies Review Detroit's Status, Standard & Poor's Offers an Upgrade," *Bond Buyer,* December 10, 1997, 1.

96. Tammy Williamson, "Detroit's Two-Year Winning Streak Continues with Moody's Upgrade," *Bond Buyer,* October 15, 1998, 3.

97. Elizabeth Carvlin, "We Didn't Screw It Up," *Bond Buyer,* August 29, 2001, 1.

presentation fits the diachronic-constructivist view of rating, wherein the application of judgment is vitally important to outcomes. Imagine a counterfactual scenario, in which judgment was not part of the intellectual framework. There would be little need for the emphasis on presentation and relationships that come across so strongly in the Detroit account. The observations of S&P's O'Keefe would not have been made otherwise.

Knowledge

As we have seen, rating judgments rely on both quantitative and qualitative information. They cannot be deduced purely by formula. Nevertheless, the knowledge structures promoted by the agencies give analytical precedence to certain types of data. Other types are disregarded or downplayed. The data that are emphasized reflect prevailing assumptions about the relationship between governments, fiscal affairs, and civil society.

The intellectual tools developed for private financial dealings are increasingly applied to public finance. Indeed, the idea of public finance as a separate intellectual and practical field, with its own assumptions and prescriptions no longer seems sustainable, just as the idea of public intervention in markets no longer has the status of policy orthodoxy. There seems to be a process that "reduces" the acceptable forms of data. From this reduction, the form of knowledge that emerges is instrumental and also static. Characteristically, it lacks an appreciation of change and development. It does not consider the broader circumstances of public investment. Consequently, this instrumental knowledge form undermines the basis of public service delivery.

Detroit's example, at first glance, contradicts this image of narrow rating knowledge. The Detroit case led to a debate between U.S. municipal government officials and the rating agencies over appropriate criteria for assessing municipal creditworthiness. A former Albuquerque, New Mexico mayor, David Rusk, suggested in his *Cities without Suburbs*, that Detroit's difficulties reflected the separation between city and suburbs.[98] Cities that have been able to hold on to or annex their suburbs have avoided polarization and have kept their bond ratings higher than cities of similar demography. Others suggested that Moody's should concentrate on financial management. It should stop looking for a "new city on the hill," with different market, government, and demographic characteristics—a "brand new Detroit [but] we don't have one to offer them."[99]

98. Rusk's *Cities without Suburbs* (Washington, D.C.: Woodrow Wilson Center Press, 1993) is discussed in William Tucker, "Annexations and Secessions: Keys to Urban Growth and Decay?" *American Banker Washington Watch*, November 29, 1993.

99. J. Chester Johnson, president of Government Finance Associates, Detroit's financial adviser in the early 1990s, quoted in Karen Pierog, "Mayor of Detroit Protests Moody's Ba1 Downgrade, Citing Unfairness," *Bond Buyer*, July 20, 1992, 1.

In an interview, Brenton W. Harries, president of S&P from 1972 to 1981, denied racism in rating judgments. He defended taking demographic issues into account, because "this particular mix of population requires more welfare payments, more housing. They're more of a drain as opposed to being more of a contributor."[100] S&P official Tillman observed that "quality of life" factors, such as education, homelessness, crime and health care, are "difficult to measure" but "have potential long-term effects" on municipalities' ability to meet their obligations. Confusingly, however, Tillman insisted that the "primary determinants" of creditworthiness remain "measurable financial and economic factors."[101]

Farnham and Cluff had previously reported a relationship between the higher rungs of the rating scales and home ownership, and the lower rungs and predominance of black Americans in the local population. But the implications of these analytics only became apparent with Detroit's experience.[102] Driven by the near-default of New York City in 1975, Moody's and S&P revised their municipal processes to include more "fiscal strain indicators."[103] Perhaps reflecting the view that the agencies' expectations are vital to municipal financing, Crowell and Sokol sought a "succinct definition" of these quality of life variables. To their consternation, they confirmed that the variables were defined subjectively. No rating officials would explain the priority rankings for the nonfinancial variables or their use in "the overall rating equation."[104]

Quality of life analysis seems to fit easily with a more societal view of bond repayment and therefore a broader, diachronic-constructivist understanding of bond-rating analytics. However, quality of life as a variable seems to be at odds with the rating myth and prevailing norms in the rating business. Hence the controversy and the suggestion that raters stick to narrower issuers of financial management. Tillman's assertion that measurable factors should stay the main determinants of creditworthiness reflects the contradiction between the reality of the rating process as indeterminate and public expectations about its supposed systematic, technical character. In this context, quality of life may be characterized as a weakly developed analytical stance that risks harming the rating myth.

100. Brenton W. Harries quoted in "Profits, Racism, Quality of Life, and Other Issues Facing Rating Agencies," *Bond Buyer*, February 26, 1993, 5.

101. Vickie Tillman, "Quality of Life and Bond Ratings: One Agency's Viewpoint," *Public Management* 75, no. 4 (April 1993): 8.

102. Farnham and Cluff, 1984, 29, 31.

103. Ester R. Fuchs, *Mayors and Money: Fiscal Policy in New York and Chicago* (Chicago: Chicago University Press, 1992), 29; John E. Petersen, "Background Paper," in Twentieth Century Fund, *The Rating Game: Report of the Twentieth Century Fund Task Force on Municipal Bond Credit Ratings* (New York: Twentieth Century Fund, 1974), 127.

104. Anthony Crowell and Steven Sokol, "Playing in the Gray: Quality of Life and the Municipal Bond Rating Game," *Public Management* 75, no. 5 (May 1993): 3. This theme is not new. Concerns about the lack of clarity of what ratings "measure" and the insistence on transparency can be found in *The Rating Game*, 1974, 3, 7.

Changing Norms About Public Goods

The mental framework of rating orthodoxy changes over time as prevailing economic and financial orthodoxies also develop and as dominant social forces are transformed. In one analysis of New York City's fiscal crisis of the 1970s, the broad sweep of change in hegemonic views was identified:[105]

> Conventional political "wisdom" now asserts the historical inevitability and absolute necessity of an austere public sector. Austerity, with its underlying ideology of scarcity and Social Darwinism, goes unchallenged, and in the process the social welfare apparatus . . . is now endangered.[106]

This consensus—which Lichten terms the "austerity state"—about the parameters of feasible policy-making reflects agreement to reduce social policy expenditures and increase the private sector's influence in the market.[107] This "neoliberalism" has two major implications for the rating of governments.[108] The first is an agenda to re-establish in the public sector a connection between remuneration and productivity.[109] The second is the privatization of services. The first consideration is ubiquitous in almost any review of government finance, and it was certainly a factor in the rating of Philadelphia and New York City. The second issue, privatization, is a global phenomenon.[110] The aims that seem to be at work are to "shrink the state, in pursuit of greater economic efficiency," and to "raise cash."[111]

The trend toward economic efficiency has developed in, among other things, garbage removal and airport management. Ominously, in the United States, this tendency has gone as far as to include law enforcement. Private spending on security amounted to $52 billion in 1992–93, overshadowing public expenditure by 73 percent, up from 57 percent in the early 1980s.[112]

The tendencies identified above have a most obvious public expression in politicians' concern with government budget deficits.[113] No fixed analytical criteria exist for determining that any particular deficit level is more troublesome than any other—except that bigger deficits are understood to be worse than smaller ones. But

105. Eric Lichten, *Class, Power & Austerity: The New York City Fiscal Crisis* (South Hadley, Mass.: Bergin & Garvey, 1986).

106. Ibid., 2.

107. Ibid., 3.

108. On neoliberalism, see Stephen Gill, *Power and Resistance in the New World Order* (London: Palgrave Macmillan, 2003).

109. "Running New York City: Rot at the Core," *Economist*, May 8, 1993, 23–25.

110. "Privatization: Selling the State," *Economist*, August 21, 1993, 18–20.

111. Ibid., 18.

112. Ralph Blumenthal, "As the Number of Private Guards Grows, Police Learn to Enlist Their Help," *New York Times*, July 13, 1993, A16.

113. Stevie Cameron, "How the Gravy Train Went Off the Rails," *Globe and Mail*, February 6, 1993, D1; Shawn McCarthy, "Canada's Debt," *Toronto Star*, March 21, 1993, B1; David Crane, "Fighting Deficit: Massive Changes Loom for Canada," *Toronto Star*, September 25, 1993, 1.

the idea that deficits are out of control and likely to compromise both public and private initiatives has dominated public discourse.[114] With a few exceptions, it is again common sense to believe, as was the case prior to the Depression, that governments must manage their affairs in the same way that individual households do.[115] Bond raters have helped to re-establish this view, despite their occasional comments to the contrary.[116] Both major U.S. raters use quantitative and qualitative information, even though their public pronouncements tend to emphasize the quantitative, objective character of their ratings.

Where, then, do public goods fit into this narrow form of knowledge? Public goods are those for which no market can exist. Any provision of them must be made by government, if they are to be produced at all.[117] However, it can be debated whether any particular good or service is really a public good or in some form can be provided by the market or some combination of market and government. These policy debates often revolve not so much around the question of provision, as such, but over the price and quantity of supply.

Different patterns of social forces lead to different resolutions of these conflicts, as is evident to anyone who has driven on freeways in southern Ontario and in western New York State. In Ontario, these roads have traditionally been free in that the driver pays no fee for traveling any particular distance. But as soon as the same driver crosses the border into the Niagara frontier region of western New York State, he or she pays to use the I-190 (Interstate 190). For a trip across Grand Island, New York, and into the city of Buffalo, the driver must disburse funds to toll operators, at several locations. Similarly, to exit Brooklyn and take the Garden State Parkway south to Atlantic City, the driver pays several dollars at the Verrazano Narrows and Goethals bridges, and for travel along the New Jersey and Pennsylvania Turnpikes— a two-hour drive. In contrast, traveling on the several thousand miles of the Trans-Canada Highway, from coast to coast, is toll free.

Bond rating agencies reinforce this more privatized provision of social goods in the United States and elsewhere. Their focus on financing arrangements and their judgments about the arrangements reinforce a particular pattern—to identify "revenue producing" projects that are not dependent on general revenue derived from

114. "Canada's Worrying Bond Spree," *Economist*, August 28, 1993, 76.

115. Thomas Walkom, "Debt Crisis? What Debt Crisis?" *Toronto Star*, March 27, 1993, D4.

116. Lisa Grogan-Green, "Moody's Analyst Says Deficit Threat 'Exaggerated,' " *Financial Post*, October 29, 1993, 28; also see Timothy J. Sinclair, "Deficit Discourse: The Social Construction of Fiscal Rectitude," in Randall D. Germain, ed., *Globalization and Its Critics* (New York: St. Martin's Press, 1999).

117. Public goods are usually thought to have three characteristics: they yield nonrivalrous consumption, in that one person's consumption does not deprive others; they are nonexcludable, in that if one person consumes it is impossible to stop all from consuming; and they are nonrejectable, because individuals cannot abstain from consuming them even if they want to; see Graham Bannock, R. E. Baxter, and Evan Davis, *Dictionary of Economics* (London: Economist Books/Hutchinson, 1987), 335.

taxation.[118] From a raters' point of view, taxation sources are perceived as less reliable than other types of income, because tax revenue is vulnerable to political gridlock and economic recession.[119] The effect of dedicating revenue sources is to specify, reduce, and allocate risk. However, the implications go beyond public finance. The public/private goods distinction also influences how costs are allocated across the economy and what access to government-provided goods is given to different social forces. Financing the Verrazano Narrows bridge from tolls rather than taxes rations access to the bridge for lower-income drivers living on Staten Island, for instance.

As was indicated in the Government of Ontario's 1993 budget, this approach to public and quasi-public goods is taking hold outside the United States.[120] Ontario officials suggested that the approach might well be the way to finance expansions of the freeway system.[121] In December 1998, the 407 ETR (Express Toll Route) opened just north of Toronto. The problem with this subsumption of public under private criteria is that, as Hayward and Salvaris argue, "governments are not like businesses." Unlike businesses, governments can still impose taxes. Moreover, the concern that governments have with economic growth means that deficits might be better viewed as countercyclical stimulation to prevent further economic deterioration.[122] Governments should not, therefore, be analyzed in debt-equity terms but in terms of the viability of their cash flows—the income-tax stream. This view entails a more societal approach to knowledge, whereby taxpayers' income levels and capacity to support more taxation become central concerns.[123] The agencies have attempted this sort of analysis elsewhere, such as in the Detroit and Philadelphia cases.

This investigation of the knowledge dimension of municipal rating suggests that a general, public benefit is no longer acceptable or even identifiable to the agencies. This change will affect social groups that have benefited in the past from subsidization by other interests. For instance, if transit fees were to increase to recover full costs, the assessment of benefit might be allowed to outweigh any wider public interest.

The scenario analyzed above depicts the rating agencies as purveyors and enforcers of a new common sense about public infrastructure and investment. Where public services must be provided, the problem seems to be how to tie the service provider into the cash nexus. Compared with ordinary tax revenue, tolls and

118. Interview with Hyman C. Grossman, managing director, Municipal Finance Department, Standard & Poor's, New York, N.Y., August 18, 1992.

119. See, e.g., "Pennsylvania Turnpike Commission," *Moody's Municipal Credit Report*, August 12, 1992.

120. "Budget Paper C: Fiscal Review and Outlook," *1993 Ontario Budget* (Toronto: Queen's Printer, May 1993), 64–66.

121. Two Ontario government officials mentioned this option in different interviews during spring of 1993.

122. . On this point, see Robert Eisner, *The Great Deficit Scares: The Federal Budget, Trade, and Social Security* (Washington, D.C.: Brookings Institution, 1997); also see Sinclair, in Germain, ed., 1999.

123. Hayward and Salvaris, December 1994, 12–13.

other forms of dedicated revenue ensure investors are more likely to get their money back. In other situations, public provision of services can be privatized. The scenario does not suggest rating agencies are the sole causal agent producing these outcomes. In an alternate scenario, the agencies would not promote a close link between new public investment and revenue sources or privatization. Then the mental framework surrounding these trends would be weaker and more inchoate. The penetration of these norms would likely be reduced and delay the timing of their introduction.

Governance

What are the governance implications of municipal rating? How does the rating process affect democratic policy choice and accountability? Here, the argument is that bond rating agencies, among other institutions, have acquired an unprecedented capacity to exercise disciplinary power over civil society and political organization. Along with other pressures, rating agencies are contributing to a narrowing or redefinition of social citizenship. Social citizenship becomes a liability within the orthodox mental framework of rating work.[124] Much of what has been discussed above, especially the political gridlock in Philadelphia and rating's impact on knowledge structures affecting government, supports this claim.

Rating New York City

New York City's fiscal troubles illustrate the trend for private institutions of governance to displace government. In the mid-1970s, the city's economy underwent massive structural change as local manufacturing activity shut down or relocated.[125] Later, in the early 1990s, the city's finances again faltered as Wall Street firms restructured.[126] In April 1975, Standard & Poor's suspended their rating on New York City bonds.[127] Two major factors contributed to the crisis. The first was the changing New York City economy and its impact on tax revenue. The second had to

124. Marshall identifies three types of citizenship within contemporary democratic society: civil, political, and social. Civil citizenship refers to freedom of speech and religion. Political citizenship refers to political expression. Social citizenship refers to the right to a certain minimum standard of life and economic security; it is associated with the rise of the welfare state (T. H. Marshall, *Class, Citizenship and Social Development* [Chicago: University of Chicago Press, 1977], passim).

125. Richard Levine, "Now Albany Gets Its Opportunity for Fiscal Delusions," *New York Times,* March 4, 1990, 6.

126. "Running New York City: Rot at the Core," *Economist,* May 8, 1993, 23–25; Todd S. Purdum, "New York City to Slash Borrowing under Pressure from Bond Raters," *New York Times,* February 28, 1992, 1.

127. Hyman C. Grossman, managing director, Municipal Finance Department, Standard & Poor's Ratings Group, "Ingredients of Municipal Payments Difficulties," New York City, February 1977.

do with the way the city administration functioned—its rigid procedures, high salary levels, and difficult labor union negotiations. The crisis challenged the position of organized labor and realigned interests within the city. Labor was increasingly confined to the margins of city authority, as austerity measures were adopted.[128]

The city's way of organizing its finances at the time later became a benchmark for change in the accounting and fiscal systems of all U.S. municipal governments. As Grossman notes, "For many years we [at S&P] had been critical of various aspects of the city's fiscal policies."[129] The problems included a substantial quantity of short-term borrowing, borrowing for operating expenses (deficit financing), and anticipation of 100 percent receipt of tax levies (when collection history really suggested a much lower rate). In the case of tax collection, S&P found that city practices made no provision for taxes not collected, canceled, or abated. In June 1975, a tax revenue shortfall amounting to $232 million placed the city's overall financial position in peril.[130]

Nevertheless, city officials used these tax shortfalls to support a further $380 million in tax anticipation notes. Given that the tax arrears were not receivable, realistically, the pledged support for the tax anticipation notes was, in S&P's words, "essentially absent."[131] Similar problems were perceived with the way the city incorporated state and federal support into its accounts. It was never acknowledged that shortfalls were the historical norm, and thus the city overborrowed against these inflated amounts.

What is interesting about S&P's analysis of New York's problems is that it gave rise to wider change to prevent this sort of debacle elsewhere. Grossman, the author of a report on municipal payments difficulties and a major figure in the world of municipal rating, was a member of the Governmental Accounting Standards Board and the National Council on Governmental Accounting after New York's mid-1970s fiscal crisis. The standards facilitated comparisons among municipal governments and introduced the accrual-type method to cash-based government accounting. Traditionally, payment obligations had only been recognized when a check was drawn.[132] The New York crisis provided an opportunity for external monitoring to be increased and municipalities' capacity for unilateral action or inaction to be reduced.

The 1970s did not, of course, mark the end of New York's financial troubles. The city experienced good economic times during the 1980s as Wall Street boomed, compensating somewhat for the loss of skilled manufacturing jobs. However, as recession set in from late 1989 through the early 1990s, fiscal problems again began to accumulate.

128. Lichten, 1986.
129. Grossman, February 1977, 26.
130. Ibid., 28.
131. Ibid., 29.
132. Interview with Hyman C. Grossman, managing director, Municipal Finance Department, Standard & Poor's, New York City, August 18, 1992.

Democrat mayor David N. Dinkins (1990–93), the city's first black mayor, had been elected to improve the lot of the disadvantaged and of organized labor, not reorganize the city's finances. The recession reduced tax receipts and simultaneously raised the cost of social programs. The Dinkins administration never tackled the long-term problems of the city's income and expenditures, but it was adept at finding ways to plug acute budget gaps, at the last minute. Downgraded by Moody's to Baa1 in February 1991, the city managed to avoid a downgrade by S&P. The mayor made skillful budget cuts and responded effectively to rating agency concerns in order to avoid further downgrades.[133] During a speech at Yale University, after his defeat by Rudolph W. Guiliani in the 1993 election, Dinkins offered a stable bond rating as one of his achievements as mayor.[134]

Rating has a special place in New York's finances, not only for the agencies' primary role in financial markets. The views of the rating agencies are also closely watched by the state's Financial Control Board and by the Municipal Assistance Corporation, established in the 1970s to monitor New York City finances.[135]

The incoming mayor declared a "fiscal emergency" in early 1994. Giuliani advocated privatization, changes in work rules to make city workers more productive, and other cost-saving exercises.[136] Although some of his agenda addressed structural problems, many of the savings came from one-time-only asset sales, a measure that did not address what the rating agencies reportedly saw as the city's long-range budget problems.[137] Giuliani concentrated on reducing "head count," because the agencies understood personnel numbers to be a key indicator of real government cuts.[138]

Giuliani's budget proposals led to protracted conflict with the city council and the city comptroller during 1994, with the mayor asserting that the city's rating was a good indicator of market confidence in his program.[139] The pattern of extreme short-term financing continued, however. S&P finally downgraded the city in July 1995, despite strenuous efforts on the mayor's part to avert the decision.[140]

133. Clifford J. Levy, "Dinkins Orders Sharp Budget Cuts to Save New York's Bond Rating," *New York Times*, July 3, 1993, sec. A1.

134. Jonathan P. Hicks, "Dinkins Spells Out Hopes for Lasting Legacy," *New York Times*, November 18, 1993, sec. B4.

135. James C. McKinley Jr., "Badillo Urges State to Study City Budget," *New York Times*, June 2, 1993, B1.

136. Steven Lee Myers, "Giuliani Outlines Budget to Cut Government Size," *New York Times*, February 3, 1994, A1.

137. James C. McKinley, Jr., "Giuliani's Budget Proposes Cuts for Spending and Work Force," *New York Times*, May 11, 1994, A1.

138. James C. McKinley, Jr., "Making Do with Less," *New York Times*, May 13, 1994, A33.

139. Jonathan P. Hicks, "Giuliani Tells Agencies to Use His Budget, Not the Council's," *New York Times*, November 29, 1994, B3.

140. Carol O'Cleireacain, "New York's Desparate Hours," *New York Times*, March 14, 1995, A25; David Firestone, "Giuliani Obtains a Delay on a Shift in Bond Ratings," *New York Times*, May 23, 1995, B3; David Firestone, "City's Bond Rating: Did Giuliani Do Enough to Help It?," *New York Times*, July 11, 1995, B4.

Giuliani subsequently claimed that S&P had held off downgrading in 1993 so as not to interfere with the incumbent's chances for re-election and that the 1995 downgrade covered up prior mistakes by S&P.[141] However, the state Financial Control Board reinforced S&P's warning about short-term financial gimmicks.[142] S&P's criticism of New York's "one-shot solutions and other manipulations" was reiterated in 1996.[143] At the time, Moody's acknowledged the dilemma New York's mayor faced: "The city can't afford to borrow more because its debt burden is high, but at the same time it can't not afford to borrow more because its infrastructure needs are so great."[144]

Things changed dramatically in New York finances at the end of Giuliani's first term, because of prosperity on Wall Street, according to the Financial Control Board.[145] The city was upgraded by S&P and Moody's in February 1998.[146] Moody's upgraded again in August 2000.[147] The good news was not to continue, however, with the onset of recession and the events of September 11, 2001. The new mayor, Michael Bloomberg, projected budget gaps of $4.7 billion in 2003, $5 billion in 2004, and $5.3 billion in 2005.[148] Bloomberg pursued a tax-raising strategy to close the gap in 2003.[149]

The experience of the Australian states also provides an example of the trend for agencies to take a view on governance. The 1990 premiers' conference decision to give states responsibility for debt the Commonwealth of Australia issued on their behalf "exposed the states' soft underbellies to the sharp teeth" of the rating agencies.[150] The intention was to make state finances "transparent" to the capital markets and the agencies. In place of democratically accountable intergovernmental forums, financial markets were now to assume the burden of regulating and overseeing the states.[151]

141. David Firestone, "In Blow to Mayor, Credit Agency Lowers New York's Bond Rating," *New York Times*, A1.

142. Vivian S. Toy, "Control Board Is Critical of Giuliani Budget Ploys," *New York Times*, A23.

143. Steven Lee Myers, "For Giuliani, Current Budget Woes Overtake Future's," *New York Times*, A25.

144. Robert A. Kurtter of Moody's Investors Service, quoted in Clifford J. Levy, "New York Fiscal Monitors Warn of Rising Debt Cost," *New York Times*, August 27, 1996, B3.

145. David Firestone, "High Marks for Giuliani from Budget Watchdogs," *New York Times*, July 18, 1997, B3.

146. Norimitsu Onishi, "Bond-Rating Agency Gives a Vote of Confidence to the City," *New York Times*, February 4, 1998, B7; Norimitsu Onishi, "Citing Improving Economy, Moody's Raises City's Bond Rating," *New York Times*, February 25, 1998, B3.

147. Eric Lipton, "Flush with Cash, New York Gets Highest Credit Rating in Nine Years," *New York Times*, August 9, 2000, B3.

148. New York City Office of Management and Budget, *Financial Plan: The City of New York, Fiscal Years 2002–2006* (New York: Office of Management and Budget, February 13, 2002).

149. Michael Cooper, "The City Budget: Overview: City Budget Deal Closes Big Deficit without Big Cuts," *New York Times*, June 26, 2003, 1.

150. Hayward and Salvaris, December 1994, 20.

151. Ibid., 21.

This new regulatory process has a distinct semantic content. It is opposed to "an activist economic role" for government.[152] Privatization of government assets is a good thing because it potentially reduces debt burden.[153] Privatization also helps to repair the problems expansionist governments created. But selling off assets, as in the case of New York City, is not a long-term solution, and the agencies want more than just a short-term fix. Hence, S&P encouraged longer-term changes in how the Australian states do business, embodied in legislation. The changes were a good thing, as S&P saw it, because they "committed governments" to prudent financial goals.[154]

The role of the rating agencies in New York's finances seem best characterized as a constant effort to challenge structures thought to have produced endemic fiscal imbalance in the city's affairs. The results of their investigations into the city's administration, which were a feature of the rating process, have been held up by the agencies as examples to other municipalities of how not to govern. In this struggle, the rating agencies were allied with other institutions, including the Governmental Accounting Standards Board and the National Council on Governmental Accounting, in trying to change how the city was governed. Counterfactually, if the agencies had not continually prodded the city, other institutions might have attempted this task. But the benchmark that the agencies could offer—an investment-grade rating—was a clearly identifiable target for the city. It was this specific prize that seemed to have been so strong a lure for Dinkins, Guiliani, and Bloomberg. Without this element, it is unlikely that New York's endemic fiscal imbalance could have been managed for more than two decades without default.

Conclusions

As the examples of Detroit and Philadelphia illustrate, rating agencies have considerable influence over investment and are able to promote neoliberal policy initiatives. The variables the agencies deploy in assessing cities are not socially neutral. They reflect a process of judgment that tends to produce socially partial policy on the bond issuer's part, other things being equal.

Rating agencies apply to the public realm forms of knowledge developed in the private world. This effort to "lock down" public goods—within private ways of thinking that narrowly specify costs and benefits—amounts to a privatization of

152. "Scope for Higher Ratings of Victoria, S. Australia: Moody's," *Asia Pulse,* March 4, 1997, accessed via Lexis-Nexis, February 20, 2002.

153. "Moody's Says South Australia's Rating Likely to Improve," *AAP News,* September 19, 1999, accessed via Lexis-Nexis, February 20, 2002.

154. Standard & Poor's, "Australian States' Strong Balance Sheets Underpin Their Ratings," June 4, 2001, available from www.standardandpoors.com, accessed February 20, 2002.

knowledge. Increasingly, the very notion of public goods seems to be under threat from rating.

At the same time as social citizenship is coming under attack, rating agencies are assuming a stronger position in the governance of communities. As in New York, established social interests are being marginalized as rating agencies pressure local governments to shape up or suffer the consequences. The diminished public governance that follows is linked to increasing attempts at rule-setting by these private agents of risk reduction. We look next at sovereign governments and the global spread of rating.

CHAPTER SIX

Global Growth of the Rating Business

> As the free capital flowing through debt markets reaches new heights,
> the American rating agencies' lever of upgrading, downgrading or put-
> ting on the "watch list" seems to have more weight than most interna-
> tional actions by the American government. But even the IMF, as the
> only global institution with the power to infringe upon the sovereignty
> of even the biggest nations by carrying out its regular surveillance,
> looks weak compared with Wall Street's mighty rating twins.
>
> KLAUS C. ENGELEN, *International Economy,* 1994

$\mathbf{B}$ond rating has a global reach in this era of international capital mobility. The previous focus on corporate and municipal rating was drawn largely from the American experience, because rating began in the United States and remains most developed there. In this look at rating outside the United States, two sets of considerations dominate. Both have to do with the implications of rating for the world order. The first consideration is the rating of national or sovereign governments. Sovereign rating raises many questions. The most important is the probable effect on national policy autonomy, where the rating agency is not domestically owned and controlled (as is the case with Moody's and S&P's rating of non-U.S. issues).[1] The second concrete phenomenon considered here is the spread of bond rating into new territory. Moody's and S&P have opened branch offices in locations outside the United States, and domestic or local rating agencies have been established in many regions, including Europe and Japan, but especially in emerging markets and the developing world. Most attention is given to the expansion of the global

---

1. In this analysis of constraints on policy autonomy, a broad conception of sovereignty is utilized. It is the popular view—the idea that when state policy autonomy is challenged, so is sovereignty. The legal conception of sovereignty, which dominates Realist international relations scholarship, is premised on a different idea—that states can still act when necessary to "defy markets." See Louis W. Pauly, "Capital Mobility, State Autonomy and Political Legitimacy," *Journal of International Affairs* 48, no. 2 (Winter 1995): 373.

agencies. As is made clear throughout this book, they are the institutions that bring change.

What is the significance of sovereign rating and the spread of rating processes? Is rating a specifically American process, whose growth reflects American interests? If so, the emergence of local agencies may be a reaction to the dominance of U.S. institutions. Alternatively, even though rating's origins are in the United States and reflect sophisticated U.S. knowledge production and capital markets, is rating actually a transnational phenomenon? Suppose that the transnational view is accurate. Then the establishment of domestic agencies could be intended to transform the way capital is allocated in developing countries, to promote liquid capital markets, and to pave the way for capital flows and full membership in the global economy.

To interpret rating as a specifically American phenomenon fits the diachronic-constructivist principles from the mental framework of rating orthodoxy (table 5). Analysts working from a diachronic-constructivist perspective seek specific historical and social origins for phenomena. But agencies take a transnational view, premised on synchronic-rationalist assumptions about the need for their services. Either scenario generates pressures for policy convergence across national boundaries.

The position taken here is that, in the first instance, rating is a U.S. phenomenon. But rating becomes transnational in character as the agencies acquire both allies and opponents in new territories. The transnational view affirms the agencies' U.S. origins, norms, and practices. Even if rating is increasingly transnational, the mental framework of rating remains largely American.

As in chapter 5, the mid-range arguments about investment, knowledge, and governance contrast rationalist and constructivist accounts, in terms of the counterfactual method introduced in chapter 1.

Investment

The form of global investment is changing. The initial mid-range argument to be made is that rating has become a key feature of an increasingly centralized investment system. Hence, the judgments inherent in rating (the mental framework of rating orthodoxy) have greater global impact.

The centralization of rating generates emphasis on "fundamental" investment analysis. This type of analysis concerns the basic macroeconomic environment and the potential of an entity to achieve its goals. The trend is seen in rating decisions about municipalities like Detroit, where long-run population growth, tax base potential, and quality of life became more important to the rating analysis than evaluation of the city's budgets. Fundamental analysis brings rating judgments much closer to the organization and operation of corporations and governments.

Raising money in the debt markets implies a much longer-term time horizon for repayment than has typically been the case with bank lending. Thus, rating agencies use different variables than banks in judging corporations and sovereign governments accessing the debt markets for the first time. These variables are increasingly economic, social, and political, not merely financial. The change is significant, because financial and economic analyses, though related, have separate purposes. Financial analysis is focused on an entity and its goals; it is therefore essentially pragmatic in orientation. Economics and related disciplines (demography, for example) focus less on individual entities than on collective situations. Much broader conclusions about the efficiency (and thus appropriateness) of institutional arrangements and about the probability of future events are common in these disciplines. The incorporation of such conclusions into analyses of creditworthiness means that rating agency scrutiny of institutions, based on these strategic models of probable outcomes, is much more pervasive.

With investment judgment centralized in rating agencies, what are the likely consequences from fundamental analyses of debtors?

The mental framework of rating orthodoxy or "rating myth" creates pressure to respond to rating issues with "cookie cutter" conceptions of problems and solutions. Fundamental analysis, as described here, assumes that societies are much the same in their essentials. They are driven by similar dynamics, such as individual self-maximization. This synchronic-rationalist assumption is at odds with a developmental view implying a world order in which societies are qualitatively as well as quantitatively differentiated.

Abstract assumptions and objectives about investment are central to fundamental analysis. But investment is actually premised on relations between different social forces (such as employees and management). Consequently, the growth of capital markets in which rating agencies provide the major information link between buyers and sellers of debt potentially change the relations between those social forces. Existing accommodations among social interests are likely displaced as technically or abstractly driven arguments, underpinned by rationalist impulses, increasingly determine investment decision-making. The breakdown of traditional financial intermediation and the centralization of investment authority inherent in rating eliminates relationships between those who have funds and those who seek them. What we see is the loss of agents that collectively absorb risk (banks and bank lending), and that act as social buffers among interests. The agents' role changes to that of market participant.

The tendency described above is evident in Europe, Japan, and in the more advanced developing countries. In London, of course, there is a long tradition of "commercial" finance distanced from productive life.[2] Europe has traditionally had strong relationship banking and finance-government interaction. Even there, how-

---

2. See Geoffrey Ingham, *Capitalism Divided? The City and Industry in British Social Development* (London: Macmillan, 1984).

ever, there are signs of change as the costs of intermediation draw European borrowers and lenders toward disintermediation.[3]

Rating is also changing emerging markets. Until the 1990s, most developing countries did not have liquid capital markets. Credit allocation was organized by "repressed" financial systems—governments maintained low interest rates and rationed capital through the banks.[4] However, rating agencies are being established in the developing world as disintermediated, market-based capital allocation spreads from the world's economic and financial centers.[5] Rating activity in the developing world was spurred by the Asian financial crisis of 1997–98, as the value of financial transparency was perceived.[6]

We have seen that large pools of financial assets are at stake in the move to a disintermediated system of capital allocation. Before the 1997–98 Asian crisis, this combined portfolio probably amounted to between $10 and $15 trillion. It easily dwarfed the value of the equity of the emerging markets, which totaled $1 trillion in 1994.[7] Many of these funds have started to invest in local currencies rather than solely in dollar assets.[8]

Major infrastructure investments are a priority for developing countries. The World Bank identified fifteen public utilities in 1994 that needed to raise $52.5 billion.[9] Banking is not able to provide this volume of cash with the long-term maturities sought, equity is too expensive, and governments are reluctant to increase their commitments. But "Moody's and S&P tend only to rate companies that borrow in dollars or in the Euromarkets," so the establishment of domestic rating agencies are a priority in investment-scarce countries.[10] Even if they are often not as creditable as the U.S. agencies, local agencies further transparent investment norms.[11] They also

3. Interview with Richard Waters, reporter, *Financial Times* (London), December 8, 1992; also see Geoffrey R. D. Underhill, "Global Capital Markets and EU Financial Integration," paper presented to the annual workshop, International Political Economy Group, British International Studies Association, Political Economy Research Center, University of Sheffield, Sheffield, England, March 31, 1995.

4. Stephan Haggard and Chung H. Lee, "The Political Dimension of Finance in Economic Development," in Haggard, Lee, and Sylvia Maxfield, eds., *The Politics of Finance in Developing Countries* (Ithaca: Cornell University Press, 1993), 5.

5. On the disintermediation trend in Asia and the forces driving it, see Peter Montagnon, "Intermediaries Find Role under Threat in Asia," *Financial Times*, December 6, 1994, 21.

6. . "On Watch: Credit-rating Agencies," *Economist*, May 15, 1999, 122, 125.

7. International Monetary Fund, *International Capital Markets: Developments, Prospects, and Policy Issues* (Washington, D.C.: IMF, 1994), 18.

8. International Monetary Fund, *Private Market Financing for Developing Countries* (Washington, D.C.: IMF, 1993), 27; also see William Glasgall, Larry Holyoke, John Rossant, and Bill Javetski, "The Global Investor," *Business Week*, October 11, 1993, 120–26.

9. William Barnes, "Emerging Markets: Thai Bond Market Set for Lift-Off," *Financial Times*, October 24, 1994, 29.

10. Nicholas Sargen, Salomon Brothers research director, quoted in Amy Barrett, "Scanning the Globe for High Yields," *Financial World* 159, no. 19 (September 1990): 2.

11. Lucy Conger, "Transition to Transparency," *Institutional Investor* (January 1994): 111–14.

provide a new means for tapping huge sources of relatively low-cost capital. At the same time, they offer assurance to investors. Risks are scrutinized, and the relative absence of volatility—a benefit that went with the economic and financial inertia of bank intermediation—is not lost altogether in the rush to disintermediation.

Agency growth is most evident in Asia and Latin America. South Africa also has its own agency.[12] There seem to be two tiers to the local agency business. The top tier is integrated with the U.S. agencies, either through technical support arrangements or some sort of ownership interest. The second tier is independent of the U.S. majors. Ownership by financial institutions is common in developing country agencies and may cause conflicts of interest where an agency rates issues being sold by its owners. Calificadora de Valores (Caval), the Mexican agency, is typical of the former type.[13]

In 1989, after an approach from the International Finance Corporation (IFC), a World Bank affiliate that sponsored a feasibility study, the Mexican securities authority, the Comision Nacional de Valores, ruled that debt issuers must obtain credit ratings.[14] Caval, with a staff of eighteen, opened in January 1990, with the assistance of Standard & Poor's. Subsequently, the number of Mexican commercial paper issuers fell from 770 in mid-1991 to fewer than 200 in mid-1993, because many low-quality issuers were forced out of the market by the agency.[15] In September 1993, Caval was acquired by S&P, which seemed to have been motivated by U.S. interest in Mexican companies after the North American Free Trade Agreement (NAFTA) came into force. Agency creation and growth also has accompanied government liberalization of capital allocation in India. The subcontinent has two agencies, the Investment Information and Credit Rating Agency (ICRA) and Credit Rating Information Services of India (CRISIL).[16] Both initially developed without major agency contact. They have been fostered by regulatory requirements mandating the rating of commercial paper and unsecured bonds.[17] CRISIL has large participation by S&P, and ICRA has Moody's as a significant shareholder and technical partner.[18]

12. Telephone interview with Roy Weinberger, Roy Weinberger and Associates, Maplewood, N.J., January 19, 1993 (Weinberger is a rating consultant and former S&P vice president); also see Richard Lapper, "Growth in Rating Agencies Serving Emerging Markets," *Financial Times,* November 2, 1994, 19.

13. "Credit Ratings, with Their Awesome Power, Come to Mexico," *Institutional Investor* (January 1994): 112–13.

14. Steven Bavaria, "Credit Rating Agencies Plan Expansion of Mexican Coverage," *Investment Dealers Digest,* August 26, 1991, 13.

15. "Credit Ratings," January 1994.

16. N. Girish Kumar and P. Dhileepan, "Credit Rating and the Capital Markets in India," *MDI Management Journal* 7, no. 1 (January 1994): 64.

17. Ibid., 68.

18. Based on information in a communication with the author from David Levey, managing director, Moody's Investors Service, April 9, 2002. Levey notes that Moody's has also invested in a Czech/Slovak agency, is rating locally in Mexico and Brazil, has formed joint ventures in China and Malaysia, and is working with Interfax in Russia.

The Asian Development Bank (ADB) also holds an equity stake in CRISIL. ADB is committed to fostering domestic capital markets and rating agencies elsewhere in Asia.[19] The bank funds feasibility studies throughout the region, including Indonesia and China, and finances staff training for the new agencies.[20] The bank seems motivated to move away from "repressed" systems, in order to remove the "element of bureaucratic discretion" from capital allocation.[21]

Major assistance in founding developing country rating agencies is provided by the IFC, "the largest multilateral source of loan and equity financing for private sector projects in developing countries."[22] IFC assistance includes ventures throughout Asia and Europe: Pakistan in 1994, the Middle East in 1995, Turkey in 1996, China in 1997, the Czech Republic and Hungary in 1998 and 1999, Sri Lanka in 1999, and the Philippines in 1999.[23]

In each case, the IFC has provided an equity stake of around 20 percent. A second-level U.S. rating company, such as Fitch, usually provided the know-how and an ownership stake of 40–60 percent. In the case of the now-defunct Inter-Arab Rating Company (IARC), the Abu Dhabi–based Arab Monetary Fund held a 20 percent stake.

Malaysia acquired a rating agency in 1990, when Rating Agency Malaysia (RAM) was formed to meet the Malaysian government's requirement that the agency rate all debt issues after May 1992.[24] The Thai rating agency, Thai Rating & Information Services (TRIS), was established in 1993.[25] Part owners are the government and the

19. Jack Lowenstein, "Will Rating Catch On?" *Asiamoney*, no. 7 (May 1990): 64. John Thornhill and Richard McGregor, "Bank to Develop Asian Capital Market," *Financial Times*, May 11–12, 2002, 3.

20. On capital market developments in China, see Scott Kennedy, "China's Credit Rating Agencies Struggle for Relevance," *China Business Review* 30, no. 6 (November–December 2003), 36–40; Paul Bowles and Gordon White, *The Political Economy of China's Financial Reforms: Finance in Late Development* (Boulder, Colo.: Westview, 1993).

21. Arvind Mathur, ADB investment banking specialist, quoted in Lowenstein, May 1990, 64.

22. "IFC—What We Do," available at www.ifc.org, accessed March 6, 2002. In a related development, since 2003 the UNDP has been cooperating on a credit-rating initiative with Standard & Poor's to provide sovereign ratings of sub-Saharan African nations, as a first step to gaining access to international capital markets ("Credit Rating Critical for Africa's Development, Senior UN Official Tells New York Business Forum," available at www.undp.org/dpa/pressrelease/releases/2004/february/pr26Feb04.html, accessed March 3, 2004).

23. "IFC Signs Agreement to Form Pakistan's First Credit Rating Agency," IFC press release, no. 94/101, June 15, 1994; "IFC Joins Forces with Arab Monetary Fund and IBCA to Launch Inter-Arab Rating Company," IFC press release, no. 96/36, October 8, 1995; "IFC Invests in Credit Rating Agency in the Philippines," IFC press release, no. 99/137, April 29, 1999; "IFC Invests in Hungarian Credit Rating Company," IFC press release, no. 99/165, June 28, 1999. These releases were obtained from www.ifc.org, accessed April 13, 2001. Information on IBAR, China Chengxin, DCRC, and DCR Lanka were taken from project data on the World Bank site, at www.worldbank.org, accessed April 13, 2001.

24. "Rating Agency Malaysia: Boosting the Corporate Bond Market," *Asiamoney*, June 1994, 17.

25. Paul Handley, "Committed to Paper: Thailand Launches Its First Credit-Rating Agency," *Far Eastern Economic Review*, August 12, 1993, 1.

ADB, as well as financial institutions, and it is licensed by the Thai SEC. TRIS has a technical assistance agreement with S&P and acts as S&P's marketing arm in Bangkok.[26]

RAM and the Central Bank of Sri Lanka both have a 10 percent share of DCR Lanka. In 2001, the IFC invested in Fitch Ratings (Thailand) Limited, the second rating company to be founded in that country.[27] Fitch also provided technical assistance and day-to-day oversight of operations. According to *Asiamoney*, the project was supposed to encourage the development of Thailand's bond market as a source of long-term finance for the private sector.[28]

In the 1990s, as we have seen, many new agencies opened in developing countries. Greg M. Gupton, an official at Moody's who runs a web page on credit risk, publishes a list of some sixty-nine agencies. He notes that the list "is very dynamic with the opposing forces of 'consolidating for efficiency' on the one hand, and 'emerging market governments putting their own spin on their company's credits' on the other," working to increase and decrease that total.[29] Apart from the quantitative dynamism, these new agencies and their governments have made concerted efforts to improve the perceived quality of their output. State-led initiatives include mandatory ratings, as in Malaysia, and efforts to regulate the rating process, as in India.[30] The Indian regulations are important in terms of quality. They include a code of conduct and ban conflicts of interest, preventing, for example, a rating agency from rating a corporation that owns or "promotes" an agency.

The agencies have led efforts to improve ratings quality. Initiatives include links with the U.S. majors and assistance from the ADB for the creation of AFCRA in November 1993. This body is the ASEAN Forum of Credit Rating Agencies, a regional industry association within the Association of South East Asian Nations.[31]

26. "Stars Line Up behind TRIS," *Banker*, October 1993, 55.

27. "Good Business," International Finance Corporation press release, no. 01/48, February 27, 2001, available at the Press Room of www.ifc.org, accessed March 6, 2002.

28. In addition to Fitch, which has 39.9 percent equity, other partners are "Government Pension Fund, an investment vehicle for retirement savings of government employees, with 10.1 percent equity; Thai Life Insurance Company with 10 percent equity; Muang Thai Life Assurance Company with 10 percent equity; Thai Farmers Asset Management Company with 10 percent equity; and TISCO Asset Management Company with 10 percent equity." International Finance Corporation, 2001.

29. Greg M. Gupton's page can be found at www.defaultrisk.com.

30. On Malaysia, see Nandkumar Nayar, "Asymmetric Information, Voluntary Ratings and the Rating Agency of Malaysia," *Pacific-Basin Finance Journal* 1, no. 4 (December 1993): 369–80. On India's regulation of rating agencies, see "Notification Securities and Exchange Board of India (Credit Rating Agencies) Regulations, 1999," available at www.sebi.gov.in, accessed August 4, 2001. On motivations for the establishment of local rating agencies, see Michael Pettis, "Latin America Needs a Bond Market," *Wall Street Journal*, September 4, 1998, A11, and "Bonds: Asia's Missing Market," *Economist*, September 2, 2000, 98, 101.

31. On links with the U.S. agencies, see "Asian Bond Markets: First Rate," *Economist*, December 24–January 6, 1995, 94–95; on AFRCA, see www.pefindo.com/afcra1.htm, accessed March 3, 2002.

Members of AFCRA, in addition to TRIS, are Malaysia Rating Corporation (MARC), Philippine Rating Services Corporation (PhilRatings), PT Kasnic Duff & Phelps Credit Rating Indonesia (DCR-Indonesia), PT Pefindo Credit Rating Indonesia Ltd. (Pefindo), and Rating Agency Malaysia (RAM).[32] In the AFCRA Code of Ethics clauses excerpted in table 7, note the emphasis on the responsibility of raters to the rated (and not to investors) and the weak conflict of interest language.

The U.S. government also promotes rating. The idea is that sovereign debt rating is the initial move in a process of moving countries away from dependence on international aid and toward markets. Pushing African nations in particular into the private sector seems to have been the agenda of a meeting in Washington during April 2002 of African finance ministers and central bankers, with Secretary of State Colin Powell and Treasury Secretary Paul O'Neill as hosts. The administration paid for new ratings of these countries by Fitch Ratings. According to Mr. O'Neill, "We believe all nations need to move in a direction where they have investment-grade debt." The administration estimated that about a dozen African regimes could attract such a rating in the foreseeable future, based on their budget balances and the transparency of their legal systems. Only four of forty-eight sub-Saharan African states had ratings in 2002.[33]

There are clear differences between the domestic agencies and the global market leaders, Moody's and S&P. The major agencies are tied to government regulation. But they are not creatures of a transition from "repressed" financial systems to market-based systems, as are the domestic agencies. The domestic agencies and responses to them reflect both the transfer of transnational norms and the particular histories and needs of their home countries.

Agencies that are in some ways comparable to the majors usually have technical or ownership arrangements with them. But in most developing countries, disintermediation has not progressed enough to make thorough financial examination by the major agencies a serious constraint. Secrecy is the norm, and comparisons are thought unseemly.[34] Hence, these local rating agencies remain primordial.

They provide a bridge, albeit tentative, between the large, liquid, and relatively low-cost pools of financial resources in the developed world and the major investment needs in developing areas. They are part of the secular trend to greater financial

32. See information on AFCRA at Thai Rating and Information Services' web page, www.tris.tnet.co.th, accessed March 3, 2002.

33. Paul O'Neill quoted in Michael M. Phillips, "U.S. to Push Credit-Rating Plan for Indebted Nations in Africa," *Wall Street Journal*, April 22, 2002, A16; on access to U.S. capital markets as a policy incentive mechanism, see Thomas Catán, Joshua Chaffin, and Stephen Fidler, "Capital Markets 'Could Be Used as Tool of U.S. Foreign Policy,' " *Financial Times*, May 24, 2001, 14.

34. Edward Young, head of Moody's office in Hong Kong, which opened in June 1994, has observed that rating in Asia is very different from rating in the West. Although many Asian companies "have the form of a western company . . . you may not know what goes on behind the scenes. There may be relationships you don't fully understand" (quoted in "Insatiable: A Survey of Asian Finance," *Economist*, November 12, 1994, 14).

Table 7. ASEAN forum of credit rating agencies (code of ethics-excerpts)

- Credit rating is a function of serious responsibility and any and all persons exercising the function must view it as a matter of great trust.

- Credit rating is a matter of personal judgment but this should not be an excuse for rash or unsupported decisions. Any credit rating must be based on adequate and accurate information.

- The credit rating process should be announced and explained to the companies or issuers whose debt securities are being rated, as a matter of minimum requirement of transparency and fair treatment.

- In case of any possible conflict of interest situation, the member of the credit rating board or the staff member shall so disclose such conflict of interest and shall not participate in formulating or arriving at a rating.

- Nevertheless, the person with a conflict of interest may be asked to be a resource person to give information or opinions, useful for the consideration of others, but such person shall not participate in the voting process itself and must not at any time have access to confidential information generated by the rating process.

Sources: The AFCRA Code of Ethics can be found at www.pefindo.com/afcra2.htm, accessed March 3, 2002.

market integration and capital mobility that is transforming developing-world capital allocation into something more closely resembling that found in the developed world.[35] Indeed, state repression of financial markets might eventually give way to "overheated expectations" of rating in a disintermediated context, especially the view that ratings provide a guarantee, signifying risklessness.[36]

The investment dimension of global rating discussed above suggests several things: that investment institutionalization is changing along disintermediated, capital-market lines; rating is becoming more important within that institutional pattern; and a wider set of judgments than budgetary analysis, conventionally conceived, informs the rating process itself. Is this pattern synchronic-rationalist, or does it reflect diachronic-constructivist principles? Certainly the pattern reflects choices that the actors involved label in synchronic-rationalist terms as sensible, given the circumstances. For example, widening the rating process to include fundamental analysis makes sense from a synchronic-rationalist point of view. To really do justice to this wider analytical agenda, however, an element of temporality—something lacking in the synchronic-rationalist framework—would have to be added.

The proliferation of domestic or emerging market rating agencies, many of which are weak, suggests that the diachronic-constructivist view is a better frame of reference. The reason these small agencies exist is not market- but usually state-driven.

35. On this secular trend, see Stephen Haggard and Sylvia Maxfield, "Political Explanations of Financial Policies in Developing Countries," in Stephen Haggard, Chung H. Lee and Sylvia Maxfield, eds., *Politics of Finance in Developing Countries* (Ithaca, NY: Cornell University Press, 1993), 325.

36. Don Noe, Moody's Investors Service, quoted in Lowenstein, May 1990, 66.

Given their extramarket origins, their existence does not fit the orthodox rating myth. In a counterfactual scenario, where rational maximization is key, they likely would not exist. But they do, even though the motivations for creating a rating system cannot be captured within a synchronic-rationalist framework.

Knowledge

The global spread of bond rating is changing the knowledge structure of financial business. Strange argued that knowledge structures shape what knowledge is created and used by reinforcing certain forms of knowledge rather than others.[37] As capital markets displace bank lending, as the U.S. rating agencies establish a wider list of rated entities in Europe, Asia, and Latin America, and as domestic agencies are established in countries that receive "technical assistance" from the major agencies, a slow transformation is occurring. Knowledge based on history, location, and tradition, exemplified by what used to be called "names" in London, is giving way to more abstract, verifiable, and "transparent" knowledge forms.

Borrowers have a strong incentive to adopt forms of knowledge such as GAAP (Generally Accepted Accounting Principles), despite U.S. agencies' assurances that they will interpret local accounting practices. Rating agencies want comparability across countries. So we see the development of an "operating system" from which rating judgments are derived, centered on hegemonic norms and values, despite explicit assertions of the value of local knowledge.[38] Because the U.S. agencies express (and reinforce) the hegemonic mental framework of rating orthodoxy most convincingly, they represent the norm around which the domestic agencies organize their analyses.

The Development of Rating in Japan

This convergence of knowledge is illustrated by rating expansion in Europe and Japan. The hegemonization of investors is more complete in Japan yet has fewer consequences than in Europe, where the view is more critical, despite greater utilization of rating. As noted previously, Japan has a handful of domestic rating agencies (not including Mikuni & Company), which compete with the global U.S. agencies. In Europe, apart from Fitch, there is little substantial competition for Moody's and Standard and Poor's. These different patterns of institutional arrangements reflect distinct histories of capital market growth.

---

37. Susan Strange, *States and Markets*, 2nd ed. (London: Pinter, 1994), 119–20.
38. Ronnie D. Lipschutz, "Reconstructing World Politics: The Emergence of Global Civil Society," *Millennium: Journal of International Studies* 21, no. 3 (Winter 1992): 418.

In Japan, domestic rating agencies were introduced as a result of financial negotiations with the U.S. The yen–dollar agreement of 1984 followed the indexing of U.S. current account and merchandise trade deficits during the early 1980s, much of that with Japan.[39] Bond issuance in Japan was tightly controlled during the Great Depression and the so-called clean bond campaign of 1933.[40] (In the United States, the Depression led to an expansion of rating, as investors took more interest in risk assessment.) But the defaults of the 1930s led to requirements for collateral on Japanese corporate bonds. The risk of default was thereby reduced simply because higher-yield issuers were excluded from the market altogether. After this change, credit risk was not a major consideration for Japanese investors for the next fifty years.

The yen–dollar negotiations brought forth a series of policy agreements that liberalized the rules for issuing Japanese securities and allowed many new issuers to raise funds in this way for the first time. A major condition for relaxing controls on disintermediation was the incorporation of ratings into bond issuance criteria.[41] The Japanese government made a "bilateral promise" during these negotiations to form domestic rating agencies.[42] Subsequently, the Ministry of Finance (MoF) "strongly persuaded" banks and securities houses to organize rating businesses. The official story suggests that MoF relations with Japanese rating agencies have been arms' length. But MoF has actually been "committed" to the existence and growth of Japanese agencies since 1984. Regulatory oversight of the ministry has slowly become more transparent since then, much as with the SEC.[43]

The crash of Japan's so-called bubble economy, with its inflated asset values, and the subsequent decade-long economic recession have weakened bank-corporate relations and increased volume in the domestic bond market. Still, there are major differences between the knowledge that informs rating in the United States and the influences on Japanese raters. The Japanese agencies have readily assumed the outward form of their U.S. counterparts and have sought SEC recognition as NRSROs[44] However, in their rating determinations they make more use of local knowledge, such as the "vague," so-called hidden financial reserves not listed on financial statements.[45] These reserves are not considered by the U.S. agencies. Japanese agencies

39. Frances McCall Rosenbluth, *Financial Politics in Contemporary Japan* (Ithaca: Cornell University Press, 1989), 68.

40. Kiyoshi Udagawa, managing director, Japan Credit Rating Agency, "Concerning the Credit Rating System in Japan," speech delivered to the Business Research International Conference, London, February 13, 1989, 2. Udagawa is now the senior Japanese official in S&P's Tokyo office.

41. Rosenbluth, 1989, 81.

42. Interview with Toshikazu Ishii, deputy director, Securities Market Division (Bond Market Office), Securities Bureau, Ministry of Finance, Tokyo, May 20, 1994.

43. Oversight of the agencies is undertaken in connection with ordinances on capital adequacy and corporate disclosure, first issued in July 1992. The designation is valid for one year, and documentation must be submitted to MoF's securities bureau at regular intervals (interview with Koyo Ozeki and Reiko Toritani, IBCA, Tokyo, May 17, 1994).

44. Interview with SEC official, Washington, D.C., March 1994.

45. Interview with Ozeki and Toritani, May 17, 1994.

"tend to judge a company by size and how much profit there is if the company sold its land and securities holdings," according to Toshiaki Nakano, a manager at Asahi Mutual Life Insurance Company's bond investment division.[46]

This different pattern for producing knowledge reflects the specific, local character of the Japanese domestic agencies. In comparison, the local agencies now developing in emerging markets have an organization and a process for acquiring knowledge that are in many ways tightly linked to the norms of Moody's and S&P. Like the developing country agencies, though, in Japan rating agencies developed not as a market response "but as an infrastructure to deregulate the Japanese direct finance market."[47] The objective was to reintroduce a risk culture into Japan, by gradually allowing creditworthiness assessments to be incorporated into investment decisions.[48]

The lone Japanese critic of rating agency ownership and the use of insider knowledge in rating determinations is Mikuni & Company. The firm exclusively uses public-domain quantitative criteria, does not charge issuers' fees, and is not licensed by the MoF.[49] Akio Mikuni, the company president, is something of a critic of Japanese business practices and the MoF. His views have been published in the *New York Times,* although an anonymous source has claimed that Karel van Wolferen, the Dutch journalist and critic of Japanese economic organization, was the actual author.[50] Mikuni argues that Nippon Investors Service is "guided" by MoF's securities bureau, whereas the Japan Credit Rating Agency is the "brainchild" of another part of MoF.[51]

Former MoF officials, such as Masao Fujioka, are senior figures in the Japanese agencies.[52] These agencies are able to sell their ratings on domestic issues. However, for Euromarket issues where Japanese issuers are seeking foreign financing, the Japanese agencies have little credibility. Non-Japanese investors want judgments that reflect a globally comparable knowledge base, which only the U.S.

46. Nakano quoted in "Standards of Japanese Credit Ratings Questioned," *Bloomberg Business News* (online service), April 8, 1994.

47. Interview with Ishii, May 20, 1994.

48. On the development of a risk culture in risk-socializing Japan, see Yoko Shibata, "Men from the Ministry Try to Fill the Hollow," *Euromoney,* March 1987, 135–38, and "A Dangerous Lack of Risk," *Economist,* July 9, 1994, 77–78.

49. In its exclusive use of quantitative data, its noncharging of issuers, and its distance from regulatory bodies, Mikuni seems to be charting a course at odds with U.S. rating norms as well as those that prevail in Japan.

50. Akio Mikuni, "Behind Japan's Economic Crisis," *New York Times,* February 1, 1993, 10; Akio Mikuni, "A New Era for Japanese Finance," *Asian Wall Street Journal,* July 2–3, 1993, 10; Gale Eisenstodt, "Saved to Death," *Forbes,* March 28, 1994, 107; David Lake, "Akio Mikuni: The Ratings Rebel," *Asian Finance,* May 15, 1989, 20–22; Karel van Wolferen, *The Enigma of Japanese Power: People and Politics in a Stateless Nation* (New York: Vintage, 1990).

51. Charles Smith, "Credit Where It's Due," *Far Eastern Economic Review,* March 2, 1989, 84.

52. N. Balakrishnan, "The Credit Minders," *Far Eastern Economic Review,* July 22, 1993, 44.

agencies can provide.[53] Their close connections with Japanese banks also trouble some observers, who see this potential conflict of interest as compromising the disintermediation infrastructure.[54] Split ratings between the Japanese agencies and Moody's and S&P reinforce the view that the two sides have significantly different judgmental frameworks.[55]

There is another interpretation of these differences in ratings. As seems to have been the case with the minor U.S. agencies, the Japanese agencies have an incentive to inflate ratings somewhat—to increase the number of institutions they rate—given that the Japanese agencies have not been profitable enterprises.[56]

By 2002, these pressures had led to consolidation among the Japanese companies. Mikuni & Co., Japan Rating & Investment, Inc. (R&I), and Japan Credit Rating Agency (JCR) were left to share the market with Moody's and S&P. Corporate failures during the late 1990s—and the failure of the Ministry of Finance to save bad institutions like Yamaichi Securities—had made the financial markets concerned about ratings for the first time since the war.[57]

Despite their problems, the Japanese agencies scored good marks with Japanese investors surveyed by the Japan Center for International Finance, a quasi-government research body set up with MoF assistance. Its third annual questionnaire, the 2001 survey, found similar respect for the local agencies and the U.S. institutions. But among investors, there was "deep-rooted distrust" of unsolicited ratings by the U.S. agencies.[58] Seventy percent of issuers claimed to give to agencies data not provided to investors or financial analysts.[59]

Japan remains an intellectual battleground between American-derived transnational knowledge structures and the local forms of knowledge nurtured in postwar reconstruction. This battle is being fought within capital markets. The state-sponsored process of disintermediation desocializes risk and establishes the need for

53. Shigeru Watanabe, Yoki Tanahashi, and Hideki Somemiya, "Credit Rating in Japan" (Tokyo: Nomura Research Institute, 1993), 29.

54. Akiyoshi Horiuchi, "Financial Liberalization: The Case of Japan," in Dimitri Vittas, ed., *Financial Regulation: Changing the Rules of the Game* (Washington, D.C.: World Bank, 1992), 115, 117.

55. Balakrishnan, July 22, 1993; Watanabe, Tanahashi, and Somemiya, 1993, 27, 29; "Credit Rating Agencies Part Ways When It Comes to Nippon Steel," *Bloomberg Business News* (online service), March 31, 1994.

56. "The Credit-Rating Agencies Should Strengthen Their Financial Base," *CaMRI*, April 28, 1994, 24.

57. "Never Mind the Quality," Japanese finance survey, *Economist*, Japanese Finance Survey, June 28, 1997, 15–16; "Japanese Bonds: Creditable," *Economist*, July 5, 1997, 98; David P. Hamilton and Bill Spindle, "Market Forces Are Staggering to Yamaichi," *Wall Street Journal Europe*, November 24, 1997, 13; Bill Spindle, "Credit Analysis Takes on Greater Role in Japan in Wake of Yamaichi Failure," *Wall Street Journal Europe*, November 26, 1997, 22.

58. Japan Center for International Finance, "Characteristics and Appraisal of Major Rating Companies 2001," available at www.jcif.or.jp, accessed March 5, 2002, 3.

59. Ibid.

more "independent" forms of knowledge, which do not reflect the implicit guarantee of risk socialization that were part of Japan's postwar system. As Pauly argues, major differences in economic and financial practices persist between nations.[60] However, the Japanese state, in cooperation with major financial interests, including banks, has been intimately involved in building the knowledge infrastructure of a different form of capital allocation in recent years. The degree to which this capital allocation transforms knowledge structures in Japan depends on the fortunes of the country's banks, the demand for financial resources there, and the ability of the Japanese-owned rating agencies to establish sustained credibility with investors, in competition with Moody's and S&P.[61]

Europe and Rating

In Europe, monetary union has generated the long-term expectation that a corporate bond market based on credit differentials spanning the continent will develop, as it has in the United States. The logic of rating analysis has seeped into EU directives on capital backing for investment banks, which "explicitly recognises the ratings of bonds," following similar incorporation of rating agencies into regulation in the UK and France.[62] The utility of credit analysis is also evident in the increasing resources devoted to consulting and in fee-based, customized credit analysis by major commercial banks in London, especially the U.S. institutions. The independence of this credit analysis is in doubt, however, because these banks trade in securities for profit.[63] Such financial innovations as derivatives and asset-backed debt are very important to the increasing use of credit analysis in Europe.[64]

The late 1990s and early years of the twenty-first century have seen the increased influence of U.S. business norms and practices.[65] The potential for a large Euro-

---

60. Louis W. Pauly, "National Financial Structures, Capital Mobility, and International Economic Rules: The Normative Consequences of East Asian, European, and American Distinctiveness," *Policy Sciences* 27, no. 4 (1994): 344.

61. Gerlach argues that the shift to capital market-based financing will not fundamentally alter the complex set of strategic interests established in Japan. He does not say so, but this shift implies that well-defined, bank-intermediated keiretsu relationships will transform themselves to incorporate the desocialized form of investment (Michael L. Gerlach, *Alliance Capitalism: The Social Organization of Japanese Business* [Berkeley: University of California Press, 1992], 17).

62. Richard Waters, "The Awesome Power of a Triple-A," *Financial Times*, May 14, 1992, 21.

63. Richard Waters, "International Bonds: Spotlight on Credit Analysis," *Financial Times*, April 27, 1992, 19; also, my interviews with Christopher Rowe, Citibank, London, December 10, 1992, and Frank Knowles, Lehman Brothers, London, December 10, 1992.

64. Declan McSweeney, "The Role and Influence of Rating Agencies," *Irish Banking Review* (Summer 1993): 28.

65. See, e.g., "Le Défi Américain, again," *Economist*, July 13, 1996, 19–21; Reginald Dale, "There Is No Anglo-Saxon Conspiracy," *International Herald Tribune*, January 16, 1996, 11; Robert Bonte-Friedheim, "Continent Embraces Anglo-Saxon Variety of Tough Capitalism," *Wall Street Journal Europe*, August 21, 1997, 1.

based capital market to develop and an awareness that European banks are weaker international competitors underpins this greater influence.[66] The new Euro capital market is shifting attention from currency risk to credit risk between European issuers.[67] A single market in sovereign, corporate, and municipal debt is developing in Euroland, "and with it the influence of formal credit assessment by independent agencies."[68]

Europe has few local rating agencies and more overt hostility to U.S. rating institutions and their ways of thinking.[69] This hostility is most strongly expressed in Germany. There, the demand for cross-border finance is growing, and practices such as Moody's unsolicited ratings are strongly disapproved.[70] Opposition to the way U.S. agencies undertake ratings seemed to grow in 1992, as the recession deepened and some major Swiss banks were downgraded.[71] In fall 1992, IBCA and Euronotation of France announced their merger.[72] Around the same time, a German rating initiative, Projektgesellschaft Rating, began preparatory work for the creation of a pan-European body. Surveys in the Netherlands and Germany had shown that European companies wanted a new agency based on the continent, with full coverage of European issues that could compare with the judgments of Moody's and S&P.[73] A Frankfurt banker interviewed by Engelen commented that Moody's and S&P "display a colonial attitude and often fail to take into account the special characteristics in European accounting, disclosure and management practices."[74] European bankers attacked the "often unpredictable verdicts" of the agencies, noting America's "rat-

66. Brian Coleman, "Euro Is Seen as a Rival to Dollar, Creating Immense Bond Market," *Wall Street Journal Europe*, April 23, 1997, 11; Charles Fleming, "European Bankers Wake Up to Threat of 'Cherry Pickers,' " *Wall Street Journal Europe*, August 22–23, 1997, 1; Michael R. Sesit, "A Common Bond: Europe Is Heading for a Fixed-Income Market That Looks a Lot Like the U.S.," *Wall Street Journal Europe*, September 22, 1997, R3; Hugo Dixon, "EMU's Capital Consequences," *Financial Times*, April 30, 1998, 21; "Much Indebted to EU," *Economist*, September 18, 1999, 119–20.

67. Nicholas Bray, "Bond Buyers Shift Focus to Spreads," *Wall Street Journal Europe*, July 28, 1997, 11–12.

68. Christopher Taylor, "Strains in the Eurozone," *Financial Times*, July 30, 2001, 17.

69. A corporate finance officer for a major British-based multinational suggested that Moody's is more centralized, bureaucratic, and New York-based as compared to S&P, which is perceived to be more European, less aggressive, and more academic, which "makes a difference" (confidential source, London, December 1992).

70. Interview with Richard Waters, reporter, Financial Times, December 7, 1992; on German antipathy to the U.S. rating agencies, see Michael R. Sesit, "Global Player: German Bonds: Fading Glory?" *Wall Street Journal Europe*, March 7–9, 2003, P1.

71. Waters, May 14, 1992. Rowe suggested that German banks did not wish to see the corporations they owned evaluated by outside interests.

72. Richard Waters, "International Capital Markets: Ratings Agencies Complete Merger," *Financial Times*, October 21, 1992, 29.

73. Ibid.

74. Klaus Engelen, "A European Nightmare: Unchecked American Rating Agencies Become Continent's New Boss-Men," *International Economy*, 7, no. 6, (November–December's 1994): 46–50, 1994, 46.

ing power." They deplored Europe's failed efforts to come up with a continent-wide agency such as Projektgesellschaft Rating. The new attempt failed because the French interests that own the new Fitch agency could not come to agreement with Bertelsmann, the German-based global media giant.[75]

Germany's interest in a local rating system revived with the implementation of the Euro. In 1999, three agencies were founded: Euroratings, Unternehmens Ratingagentur (URA), and Ratings Services A.G.. They focused specifically on the Mittelstand, the largely family-owned medium-sized industrial companies in Germany.[76] These German companies are premised on the idea that German industrial managers do not believe they can get a fair hearing from Moody's and S&P. One individual, in discussions with Oliver Everling, a German rating consultant and managing director of Everling Advisory Services (a Frankfurt-based company established in 1997), is reported to have "insisted he only wanted to talk to a small national agency as he didn't believe an American would understand his market or the way his company ticks."[77] Everling further suggested the U.S. agencies were reluctant to "serve" the Mittelstand, not wanting to risk their reputations on many small companies promising low fees. Everling, "Mr. Rating Agency in Germany," is also the chairman of the German rating agency association, RatingCert eV, located in Berlin.[78] A credit-analyst training program at the University of Augsburg backed by Rating Services A.G., is one measure for addressing the "political question" of getting the rating business moving in Germany, according to Hans Loges, the firm's proprietor.[79]

Besides this focus on small- and medium-sized company ratings, a renewed effort to establish a pan-European agency to compete with Moody's and S&P directly was launched in 1999. The initiative came from a group of high-profile German financiers, again with the help of German publisher Bertelsmann.[80] According to a Deutsche Bank official, "There's overwhelming support from the institutions" in Germany for these intitiatives.[81] Changes to Germany's system of state-backed guarantees to the 12 Landesbanks and 560 Sparkassen will take away the commercial advantages these banks have, making German capital markets more attractive and ratings more important information.[82] The changes to accounting law forced by EU initiatives, which currently lets German companies understate

75. Ibid., 48–49.

76. Quoted in Sarah Althaus, "Minnows' Needs Met by Locals," *Financial Times,* survey of Germany, October 25, 1999, viii.

77. Everling quoted in ibid.

78. David Shirreff, "If It Moves, Rate It," *Euromoney,* November 1999, 77.

79. Loges quoted ibid., 77.

80. Ibid.

81. Stephan Schuster, head of capital markets policy issues at Deutsche Bank in Frankfurt, quoted ibid.

82. Tony Barber, "Level Playing Field Coming," survey on German banking and finance, *Financial Times,* October 15, 2001, 4.

profits, reduces companies' tax liability and allows them to build up reserves for bad times. The accounting changes will also expand the scope for rating activity. Under pressure from the proposed Basel II rules, banks may become less willing to accept the low returns commonly accrued from loans and credits. That would push up interest rates charged to German corporates and encourage capital market financing.[83]

With the advent of financial globalization, raters have been trying to reinforce their claims to knowledge. Although ratings promise to cut through constraints established in the past by local financial elites, they offer their own mystification. Because ratings are fundamentally highly subjective stories about enterprises and governments, they drive the rating agencies to support ratings with what Wall Street calls "rocket science" (quantitative and formal modeling approaches to financial market behavior).[84] However, it is unclear whether there has been substantial progress in this effort. The global spread of rating and the emphasis on comparability of ratings has stretched the credibility of rating judgmental frameworks to the limit.[85] In contexts where ratings are less traditional, their contested introduction is typically met with earnest attempts by the agencies to invoke expertise and reputation. Hence, U.S. agencies in Europe tend to focus on very sophisticated financial instruments such as structured financings, which require legal knowledge of an issue's indenture.[86]

There is a paucity of this "rocket science" at the agencies—what the International Monetary Fund referred to as the "almost complete lack of a probabilistic approach to risk analysis" in rating. Consequently, the agencies have problems justifying their ratings in a world that gives quantitative analysis high status.[87] Although Moody's and S&P remain committed to both quantitative and qualitative data, the agencies are actively involved in developing and selling quantitative credit risk services. Moody's Corporation founded Moody's Risk Management Services (MRMS) in 1995 as a sister company to Moody's Investors Service, just for this purpose.

83. Standard & Poor's, "Exploring the Link between Accounting Principles and Ratings Penetration in Germany," available at www.standardandpoors.com, accessed February 9, 2002; for an analysis of related issues, see Susanne Lütz, "From Managed to Market Capitalism? German Finance in Transition," *German Politics* 9, no. 2 (August 2000): 149–70.

84. See "Rocket Scientists Are Revolutionizing Wall Street," reprinted from *Business Week*, April 21, 1988, in Zvi Bodie, Alex Kane, and Alan J. Marcus, *Investments* (Homewood, Ill.: Irwin, 1989), 7–9.

85. Evidence for this can be seen in the disagreements among the global agencies on the creditworthiness of major sovereign borrowers ("Sovereign Debt: The Ratings Game," *Economist*, October 30, 1993, 88–90).

86. "Credit Rating Agencies: Beyond the Second Opinion," *Economist*, March 30, 1991, 80.

87. Charles Adams, Donald J. Mathieson, Garry Shinasi et al., *International Capital Markets: Developments, Prospects, and Key Policy Issues* (Washington, D.C.: International Monetary Fund, 1999), 198.

Moody's bought KMV in 2002 to bolster MRMS activities, expecting $100 million in revenue from the two in 2002 and $200 million by 2005.[88]

The argument developed above is that rating spreads an instrumental form of knowledge as it grows with capital markets. Instrumental knowledge challenges established diachronic-constructivist norms and practices in emerging markets and in rich countries, like Japan and Germany. The synchronic-rationalist rating myth is the secular trend, but resistance to these norms do arise, as is evident in Europe and especially in Japan. In these places, local actors highlight the weaknesses of the mental framework of rating orthodoxy, sustaining alternative forms of knowledge and denying endogeneity to newly arrived embedded knowledge networks.

Counterfactually, the synchronic-rationalist view denies that different forms of rating knowledge exist. In this framework, knowledge is objective, cross-cultural, and instrumental. If it is not these things, it is not knowledge. The influence of the agencies aside, the spread of knowledge in this specifically rationalist sense would likely still take place in emerging countries, in Europe, and in Japan. Many forces support its slow spread. But without the agencies, would instrumental knowledge be so pervasive in the capital markets of these places, dominated for decades by tradition, "names," and other informal reputational shortcuts?

Rating agencies, especially the U.S. agencies, challenge established forms of knowledge. The agencies seem to be devices of modernity, through which governments can influence their capital markets. Accordingly, the most persuasive view here is that the agencies spread instrumental knowledge and marginalize traditional knowledge. A broad trend toward rationalist, instrumental knowledge exists, but rating agencies help to substantiate that trend in the financial markets.

Governance

Isak Antika, vice president of Chase Manhattan, Istanbul, noted that:

> Turkey has to improve its fiscal deficit. This is behind almost all the problems. No party taking power has a choice. The country has to balance its budget. The continuation of the deficit will hurt Turkey's rating and its ability to raise finance.[89]

Rating agencies challenge established governance norms and practices around the world. The governance dimension can be appreciated through an examination of sovereign credit analysis. Sovereign issuers are national governments. The degree to

88. Moody's Corporation, "Moody's Has Reached a Definitive Agreement to Acquire KMV, the Leader in Market-based, Quantitative Credit Risk Management Tools, in an All Cash Transaction for $210 million," press release, February 11, 2002, available from www.moodysrms.com.

89. These comments were quoted in Nick Kochan, "Moody's Puts Istanbul in a Bad Mood," *Euromoney*, November 1993, 79.

which their policy outputs or ways of doing things are influenced by the two major U.S. agencies illustrates the governance power of these nonstate institutions.

A central factor that influences the rating of sovereigns is what can be called managerial capacity. Because credit rating assumes a relatively long time from issue of debt to repayment, raters are concerned with the ability of those persons who run governments to keep them a going concern. Debt repayment is premised on both *capacity* and *willingness* to repay. Thus, judgments about officials' ability to manage and govern—and the likelihood of them being willing to repay—are central. As Moody's notes,

> Countries as diverse as Poland, Argentina, South Africa, and the Philippines have defaulted on or have rescheduled their foreign debts to commercial banks for other than strictly economic or financial reasons. Very often, an admixture of political, social, and cultural considerations—such as the inability to impose austerity, radical or political uprisings, or lack of public confidence in the central authorities—were at the root of a country's liquidity crisis.[90]

Rating agency views of management and policy change over time as prevailing views of economic and financial orthodoxy change. The agencies have become enforcers of the new orthodoxy, which places a premium on the separation of economic and financial institutions from "political" institutions, narrowly defined. This role as constitutional advocate and transmitter of new policy norms and practices has been magnified, because credit rating is so thoroughly centralized in comparison to bank intermediation. The implications of separating the ostensibly political from the economic are therefore much greater. An analysis of sovereign rating methodology in *Global Credit Analysis* reveals Moody's attachment to this governance model: "Especially important [in their rating determination] is the institutional pattern of decision-making power with respect to economic policy." Moody's cites such examples as the "degree of independence on critical monetary policies that the central bank has over the treasury."[91]

This stance may, at some time, have given rise within the rating agencies to a more favorable view of certain ways of governing some societies. For example, Asian countries may have been favored in comparison to those in Latin America, according to John F. H. Purcell, a former director of emerging markets research at Salomon Brothers, the New York investment bank.[92]

Sovereign Rating

Sovereign borrowing has a long tradition going back to at least the Middle Ages, when kings borrowed to finance wars and trade. More recently, newly emerging

---

90. Moody's Investors Service, *Global Credit Analysis*, (London: IFR, 1991), 163.
91. Ibid., p. 162.
92. "Sovereign Debt: The Ratings Game," *Economist*, October 30, 1993, 88–90.

states have sought to finance development. Classic cases are the new Latin American republics, which borrowed some 20 million pounds in London between 1822 and 1825. By 1829, nearly 19 million pounds' worth of these bonds were in default.[93] The Latin debt crisis that emerged in the interwar years generated U.S. interest in a credit clearinghouse, to vet these countries' creditworthiness and protect interests in the creditor nations.[94] After World War II, $14 billion in foreign sovereign bonds were sold in New York between 1945 and 1963.[95] However, sovereign rating as such was a very minor area of the rating agencies' work until the 1980s. Deficit problems then began to emerge in the advanced industrialized countries, and some of the developing countries in Latin America began to repackage their floating rate bank loans into Brady bonds that lowered their repayment costs.[96]

Contrary to the common view, sovereign rating is not merely a judgment of the finances of national governments. Instead, it comprises the ability and willingness of authorities (such as the central bank) to make foreign currency available to service the debts of all issuers, public and private, including the national government.[97] However, both Moody's and S&P take the view that the probability of repayment is different when debt is issued in the local currency. These local currency ratings tend to be higher as a consequence.[98]

This type of debt was once unsaleable outside the country, but financial globalization and pension managers' demand for yield now make local currency debt a more feasible international purchase. Periodic financial crises reduce this tendency, by creating "flights to quality" to rich-country currencies, especially the U.S. dollar. The Asian financial crisis of 1997–98 is the most dramatic recent example.

What is distinctive about contemporary sovereign rating is that it is no longer a realm of AAA countries only, as it once was.[99] Countries with little financial depth now want ratings. Conventional advice had been for lesser-income countries to approach

93. Frank Griffith Dawson, *The First Latin American Debt Crisis: The City of London and the 1822–25 Loan Bubble* (New Haven: Yale University Press, 1990), 1–2.

94. This was discussed during congressional questioning of Commerce Department officials in 1932; see testimony of James C. Corliss, specialist, Latin American Finance, Department of Commerce, *The Sale of Foreign Bonds of Securities in the United States,* hearings before the Committee on Finance, U.S. Senate, pt. 2, January 4–7, 1932 (Washington, D.C.: U.S. Government Printing Office, 1932), 851.

95. Richard Benzie, *The Development of the International Bond Market,* Economic Papers no. 32 (Basel: Bank for International Settlements, 1992).

96. "Sovereign Debt," October 30, 1993; also see Neil Osborn, "Can This Dream Come True?" *Euromoney,* September 1987, 74–79; telephone interview with John F. H. Purcell, Salomon Brothers, New York, August 1992.

97. Moody's, 1991, 157.

98. S&P argues that governments can always raise taxes and print money to service local debts. Moody's sees a close link between external and domestic defaults and considers that monetization of local currency debts is a good way to trigger hyperinflation. Accordingly, Moody's is less generous with its local ratings ("Sovereign Debt," October 30, 1993).

99. Ibid.

sovereign rating with caution, to avoid the problems associated with downgrades.[100] However, in the 1990s, "countries are coming under increasing pressure to be rated." Among other things, "Investors looking closer at putting their money into out-of-the-way corners of the world want the comfort of a rating agency assessment."[101] The business can be lucrative for the U.S. agencies, both of which are rumored to charge up to 2 percent of the face value of the sovereign debt issue in fees.[102]

Sovereign rating is one of the most subjective areas of credit rating.[103] Like municipal rating, it incorporates opaque, quality of life factors and what seem to be many overtly political variables. As noted above, there is an inclination to institutional arrangements of a neoliberal form. Moody's acknowledges that the analytics of sovereign rating are contested and that much of what is considered has to do with the analysis of power rather than more obvious financial dynamics.[104] Several political variables follow from this focus on power: the degree and nature of political intrusiveness in the cultivation of wealth, the depth and experience of government bureaucrats, political intrusiveness in economic management, political links with foreign partners, past behavior under stress, and regime legitimacy.[105] These "credit-related political fundamentals" reflect the mental framework of rating orthodoxy (table 5). The first dynamic assumes that politics and wealth creation are inherently distinct, rather than a separation characteristic of U.S. arrangements. The issue of political intrusiveness in economic management, of course, is where the new governance model is locked into the rating process. Political links with foreign partners is the analytic category in which Moody's assesses the degree of integration with financial globalization.

Sovereign ratings became controversial after the Asian economic and financial crises of 1997–98. Like the controversy in municipal rating over "quality of life," sovereign ratings were considered less supported by the sort of replicable, quantified data that was "supposed" to underpin ratings. The scope for judgment therefore went well beyond data for, say, corporate ratings. Recent research has added extra importance to this issue. Sovereign ratings do add new information to markets,

100. Alan Roe, Nicholas Bruck, and Marcus Fedder, *International Finance Strategies for Developing Countries*, (Washington, D.C.: World Bank, 1992), 20.

101. Ann Monroe, "Better a Low Rating Than None at All," *Global Finance*, September 1992, 46.

102. Ibid, 50. Comments in the financial industry press and financial reports of McGraw-Hill, Dun and Bradstreet, and Moody's Corporation suggest fees are highly lucrative for the major agencies.

103. Ronald A. Johnson, Venkat Srinivasan, and Paul J. Bolster, "Sovereign Debt Ratings: A Judgemental Model Based on the Analytic Hierarchy Process," *Journal of International Business Studies* 21, no. 1 (1990): 95–117. This study suggests "considerable reliance on informal judgement," "serious inconsistencies" in the way things are judged, and "biased ratings" (90). On differences between the Japanese and American agencies on sovereign rating (where the Japanese agencies tend to be more favorable to Asian countries), see Watanabe, Tanahashi, and Somemiya, 1993, 27.

104. Moody's 1991, 161.

105. Ibid., 164–65.

and the effect of downgrades on speculative-grade sovereigns (typically, developing countries) are more severe than expected.[106]

Australia's Rating

Sovereign rating has not been free of debate and controversy. The Commonwealth of Australia was downgraded in 1986 and again in mid-1989, much to the distress of Paul Keating, the country's combative minister of finance at the time:

> Australia's never been in a position of defaulting on debt so it should never have lost a triple-A. I think that was an incompetent judgement by Moody's. . . . Does anyone seriously believe that Australia would have at any stage defaulted on its debt obligations—public or private? And the answer's no. Therefore, the triple-A shouldn't have gone.[107]

Keating banned contact with Moody's officials after the second downgrade. His exasperation seems to have come from much the same difference of opinion about relevant variables that, during the 1990s, characterized U.S. municipal rating. The 1989 rating review came when Australia's sovereign debt, in both local and foreign currency, was falling rapidly. In June 1989, outstanding Commonwealth bonds had fallen to A$30 billion, from a peak of A$34.3 billion two years before. Overseas debt had dropped to A$9.4 billion from A$15.1 billion. At these rates, Australia was forecast in 1989 to have no sovereign debt at all by 1995.[108]

What seems to have been crucial to Moody's judgment was the fear that the Commonwealth might have to act as lender of last resort for major corporate debts and that reimposition of exchange controls was still a possibility.[109] Both of these considerations (neither were very plausible to the people Lowenstein interviewed), move the analysis of creditworthiness well away from narrow, balance-sheet-type considerations. They suggest, first, that governments would be well advised to insulate themselves from lender-of-last-resort tasks, and second, that governments suspected of wanting to return to the Bretton Woods capital-control policies will be disciplined by the agencies.

Since the mid-1990s, Australia's financial position has benefited from what S&P calls "the climate of fiscal conservatism that has characterized public finances in

---

106. Richard Cantor and Frank Packer, "Determinants and Impact of Sovereign Credit Ratings," *Federal Reserve Board of New York Economic Policy Review* (October 1996): 37–53.

107. Quoted in "Combative Keating Counters the Jabs and Jibes," *Euromoney*, April 1989, 33.

108. Jack Lowenstein, "Should the Rating Agencies Be Downgraded?" *Euromoney*, February 1990, 35.

109. Ibid., 36. Also see Michael Malik, "On Borrowed Time," *Far Eastern Economic Review*, June 15, 1989, 48–49; Anthony Rowley and Charles Smith, "The Hazard of Oz," *Far Eastern Economic Review*, December 14, 1989, 92; and Glenda Korporaal, "Tap Turned Off," *Far Eastern Economic Review*, February 14, 1991, 53–54.

Australia and New Zealand."[110] This conservatism includes debt reduction through surplus budgets and asset sales. Australia's outlook was lowered by Moody's from "positive" to "stable" during the Asian financial crisis in early 1998, but there was no subsequent ratings downgrade. New Zealand, however, was downgraded to the same rating as Australia in September 1998.[111] For nearly ten years prior, the country's sovereign rating for foreign currency had been one notch higher than Australia's. Fiscal orthodoxy was deeply embedded in New Zealand from the mid-1990s on. For instance, when the opposition Labour Party tried to modify the government's draft Fiscal Responsibility Act, it proposed that attainment of an AAA rating become a legislatively mandated objective of fiscal policy.[112]

Today, "extremely conservative financial settings" are the norm for both the Australian states and the Commonwealth, according to Dr. David Hayward, executive director of the Institute for Social Research, Swinburne University of Technology in Hawthorn, Victoria, Australia.[113] Hayward observes that for Australia, "the AAA [on debt issued in Australian dollars] has become institutionalized as the benchmark for financial settings which everyone complies with quite willingly." Both Australia and New Zealand were upgraded to Aaa by Moody's on October 20, 2002. The two countries were thought "extremely unlikely" to impose a debt moratoria policy or to socialize debt by taking on the foreign currency risk of the private and public sectors.[114]

Canada's Rating

The most recent downgrading of the Government of Canada took place in April 1995, when Moody's reduced Canada's foreign currency rating to Aa2 from Aa1. (S&P downgraded Canada's foreign currency rating in October 1992 to AA+, with local currency debt still earning the AAA.)[115] Canada was an OECD leader in gross government debt, at around 96 percent of total GDP.[116] When Canada was placed on watch by Moody's for possible downgrade on February 16, 1995, this action

110. Standard & Poor's, "Australian and New Zealand Ratings Downgrades Almost Double Upgrades in 2001," available at www.standardandpoors.com, accessed February 9, 2002.

111. V. Jayanth, "Moody's Lower Ratings for Australia and S'Pore," *Hindu*, February 5, 1998, n.p., accessed via Lexis-Nexis, February 20, 2002.

112. McKinnon, 2003, 407–8. The amendment was unsuccessful.

113. Private communication to the author, March 4, 2002.

114. Moody's Investors Service, "Moody's Upgrades Foreign Currency Ratings of Australia, New Zealand, and Iceland to Aaa," October 20, 2002, available at www.moodys.com, accessed August 4, 2003.

115. John Urquart and Rosanna Tamburri, "Moody's Downgrades Canada's Rating, Pressuring Government to Reduce Debt," *Wall Street Journal*, April 13, 1995, A2; Richard Gwyn, "Moody's Delivers Cheap Shot to Recovering Economy," *Toronto Star*, April 16, 1995, E3; Dalton Camp, "Only Our Slow Death Would Satisfy Moody's," *Toronto Star*, April 16, 1995, E3.

116. Bruce Little, "Why Canada Is Doing Poorly in the Ratings," *Globe and Mail* (Toronto) February 20, 1995, A11.

reduced the value of the Canadian dollar and increased the interest rates on Government of Canada bonds sold in foreign and domestic currencies. Sweden and Italy have experienced similar warnings and downgradings.[117]

Like Australia, Canadian public finances improved at the end of the 1990s and into the new century, winning praise in 1998 and an upgrade from Moody's in June 2000.[118] As in the Australian case, a rating downgrade seems to "concentrate minds," assisting in the subsequent reshaping of public policy.[119] One Canadian commentator implied that the credit rating agencies had been institutionalized in Canada, just as Hayward suggested in the Australian case, and their output had assumed the role of a "Doomsday Book of debtors, a kind of curia in the ranks of free marketers."[120]

Japan's Rating

Unlike other rich OECD states, whose creditworthiness improved during the late 1990s, Japan's deteriorated sharply. Repeated efforts to lift the country out of its decade-long economic malaise failed. Moody's first signaled a possible downgrading for Japan in April 1998.[121] In July of that year, Moody's commented on the governance problems that frustrated solutions to structural problems: "an apparent lack of consensus among policy makers on a medium-term strategy" exists in Japan.[122] This warning led to a three-day yen depreciation on the currency exchanges.[123] Moody's followed through with a downgrade in November 1998, its first G7 downgrade since Canada's in 1995.[124]

Japan's loss of an AAA rating from Moody's led reportedly to a "strong feeling of displeasure" from the finance minister, Miyazawa Kiichi.[125] In Japanese terms, this was a strong statement. Some commentators accused Moody's analyst of being biased against Japan. Others suggested the rating of Japan was unsolicited and

117. "Moody's Cuts Its Rating on Italian Obligations," *Wall Street Journal*, August 17, 1992, C11; Moody's Puts Swedish Foreign Currency Debt under Review," *Wall Street Journal*, October 5, 1992, A7E; Conner Middelmann, "World Bond Markets: Spotlight Falls on High-Deficit Countries—Capital & Credit," *Financial Times*, July 11, 1994, 24; Hugh Carnegy, "Survey of Sweden: A Watershed Decision—The Vote to Join the EU Now Settled, Attention Will Turn Again to Urgent Budgetary Problems," *Financial Times*, December 19, 1994, 1.

118. Brian Milner, "Budget Fails to Boost Canada's Credit Ratings," *Globe and Mail*, February 26, 1998, B11; on Canada's ratings record, see www.moodys.com.

119. Peter Cook, "At the Mercy of Markets and the U.S.," *Globe and Mail*, February 20, 1995, B2.

120. Dalton Camp, "Common Sense Revolutionaries Run into a Wall St.," *Toronto Star*, December 27, 1995, A31.

121. "The Markets: Currencies," *New York Times*, April 4, 1998, D3.

122. "Moody's to Review Some Japanese Debt," *New York Times*, July 23, 1998, D5.

123. "The Markets: Currencies," *New York Times*, July 24, 1998, D6.

124. Bloomberg News, "Moody's Decides to Downgrade Its Financial Ratings for Japan," *New York Times*, November 17, 1998, C2.

125. Sakamoto Sakae, "Japan's Downgrading Fans Criticism of U.S. Rating Agencies," *Journal of Japanese Trade & Industry*, August 19, 1999, n.p., accessed via Lexis-Nexis, February 26, 2002.

therefore "may be considered a kind of intimidation." Some parliamentarians reportedly wanted to summon the CEOs of the U.S. rating agencies to the Japanese Diet. More sober comment came from the government-financed Japan Center for International Finance. The center cited Japan's large foreign reserves, trade surplus, and savings rate, and suggested that only the narrow capacity to service debt should be considered in rating.[126] A Japanese scholar, Kurosawa Yoshitaka of Nihon University in Tokyo, pointed out that the U.S. agencies do credit ratings "on the basis of their home standards."[127] Sakae observes that for Japanese used as they are to trusting legal authority, the value of ratings is hard to understand. He notes that the Japanese media—like some U.S. congressmen—initially described the rating agencies as public-sector agencies.[128]

The effect of the downgrade was evident in 2000, when the Japanese government sought financing from banks rather than the capital markets, as had been the usual procedure during the postwar era. Jesper Koll, chief economist at Merrill Lynch Japan, observed that a recourse to banks meant "one of two things: either you don't believe in the efficiency of the financial markets or you're admitting you have a credit problem."[129] Strom suggested the government wanted to avoid "drawing additional scrutiny from Moody's and S&P."

The Japanese government did not avoid this scrutiny. S&P began to signal in early 2000 that governance failure—allowing the pace of structural reform to decline—risked a downgrade.[130] Moody's downgraded Japan for the second time in September 2000.[131] S&P finally lowered its rating on Japan to AA+ in February 2001, in what was seen as a "clear criticism" of Japanese politicians and their ability to tackle reform.[132] Financial Services Minister Hakuo Yangisawa, "dismissed the downgrade, saying the move was nothing but interference," and " 'unnecessary meddling.' "[133] S&P cited Japan's diminished fiscal flexibility, debt levels, and the government's "protracted approach" to reform, which amounted to a "political reluctance to address rigidities in the economy."[134] The government must embrace structural reform more aggressively, S&P said.

Moody's began to contemplate a third downgrading in late 2001.[135] S&P downgraded again on November 28, 2001. Demonstrating a more receptive attitude,

126. Ibid.
127. Kurosawa Yoshitaka quoted in ibid.
128. Ibid.
129. Stephanie Strom, "Japan to Turn to Direct Loans from Its Banks," *New York Times,* January 29, 2000, A1.
130. Stephanie Strom, "S&P Concerned about Prospects for Recovery in Japan," *New York Times,* February 23, 2000, C4.
131. Gillian Tett, "Growth at Last," *Financial Times,* September 12, 2000, 24.
132. "S&P Lowers Its Rating on Japanese Debt," *New York Times,* February 24, 2001, C4.
133. Hakuo Yanagisawa quoted in "Japan Blasts S&P for Cutting Long-Term Credit Rating," *Bangkok Post,* February 24, 2001, n.p., accessed via Lexis-Nexis, February 26, 2002.
134. S&P quoted in ibid.
135. "Review of Japan Debt Rating," *New York Times,* September 7, 2001, W1.

Prime Minister Koizumi's finance minister, Masajuro Shiokawa, observed, "We will have to work to regain trust in government bonds."[136] Moody's downgraded yen-denominated debt soon after to Aa3 (for the second time in three months) and suggested further rating cuts might occur.[137]

Moody's announcement that the firm was considering lowering Japan's rating again, in February 2002, led the Council on Economic and Fiscal Policy, a Japanese government committee, to accuse the agency of making a "serious government debt problem worse."[138] The *Financial Times* observed that a downgrade from Moody's would put Japan below the rating of Botswana, the African state, "where a third of the population is infected with HIV/Aids."[139] Such bonds would carry a 20 percent risk weighting under the proposed Basel II capital adequacy rules.[140] Accounting rules, which now force Japanese banks to "mark to market," would magnify the domestic impact of a sell-off of Japanese government bonds.[141]

The country's local-currency national debt was downgraded two notches by Moody's on May 31, 2002.[142] In the weeks leading up to this event, a veritable "war of words" was launched by senior Japanese government officials. They were adamant that Japan's current account surplus, foreign exchange reserves, and international creditor status made comparisons with developing countries implausible.[143] The government "began jawboning" the agencies. Then, on April 26, a letter from Vice Finance Minister Haruhiko Kuroda criticized the agencies.[144] The letter attacked the qualitative explanation of Japan's ratings, noting the absence of "objective criteria."[145] Subsequently, an issue of Japanese government bonds was under-subscribed for the first time.[146]

136. Masajuro Shiokawa quoted in Ken Belson, "S&P Cuts Credit Rating of Japan," *New York Times,* November 29, 2001, W1.

137. Ken Belson, "Moody's Lowers Debt Rating on Government Credit in Yen," *New York Times,* December 5, 2001, W1.

138. Council on Economic and Fiscal Policy, quoted in Ken Belson, "Japan's Debt under Study for New Cut in Rating," *New York Times,* February 14, 2002, W1.

139. David Pilling and Bayan Rahman, "Japan's Debt Rating May Fall below Botswana's," *Financial Times,* February 14, 2002, 12.

140. Bayan Rahman, "Downgrade Fears Cast Shadow over Japan: Moody's Is Considering a Drop of Two Notches to A2," *Financial Times,* February 14, 2002, 33.

141. On the impact of mark-to-market rules on Japanese banks, see "The Non-Performing Country," *Economist,* February 16, 2002, 24–26.

142. Ken Belson, "Despite Protest, Moody's Cuts Japan's Rating," *New York Times,* June 1, 2002, B2.

143. Arran Scott, "Japan Rebukes Ratings Agencies for Falling Grades," *Wall Street Journal,* May 1, 2002, A14; Michael Williams and Phred Dvorak, "Japan Seethes over Comparisons to Botswana," *Wall Street Journal,* May 13, 2002, C1; David Ibison, "Japan Hits out as Rating Downgrade Looms," *Financial Times,* May 25–26, 2002, 3; Michael Williams and Phred Dvorak, "Tokyo Fears Ratings Downgrades to Hit Borrowing," *Wall Street Journal,* May 28, 2002, A16.

144. Williams and Dvorak, May 13, 2002; a summary of the correspondence can be found at www.mof.go.jp/jouhou/kokusai/p140430ecov.htm, accessed May 21, 2003.

145. Haruhiko Kuroda quoted in ibid.

146. Mariko Sanchanta, "Confidence in Japan Hit as Bonds Fall from Favour," *Financial Times,* September 21–22, 2002, 7.

Deficits and Rating Agencies

What is interesting about these developments is that they reflect a definite policy line about deficits. These events also reveal how the rating agencies' pronouncements help to transform public consciousness about the appropriate scope and purposes of state action.[147] Deficits are not self-evidently bad.[148] In fact, though not risk free, their perpetual rollover can make every generation better off.[149]

Eisner has demonstrated some of the benefits of even structural deficits. He concludes that deficits have "helped and not hurt output, employment, consumption, and well-being in the present. They have also entailed more, not less investment."[150] Nevertheless, almost everywhere, government budget deficits have been identified as one of the leading causes of lower growth rates and persistent unemployment.

Warning of debt "walls" and bankruptcy, governments made their own deficit reduction a leading priority during the 1990s. Significant elements within civil societies were persuaded to support this objective.[151] The rationale for a deficit reduction doctrine was that in countries with many beneficiaries of state intervention, like Canada and Sweden, "democracy no longer work[ed] in the public interest." A bond rating downgrade would "[hold] the feet of recalcitrant policitians to the fire."[152] Friedman observed that Moody's was "imposing on democracies economic and political decisions that the democracies, left to their own devices, simply cannot take."[153]

Rating, Emerging Markets, and Developing Nations

Along with the sovereign rating of developing countries, a relatively recent phenomenon, rating governance is slowly expanding to a new group of former bank borrow-

---

147. Greg Farrell and Charles Davies, "Masters of the Universe," *Financial Post Magazine,* June 1991, 20–23; Zuhair Kashmeri, "Credit Dictators," *NOW Magazine,* April 22–28, 1993, 12, 20, 20–24; also see Andrew Coyne, "Balancing the Budget," *Globe and Mail* (Toronto), December 3, 1994, D1, D5.

148. Laurence Ball, Douglas W. Elmendorf, and N. Gregory Mankiw, "The Deficit Gamble," National Bureau of Economic Research, Working Paper no. 5015 (Cambridge, Mass.: National Bureau of Economic Research, 1995); see also chap. 5.

149. Ibid., 1.

150. Robert Eisner, *The Misunderstood Economy: What Counts and How to Count It* (Boston: Harvard Business School Press, 1994), 119; on this theme, also see Robert Heilbroner, "Anti-Depression Economics," *Atlantic Monthly,* April 1993, 100–108; Robert Heilbroner and Peter Bernstein, *The Debt and the Deficit: False Alarms/Real Possibilities* (New York: Norton, 1989).

151. A compelling exploration of this process is Linda McQuaig, *Shooting the Hippo: Death by Deficit and Other Canadian Myths* (Toronto: Viking, 1995).

152. Peter Cook, "The Illogical Left and the Logic of Debt," *Globe and Mail* (Toronto), March 2, 1995, B2, and "Is Canada Now a Serious Country?" *Globe and Mail,* April 14, 1995, B2; also see his "Sweden's Plight Resembles Canada's," *Globe and Mail,* February 6, 1995, B9.

153. Thomas L. Friedman, "Don't Mess with Moody's," *New York Times,* February 22, 1995, A15.

ers, including Poland.[154] These countries, as has been noted, are eager to tap the debt markets for infrastructure investment.[155] They are capital importers, and hence their situation is different from that of the developed countries: they have stronger incentives to cooperate with the rating agencies to build their credibility. The agencies have had a major impact on the developing countries' prospects for attracting mobile financial capital, as Turkey discovered in January 1994. That was when its rating was reduced to below investment grade, and "confidence evaporated."[156] Mexico discovered much the same thing in February 1995, although its downgrade was during an ongoing currency crisis.[157]

The rating upgrade of Argentina in 1992 provided evidence of the agencies' concern with management and policy in developing countries. In upgrading its rating to B1 (from B3), four notches below investment grade, Moody's pointed to Argentina's "significant steps in dismantling administrative and regulatory controls within the country."[158] At the same time, Moody's did not upgrade Brazil, despite a recently concluded debt accord between that country and its bank creditors.

The anxiety that a potential rating action produces in developing countries makes good sense. Recent work by Larrain, Reisen, and von Maltzan suggests a "highly significant announcement effect" when emerging-market bonds are reviewed by rating agencies with a view to a downgrade.[159] This is one reason financial newspapers contained so many articles in the late 1990s speculating on the direction of emerging market ratings and the meaning of rating actions.[160]

In the first sovereign rating in sub-Saharan Africa other than for South Africa, S&P awarded Senegal a B+ in 2000, praising the country's "political institutions [which] set Senegal apart from some other sovereigns in sub-Saharan Africa."[161] Senegal was constrained, S&P commented, by "weak human development indicators," low income, and deficiencies in its social and physical infrastructure. But the agency's praise reflected its confidence in the commitment to specific policy lines

154. John Reed, "Finance Chief Puts on Brave Face as Poland Is Downgraded," *Financial Times*, August 1, 2002, 5.

155. On the rating experience of developing countries, see Friedrich Ebert Foundation, "Credit Ratings and Emerging Economies: Building Confidence in the Process of Globalization," Fall 1999, available at www.fesny.org/finance.html, accessed August 1, 2003.

156. David Barham, "Survey of Turkish Finance and Industry: Consume Less, Borrow Less," *Financial Times*, November 3, 1994, 1.

157. Anna Szterenfeld, "It's Not Over Yet," *Business Latin America*, February 6, 1995, 1.

158. Richard Waters, "Moody's Upgrades Argentina," *Financial Times*, July 14, 1992, 21.

159. Guillermo Larrain, Helmut Reisen, and Julia von Maltzan, "Emerging Market Risk and Sovereign Credit Ratings," OECD Development Center, Technical Paper no. 124, Paris, April 1997.

160. E.g., see Thomas T. Vogel Jr., "Latin American Nations Maintain High Debt Ratings from Agencies," *Wall Street Journal Europe*, June 18, 1998, 2, and "Bond Ratings: B for Brazil," *Economist*, July 15, 2000, 107.

161. S&P quoted in William Wallis, "Senegal First in Ratings Game," *Financial Times*, December 19, 2000, n.p., available at www.business.com, accessed June 1, 2001.

that the government of Senegal had adopted. In particular, S&P noted the adherence to a "program of structural reforms, which includes selling many of the assets that still remain in state hands." Similarly, when S&P upgraded Mexico in February 2002, causing the country's stock exchange index to jump more than 2 percent within minutes of the announcement, the reasons the agency gave for the upgrade were Mexico's "improved transparency"—meaning its legal and political infrastructure—and "ever deepening integration with the US economy."[162] S&P has even developed a separate rating scale to rate Russian corporates specifically on their internal corporate governance standards.[163]

At first glance, this argument about governance and sovereign rating seems a synchronic-rationalist one. In rating governments, the agencies protect investors' interests, acting through warnings and downgrades when conditions deteriorate. But more is involved here. First, the link between the specific policy orthodoxies rating agencies promote and financial prudence is not functional and rational but rather socially constructed. Privatization, for instance, may or may not bring fiscal balance. Second, there is considerable room for judgment on sovereign governments' willingness to repay their debts. Thus sovereign rating is as much about governance—and therefore about politics—as it is about the usual narrow means-ends calculations of the synchronic-rationalist school.

If diachronic-constructivist principles were removed in a counterfactual scenario, the emphasis on broader programs of policy and the issue of debtor willingness to repay would disappear. Those broader considerations reflect a more social framework of thought and the heterodox principles of a diachronic-constructivist position. In such terms, rating can be understood as a feature of developed country "government-at-a-distance" over developing countries.

Conclusions

A key conclusion from this investigation of rating agencies' effect on governments is that "sovereignty-free actors" enter into complex relations with the "sovereignty-bound."[164] Evaluating the role of rating agencies brings into relief the relations between these mechanisms of regulation and national states. The case is most clear in the developing world, where governments are busy setting up rating agencies and mandating that issuers obtain ratings (often from designated local agencies), as part

162. On the index jump, see John Authers, "Mexico Sees S&P Ratings Upgrade," *Financial Times*, February 8, 2002, 27, and John Authers and Sara Silver, "Debt Rating Upgrade Gives Boost to Mexico," *Financial Times*, February 8, 2002, 6.

163. Arkady Ostrovsky, "S&P Plans New Type of Rating for Russian Groups," *Financial Times*, October 11, 2000, 37.

164. James N. Rosenau, *Turbulence in World Politics: A Theory of Change and Continuity*, (Princeton: Princeton University Press, 1990), 36.

of a wider campaign to reform capital allocation across their economies. Some of these processes are also seen in the United States, France, and Japan.

States seem to coexist uneasily with rating agencies, as sovereign downgradings demonstrate. The agencies helpfully offer states a vehicle through which parts of society, such as capital allocation, can be separated off as "not political." But they also discipline states by conducting surveillance and sending signals about policy and performance to internationally mobile capital.

Bond rating propagates globally many of the American-derived practices and expectations developed in corporate and municipal rating, such as the "fundamental analysis" familiar from the Detroit case. But even more than corporate or municipal rating, this consideration of the growth of global rating highlights the subjective, judgmental nature of rating. The U.S. agencies acknowledge the legitimacy of local knowledge but from within the context of a highly centralized system of global comparison, premised on instrumental, synchronic knowledge. The universality of the agencies' way of thinking is most questionable when it comes to "credit-related political fundamentals," but this specific problem reflects the subjectivity inherent in bond rating more widely.

The financial crises of the past decade have reinforced efforts toward "transparency," playing into the hands of the major U.S. agencies. Still, different forms of knowledge persist, for example, in the local Japanese rating agencies. These knowledge forms are evidence of resistance to the process of centralization identified here and challenge the influence of the global bond rating agencies.

CHAPTER SEVEN

Blown Calls: Rating Challenges and Crises

Rating companies is not unlike umpiring a baseball game. To partisan
fans, a single blown call easily outweighs a hundred irreproachable
judgments. . . . So it goes for the rating agencies, too. When a company
or sovereign nation repays its debt on time, the market barely takes
momentary notice and quickly moves on. But let a country or corporation unexpectedly miss a payment or threaten default, and bondholders,
lawyers and even regulators are quick to rush the field to protest the
credit analyst's lapse.

ROBERT CLOW, *Institutional Investor,* 1999

This book has presented a case for taking the bond rating agencies
seriously as political economy actors. The central argument is that rating agencies
help to construct the context in which corporations, municipalities, and governments make decisions. Rating agencies are not, as often supposed, "neutral" institutions. Their impact on policy is political first, in terms of the processes involved,
and second, in terms of the consequences for competing social interests. In terms of
processes, the rating agencies are not objective, in a scientific sense. The rating
process incorporates information-gathering and judgment-determination elements,
which are socially and historically conditioned. Contrary to claims to objectivity,
what rating agencies produce—a rating judgment—is inherently subjective: it
incorporates some values and excludes others. Yet, these judgments help to shape
decision-making inside bond issuers and affect communities all over the world. A
mental framework of rating orthodoxy, in large part derived from U.S. norms, is the
moral compass of this subjectivity.

The second reason for thinking the work of the agencies is political is that their
judging of creditworthiness has effects distributed throughout society, by shaping the
policy of corporations, municipalities, and governments. Some groups are affected
by road or bridge tolls, say, more than other groups. Because the agencies are so consequential and their views can potentially advantage or disadvantage interests, we

cannot see them as other than important actors through which resources—increasingly internationally—are carved up.

It may seem that this book presents rating agencies as all powerful, that the agencies quietly get their way on everything, that they rule without opposition. But the rated world doesn't work that way. In this chapter the image of rating agency power and authority is examined, in particular the ways in which rating is contested and yet, despite opposition, continues to expand to new areas of influence.

There are three types of challenge to the power and authority of rating agencies. The first challenge—problems in rating organization—is about the public discussion of problems that market actors (including government officials and financial reporters) see in the way the agencies are organized and do their business. The key elements are perceived conflicts of interest in how ratings are paid for and the question of unsolicited ratings.

The second challenge concerns performance issues and is more serious than the first. The major issues are the dated quality of ratings, concerns about "split" ratings, and the absence of probabalistic quantitative analysis models in the rating process.

The third and final challenge, rating crises, emerges from a series of high-profile failures on the agencies' part. Three cases of sudden bankruptcies or collapses of credit quality that the agencies failed to predict are investigated: Orange County's mid-1990s financial crisis, the Asian financial crisis of 1997–98, and the Enron collapse of 2001–2002.

The counterfactual method is not explicitly deployed in this analysis. The value of a constructivist-economic sociology perspective to the political economy analysis of rating was established in chapters 4–6. Here, rationalist and constructivist explanations are deployed as required.

At the heart of all these challenges lies the key reality of the rating process: reputation cannot be bought off the shelf. The reputation of Moody's and S&P has been constructed over time, through a combination of serving a need by offering information to solve problems between buyers and sellers and by providing reliable information, thus generating epistemic authority. Since the reputational assets of the rating agencies reflect a process of construction, the degrading of those assets is of vital importance. In what ways is an agency's reputation susceptible to attack? Is rating reputation vulnerable to falling apart, or does it decline incrementally? The view offered here is that the rating agencies are embedded knowledge networks, with a robustness that makes them resilient in the face of problems, issues, and crises. But in an increasingly volatile world, a program of reputational reinforcement makes sense.

Rating Organization

One commonplace of the rating world is repeated in newspaper and magazine articles wherever the raters are a presence: that a conflict of interest is inherent in charging bond issuers for work undertaken by the agencies. The problem with fees is that issuers are not actually the principals in rating. The principals—those for whom the work is done—are investors. So making issuers pay introduces the potential for issuers to influence the agencies' judgments and undermine their commitment to giving investors a true account.

Ratings are like the news—public goods. Once a rating is released, there is no way for the agency to prevent investors or intermediaries like banks, which have not paid for the rating, from free riding on the rating. That is why it is difficult for the agencies to get investors to pay the full rating costs. The dilemma for the agencies is to reconcile the public-good aspect of ratings with the need to earn revenue and make an appropriate return. All the while, they must minimize perceived conflicts of interest that degrade the agencies' reputation.[1] The solution agencies arrived at was to charge issuers, because investors will free ride. But the agencies still have to ensure issuers do not shape the rating process—that would destroy the reputational value of ratings (and thus the rating franchise).

The major agencies have been very successful in managing this dilemma. Smith and Walter suggest that internal operating procedures—and analyst compensation policies that avoid linking salary to fee revenue—are designed to avoid conflict.[2] If agencies were to give in to the conflict of interest inherent in issuers paying rating fees, they would probably find their franchise as embedded knowledge networks seriously impaired. The best evidence for the viability of their position is the absence of any scandal related to conflict of interest, despite frequent comment about the issue in the financial and mainstream press.

A more dynamic view of the industry suggests that conflicts could arise from increased rating competition, opportunities in emerging markets, and negative stock market sentiment about the agencies themselves.[3] Smith and Walter suggest that Moody's and S&P's efforts to generate business in Mexico during the mid-1990s can be interpreted in ways that call into question the veracity of their Mexico ratings.[4] There is also the broader question of conflicts of interest with emerging market agencies in which S&P and Moody's have an interest. The potential these new enterprises have for degrading the central rating franchise remains to be seen.[5]

The impetus to growth that is pushing the rating agencies into new products and services in their home markets may heighten the potential for rather than militate

1. For an excellent discussion of the conflicts of interest problem, see Roy C. Smith and Ingo Walter, "Rating Agencies: Is There an Agency Issue?," Stern School of Business, New York University, February 18, 2001.

2. Ibid., 43–44.

3. "In Their Drive for New Revenues, Credit-Rating Agencies Are Opening Themselves Up to Conflicts of Interest," *Economist*, April 12, 2001, n.p., accessed from www.economist.co.uk, December 4, 2001.

4. Smith and Walter, February 18, 2001, 40–41.

5. Ibid., 42.

against conflicts of interest. Specifically, the agencies have gone into the business of risk consulting. S&P's "Risk Solutions," launched February 2001, offers consulting and off-the-shelf quantitative credit risk models. Reportedly, these models are designed to take advantage of Basel II's promotion of internal risk rating by banks. A problem arises if banks, which are rated by the agencies, feel obligated to purchase these products. More troubling potential for conflict of interest is presented by Moody's "Rating Assessment Service," launched in late 2000. The service tells an issuer, in confidence, "what its credit rating would be if it undertook a particular course of action," such as a merger or share buyback. A problem arises, of course, if Moody's or S&P subsequently take a different view—much to chagrin of customers who think that they have taken steps to avoid precisely this outcome. If Moody's and S&P are really offering rating advice here, have they compromised their role as judges of creditworthiness?

It is not often that an event in the rating world can be called spectacular or dramatic, but these labels certainly apply to Moody's unsolicited ratings in the mid- to late 1990s.[6] The controversy involved a major court case, an investigation by the U.S. Justice Department, a reorganization within Moody's, and—years later—a refinement of what Moody's told the market about unsolicited ratings. Two things seem to have triggered the Justice Department investigation. One was the 1994 issue of $1 billion in bonds by GPA Group, an Irish aircraft-leasing corporation. Lehman Brothers, the underwriters, arranged for S&P and Fitch to rate this asset-backed deal. Moody's decided it had "an obligation to bondholders" to rate the bonds and persuaded Lehman's to include Moody's, too. According to Gasparino, "The bankers say they feared that without all the available information, Moody's would issue a low unsolicited rating and drive up borrowing costs." Gasparino says word of Lehman's dealings with Moody's reached the Justice Department. Lehman officials subsequently met with investigators from Justice during their probe of Moody's.[7]

The second thing that seems to have triggered the investigation was a rash of complaints in the mid-1990s about Moody's unsolicited municipal ratings. The complaints were capped by a lawsuit that Jefferson County School District of Colorado filed in 1996 over Moody's unsolicited rating on a county bond issue from 1993. The concern of the Justice Department's antitrust division was that unsolicited ratings were, in effect, anticompetitive. Rating firms could use the practice to "improperly pressure" issuers in order to win business.[8] Indeed, Shamosh suggests raters are supposed to be "green-eyeshade types." If they come to be viewed

---

6. *Economist*, for example, addressed the issues in an editorial, "The Use and Abuse of Reputation," April 6, 1996, and in "Credit-Rating Agencies: AAArgh!," *Economist*, April 6, 1996, 94–95.

7. Charles Gasparino, "Triple-A Dispute: Unsolicited Ratings from Moody's Upset Some Bond Issuers," *Wall Street Journal*, May 2, 1996, 1.

8. Charles Gasparino, "Antitrust Probe of Moody's May Spur Tougher Regulation of Rating Agencies," *Wall Street Journal*, March 28, 1996, sec. C, 19.

as "shakedown artists," using ratings to generate business, this will undermine credit markets.[9]

Although the Justice Department investigation was a domestic affair, according to Bransten, there was support outside the United States for addressing the unsolicited ratings issue. Some hope for a "chilling effect" on the practice internationally.[10] Waters also noted "concerns which have been raised in other countries about the way Moody's builds an influential position in bond markets."[11]

Moody's won dismissal of the case Jefferson County filed in Denver federal court, based on First Amendment guarantees of free speech.[12] But this outcome still left regulators uncomfortable with unsolicited ratings. SEC and Justice officials discussed mandating disclosure of the unsolicited status of bonds via court order or rule change.[13] In 1998, Justice's antitrust division made a submission to the SEC recommending that, in the interests of accuracy, the SEC require ratings agencies to disclose when ratings are unsolicited. The implication was that unsolicited ratings may lack all the inputs of solicited ratings.[14] A year later, the Justice Department abandoned the antitrust investigation, taking no action.

Moody's subsequently signaled it was considering identifying unsolicited ratings to investors.[15] It did just that in November 1999, in the interests of "greater transparency." At the time, Moody's claimed that the controversy over unsolicited ratings had missed an important fact—that most unsolicited ratings had always been made with input from debt issuers. Further defending the practice, the company said that it had been assigning unsolicited ratings since 1909, when Moody's Investors Service began to rate debt. The agency also claimed that unsolicited ratings are "the market's best defense against rating shopping," because issuers search for higher ratings and try to suppress lower ratings.[16]

9. Michael Shamosh, municipal-market strategist at Corby North Bridge Securities, quoted in Gasparino, May 2, 1996.

10. Lisa Bransten, "Pay Us—Or Pay the Price," in "Survey—International Capital Markets '96," *Financial Times*, March 21, 1996, 6.

11. Richard Waters, "Moody's Unsolicited Ratings to Be Investigated," *Financial Times*, March 28, 1996, 29.

12. Charles Gasparino, "SEC Won't Act to Regulate Raters of Bonds," *Wall Street Journal*, May 10, 1996, sec. A, 4B. The U.S. District Court dismissed a second antitrust aspect of the Jefferson County case in April 1997; see Gregg Wirth, "Court Dismisses Moody's Case on Unsolicited Ratings," *Investment Dealers' Digest* 63, no. 15 (April 14, 1997): 12.

13. Charles Gasparino, "Bond-Rating Firms May Be Required to Disclose When Work Is Unsolicited," *Wall Street Journal*, July 11, 1996, sec. B, 12.

14. "SEC Rule Is Urged That Would Govern 'Unsolicited' Ratings," *Wall Street Journal*, March 9, 1998, A11.

15. Charles Gasparino, "Inquiry into Moody's Ratings Practices Ends as U.S. Agency Takes No Action," *Wall Street Journal*, March 12, 1999, A4.

16. Moody's Investors Service, *Designation of Unsolicited Ratings in Which the Issuer Has Not Participated* (New York: Moody's Investors Service, November 1999).

The conclusion to the controversy over unsolicited ratings was that the courts had defended the principle of free speech for rating agencies, Moody's had not engaged in antitrust behavior, and the aggressive expansion of the rated universe to incorporate the nonrated would continue. There was more change than these observations reveal, however. Things were different now. Issuers had stood up and made it clear they were customers, too, and would make trouble if Moody's or other rating firms ignored their needs entirely. The "hidden transcript" of credit rating—that issuers actually see themselves as customers—had finally received official attention.

The change is subtle, but what we see during this period is a significant shift in Moody's internal culture and organization away from a perceived hostility to issuers, who were firmly not understood to be customers.[17] Transparency, cited in Moody's reform of the unsolicited ratings system, became central to the way the organization presented itself to the world. Where access to Moody's raters was always difficult in the early 1990s, it suddenly became much easier. So, although the unsolicited ratings episode can be a victory for Moody's and the notion that investors are the principals, issuers were able to challenge their relationship to Moody's, in their favor. Moody's was not the organization it had been prior to this ratings saga.

Rating Agency Performance

There was little innovation during the era of rating conservatism that followed World War II. The biggest development was the introduction of issuer fees during the late 1960s by S&P (1968) and Moody's (1970).[18] Even then, however, as former S&P president Brenton W. Harries noted, Congress discussed the agencies' performance and questioned rating officials about their work.[19] Raters were never left alone to enjoy a sinecure. The "hidden transcript" may have been more hidden during these years, but it was still there. Raters knew about it then, too. Today, expressions of concern about rating performance—how good the rating agencies are at their business—have become the norm. Newspapers, magazines, and online sites talk continuously about the agencies and their failings.[20]

---

17. On Moody's pre-1996 corporate culture, see Ann Monroe, "Rating Rating Agencies," *Treasury & Risk Management* (July 1995): n.p., accessed from www.cfonet.com, March 29, 1999.

18. "Profits, Racism, Quality of Life, and Other Issues Facing Rating Agencies," *Bond Buyer*, February 26, 1993, 5.

19. Ibid.

20. A few good examples from the past decade are Lynne Kilpatrick, "Debt-Rating's Flaws," *Financial Times of Canada*, March 30–April 5, 1992, 1; "Rating the Rating Agencies," *Economist*, July 15, 1995, 53–54; Richard House, "Ratings Trouble," *Institutional Investor*, October 1995, 245–49; Patience Wheatcroft, "Don't Give Raters Too Much Credit," *The Times*, April 5, 2001, n.p., accessed via Lexis-Nexis, February 3, 2002.

Three things are central to this discourse of discontent. First, because there is a discourse at all, we have further confirmation of the agencies' role in financial globalization. The expression of discontent happens because the agencies cannot be ignored in these circumstances. The role of the agencies has a certain logic. They "fit" in the capital markets, even if they have made that place for themselves. Perceived failings in their work are too important to be overlooked. Second, the rating discourse is very much framed within this logic of agency function. It is about improving rather than replacing them. Third, the agencies have to deal with the "hidden transcript" but can fall back on their role to stiffen their resolve, especially versus issuers, who seem constantly engaged in efforts to direct the agencies' activities.

As we have seen, a common criticism is that the rating agencies are too "slow." They apply the lessons of the past to the present, a bit like a general re-fighting the wars of his youth, even though technology and tactics have moved on substantially in the subsequent years. Market participants worry that the ratings they are looking at do not have much to do with the company whose balance sheet can move by billions in either direction, in just a few hours. The agencies' traditional defense against this problem of timeliness was that they took a longer view: they wanted to offer ratings that were not just for today but would have some ability to withstand the normal business cycle. They would cite their track record on defaults of rated debt.[21]

Increasingly, "event risk," such as a merger or acquisition, came to be perceived as a vital ingredient in creditworthiness, and the agencies were expected to become more sensitive to it. More recently, because of the Enron bankruptcy, the agencies have begun to discuss the impact of market sentiment on issuers. Agencies are also exploring how sophisticated quantitative analysis may be useful in understanding this dimension of credit risk.[22]

A less obvious but interesting performance issue arises when the agencies decide to treat specific financial instruments differently in their work and split on rating an issuer.[23] In a world of increasingly sophisticated asset-backed securities and derivatives, differing views of these instruments' credit implications calls into question a bedrock assumption of the mental framework of rating orthodoxy—that there is a right way and a wrong way to understand specific economic and financial matters. Investment banks, regulators, and other parties may also have different understandings of financial innovation. But this divergence might have less negative impact on the agencies than situations in which the agencies give different ratings for the same issuer or bond issue.[24]

21. E.g., *Historical Default Rates on Corporate Bond Issuers, 1920–1999* (New York: Moody's Investors Service, 2000).

22. "Quant Argue with That," *Economist*, February 16, 2002, 69–70.

23. For an example of the differences of view between the agencies on financial innovation, see Jeff French, "Securitization Wrinkle Complicates Ratings," *Wall Street Journal Europe*, April 23, 1998, 12.

24. On split ratings, see Richard Cantor, Frank Packer, and Kevin Cole, "Split Ratings and the Pricing of Credit Risk," *Journal of Fixed Income* 7, no. 3 (December 1997): 72–82.

Split ratings are sometimes reported sensationally in the financial press, so it might seem that they are very rare. In fact, split ratings are quite common. According to Cantor, Packer, and Cole, 50 percent of all corporate bonds had different ratings from Moody's and S&P when issued. Nonetheless, split ratings challenge the idea of a knowable rating universe that the agencies are trying to reflect in their work. There are only a few diviners of this knowledge, and if the agencies cannot "get it right" with an accurate rating, what does this say about the quality of their staff or management? If some agencies are less strict than others, do the less stringent agencies reduce the reputational assets of the rest?

Even if we grant a static logic to the role of the agencies, financial globalization poses threats that agencies must adapt to or confront in some way. As Strange noted in *Casino Capitalism* and subsequently in *Mad Money*, market volatility brings new risks for market institutions.[25] Like an aging sports champion eyeing the competition, the agencies cannot predict when a new way of doing things will come along and steal their franchise. Nor do they know what failure or accretion of perceived incompetence or mediocrity will destroy issuers' willingness to secure a rating from them.[26] Raters have to adjust their practices with care and listen to what the market is saying and doing. Even if raters present themselves as unmoved by market turmoil, like any purveyor of symbols or professional knowledge, they must attend to their audience at all times. In this regard, rating agencies are like an academic who has become recognized for expertise, but must always look over his or her shoulder, anticipating the arrival of a new scholar determined to "go beyond" the work of the established professor. As with academics, in rating agencies there is an anxiety belied by a calm, stoic exterior.

Rating Crises

The most substantial challenge to the agencies' power and authority occurs when there is a failure to predict a sudden financial deterioration. At a minimum, people expect rating agencies to warn investors if companies, municipalities, and governments have problems that perhaps are not immediately obvious. The agencies often get this right. They warned investors in 2001 that Argentina's finances were deteriorating. To the ire of the Japanese government, they have warned investors again and again of Japan's growing indebtedness. They aggressively downgraded the telecommunications industry when problems began to develop.

25. Susan Strange, *Casino Capitalism* (Oxford: Blackwell, 1986), and Strange, *Mad Money: When Markets Outgrow Governments* (Ann Arbor: University of Michigan Press, 1998).

26. How many errors like the one reported in the following item are needed to destroy a reputation? Julie Earle and Peter Thal Larsen, "S&P in Setback over Calpine Error," *Financial Times*, February 26, 2002, n.p., accessed from www.ft.com, March 4, 2002.

Unfortunately for the agencies, they also get it wrong. When that happens—when an investment-grade rating fails to anticipate a bankruptcy, for example—the accusations fly, and we have a rating crisis. But rating crises are nothing new. The first major rating crisis of modern times was the Penn Central Railroad bankruptcy of June 1970.[27] The failure of Franklin National Bank, the bank that created the credit card in 1951, sparked another significant rating crisis in 1974.[28] What is new is that rating crises—the public perception of acute rating agency failure—have become more common since the onset of financial globalization during the late 1970s.

Three episodes examined below tell us a great deal about these crises, what they mean for rating power and authority, and how the agencies try to cope with the fall-out. The first is a municipal crisis, the bankruptcy of Orange County, California, in the mid-1990s. The second episode is a sovereign rating crisis, the Asian financial crisis of 1997–98. The last event is a corporate rating crisis, the bankruptcy of Enron Corporation in late 2001.

Orange County

Credit ratings of Orange County proved worthless in the mid-1990s. How reliable, then, are the rating companies' assertions that no similar situation is lurking out there, especially given the subsequent Asia crisis and Enron bankruptcy? But because of Orange County, raters' policies and processes were subjected to tougher internal scrutiny and improvement.[29]

Orange County is a wealthy California municipality, located between Los Angeles and San Diego. Solidly Republican, the characteristically suburban county has a diverse economy in high-value-added, knowledge-intensive fields.[30] Unfortunately, all that know-how did not prevent the financial meltdown in December 1994. That was when officials found that the investment strategies of the county's long-serving Treasurer, Robert L. Citron, had created potential losses of $1.5–2 billion. Citron, an elected official, had pooled funds from two hundred school districts and other agencies. He had borrowed a further $12 billion to create an investment portfolio worth $20 billion in 1994.[31] But Citron had bet that interest rates would remain stable for the rate-sensitive mortgage-backed securities he had bought for the fund.

27. Joseph R. Daughen and Peter Binzen, *Wreck of the Penn Central*, 2nd ed. (New York: Beard Books, 1999).

28. Joan Edelman Spero, *The Failure of the Franklin National Bank* (New York: Beard Books, [1980] 1999).

29. Barry B. Burr, "Credit Raters Miss Many Danger Flags," *Pensions & Investments*, January 23, 1995, 11.

30. For an outline of the prosperity of Orange County, see "Orange County: Virtually Back," *Economist*, March 7, 1998, 59–60.

31. Sallie Hofmeister, "Fund Head Resigns in California," *New York Times*, December 6, 1994, D1.

Instead, interest rates rose in 1993 and 1994, accumulating substantial losses for his investment pool.[32] The county filed for bankruptcy on December 6, 1994.[33] This was a stunning event in such a stable, sound credit market, where creditworthiness is typically good and has improved since the mid-1980s, when only 1.5 percent of bonds were below investment grade.[34]

Through much hard work, Orange County rapidly returned to financial health. The new treasurer—tax collector, John M. W. Moorlach, lawyers, and other officials oversaw the transfer of assets from county agencies (dubbed Operation Robin Hood), refinancing, budget cuts, and $860 million in settlements with investment banks and other financial institutions. Moody's reinstated investment-grade ratings in late 1997, and S&P followed suit in early 2000.[35]

The Orange County events were definitely a crisis for the rating agencies. According to Partnoy, the agencies should have heeded indications that Citron's investment strategy was too dependent on stable interest rates.[36] Were the agencies overstretched, with only a vague picture of what was going on inside the municipalities they were rating? Did they understand the complex financial instruments Citron was using?[37] How could investors have confidence in investment-grade ratings one day that turned into default grade the next? Perhaps most significantly, the Orange County bankruptcy highlighted the issue of willingness to pay. As Richard Larken of S&P noted at the time: "Yes, they've got the ability to pay. But that is a moot issue. What matters is their willingness to pay."[38]

Here was a county deciding to go down the bankruptcy route rather than impose new taxes on its residents—a route that its Republican county supervisors had vowed never to take. This unwillingness to resort to new taxes, to make investors wait, was unprecedented according to Daniel Heimowitz, Moody' public finance

32. Leslie Wayne, "Orange County's Bankruptcy: The Temptations," *New York Times*, December 8, 1994, D1.

33. Floyd Norris, "Orange County's Bankruptcy: The Overview," *New York Times*, December 8, 1994, D1; on the fiscal motivations for Citron's exotic financial strategies, see Sallie Hofmeister, "A Bankruptcy Peculiar to California," *New York Times*, January 6, 1995, D1.

34. Standard & Poor's, *Municipal Rating Transitions and Defaults* (New York: Standard & Poor's, June 13, 2001).

35. On the lawyer for Orange County, see Leslie Wayne, "Orange County's Artful Dodger; The Creative Bankruptcy Tactics of Bruce Bennett," *New York Times*, August 4, 1995, D2, and Wayne, "Analysis: Orange County out of Debt, But Faith Shaken," *New York Times*, June 13, 1996. I met with Moorlach in April 1996, at the Laguna Hotel in Laguna Beach, California. Moorlach invited me to a speech he gave to the local Rotary Club.

36. Frank Partnoy, *Infectious Greed: How Deceit and Risk Corrupted the Financial Markets* (London: Profile Books, 2003), 118–19.

37. On Citron and his strategies, see Sarah Lubman and John R. Emshwiller, "Before the Fall: Hubris and Ambition in Orange County: Robert Citron's Story," *Wall Street Journal*, January 18, 1995, A1.

38. Richard Larken, director of municipal finance at S&P, quoted in Leslie Wayne, "County's Crisis Is Conservatives' Lab," *New York Times*, January 10, 1995, D1.

director at the time. He cited New York City's dedicated sales tax, which backed the bonds issued during the city's fiscal crisis of the 1970s, additional income taxes that averted a default in Philadelphia, and two property tax increases that had prevented defaults on school bonds in Chicago.[39] This was a "new game" and according to Heimowitz, it threatened "the trust that holds up this market."[40]

As if the unwillingness to play by the rules was not bad enough for the rating agencies, when the county emerged from bankruptcy in mid-1996, it decided to sue S&P in addition to going after Merrill Lynch and several other investment firms in the courts. Merrill Lynch, the main seller of financial products to Orange County during Citron's tenure, subsequently settled with the county and other claimants for $467 million. The firm also paid $2 million to settle with the SEC. The SEC case revolved around the disclosure responsibilities of a securities firm.[41] The SEC issued a proposed rule on the disclosure of the potential risks of derivatives holdings in 1995, a year after the bankruptcy.[42] A "blistering" California state senate report on the county's financial affairs reportedly largely blamed the city's officials and residents. However, it did criticize the rating agencies for not warning investors of the problems.[43]

Orange County's suit alleged that S&P "gave the county too good a grade in early 1994, failing to blow the whistle on the county's teetering finances."[44] Unlike the other suits, which had targeted businesses that had sold the county tangible things like securities, legal or accounting work, S&P sold reputation. But that reputation was key. Zane Mann, publisher of the *California Municipal Bond Adviser*, noted that the rating agencies "are the single most important force in the municipal bond industry."[45] S&P deployed the well-used First Amendment defense and pointed out that they did not undertake their own audits. They were not responsible if they were being lied to. They were not, in other words, financial detectives.

After three years of hearings, the county settled. It had sued for more than $2 billion, but "in the end, S&P admitted no wrongdoing and agreed to pay just $140,000, representing a partial repayment of fees it charged the county for rating services in

39. Ibid.; on willingness to pay, also see Joe Mysak, "Winking at Debt," *New York Times,* June 23, 1995, A31.

40. Heimowitz quoted in Leslie Wayne, "Banging a Tin Cup with a Silver Spoon," *New York Times,* June 4, 1995, sec. 3, 1; on the new game's architect, see Wayne, August 4, 1995, sec. D, 1.

41. Leslie Wayne, "Merrill Lynch to Pay $2 Million in Orange County Case," *New York Times,* August 25, 1998, C2; also see "Orange County: Seller Beware," *Economist,* June 6, 1998, 111.

42. "SEC Formally Issues Rules for Disclosing Risks of Derivatives," *Wall Street Journal,* December 29, 1995, C15.

43. Roger Lowenstein, "Intrinsic Value: As Orange County Blames Others, Guess Where the Latest Report Points," *Wall Street Journal,* September 7, 1995, C1.

44. Ronald Campbell, "Standard & Poor's Gives Orange County, Calif., a Second Low Grade," *Orange County Register,* October 31, 1997, n.p., accessed via Lexis-Nexis, February 20, 2002.

45. Mann quoted in Ronald Campbell, "Standard & Poor's Requests Dismissal of Orange County, Calif., Lawsuit," *Orange County Register,* October 4, 1996, n.p., accessed via Lexis-Nexis, February 20, 2002.

1994."[46] S&P had won a ruling that it was protected by the First Amendment, unless it was shown to have "issued false ratings intentionally or in reckless disregard for the truth." Although S&P won in the end, Orange County's aggressive pursuit of investment advisers, including S&P, had adjusted the norms of the rating world. In the future, raters would have to anticipate strategies like these from smart, resourceful people in municipal finance. Steps would have to be taken not to give them ammunition.

Asia's Financial Crisis

The Asian financial crisis of 1997–98 is surely one of the most searing events of the late twentieth century and a disappointment to millions counting on growth to expand their personal opportunities and lift their nations into the developed world.[47] A lot of ink was spilled at the time about who was to blame.[48] That is not the purpose here. What is intriguing is the way in which the Asian financial crisis, like the crisis in Mexico in 1994–95, threatened the agencies' legitimacy.[49]

Although commonly thought of as one event, following King, the crisis may be seen to have two stages.[50] The first began in July 1997, with the initial panic in Thailand. This panic ran until the end of the summer, also affecting Malaysia, the Philippines, and Singapore. The second stage began at the end of October 1997, hitting Indonesia, Hong Kong, and Taiwan, then spreading to Japan before badly affecting South Korea in late December 1997. This second crisis had the global impact, causing stock market falls in the U.S. and Europe, "infecting" emerging markets as diverse as Russia and Brazil.

The capital flight in Thailand was triggered by the Thai government, which reversed a public undertaking to support an ailing finance company. Once the extent of its liabilities became clear, the corporation was allowed to fail. Consequently, the Thai baht was devalued and IMF assistance sought. Institutional investors reconsidered their investment positions in the region, putting pressure on other currencies. Hong Kong and South Korea used interest rate increases to ward off speculative attacks that summer. In late August, the IMF announced a rescue plan for Thailand, thus calming investors' fears.

46. E. Scott Reckard and Jean O. Pasco, "O.C. Closes the Legal Books on Fiscal Fiasco," *Los Angeles Times*, June 16, 1999, C1.

47. For an excellent discussion of the varying capacity of states in the region to cope with crisis and the post-crisis consequences, see Natasha Hamilton-Hart, *Asian States, Asian Bankers: Central Banking in Southeast Asia* (Ithaca: Cornell University Press, 2002), 129–70.

48. See, e.g., Morris Goldstein, *The Asian Financial Crisis: Causes, Cures, and Systemic Implications* (Washington, D.C.: Institute for International Economics, 1998).

49. Lisa Bransten, "Mexican Crisis Underlines Agency Pitfalls," *Financial Times*, February 27, 1995, 22.

50. This account is based on the narrative presented in Michael R. King, "Who Triggered the Asian Financial Crisis?" *Review of International Political Economy* 8, no. 3 (Autumn 2001): 441.

Currency pressures returned in October, when Indonesia announced a resort to IMF assistance.[51] Late that month, the Korean government nationalized Kia Motors, leading to a downgrade of Korea's foreign debt. Hong Kong raised overnight rates the same day, from 7 to 300 percent, to defend its currency peg against speculation. That move caused a sell-off of 25 percent of Hong Kong's stock market. U.S. and European markets also fell sharply. Several Indonesian and Japanese banks and securities firms failed in November.

In mid-November, the South Korean government stopped defending the currency as it continued to fall below 1,000 to the dollar and called in the IMF. In December, Korea signed a $57 billion bailout package. Thanks to rollovers by foreign banks, the country narrowly avoided a default at the end of the year, when it became clear that short-term foreign currency liabilities amounted to as much as $100 billion.

For the trustees of normally conservative U.S. and European funds, the ratings turmoil was a sobering experience.

> If you want to see a grown man cry ask him about Thailand's 7.75 percent issue of 2007, rated A/A3 back in May [1997]. The more conservative funds that held this paper did so under investment criteria that permitted A minus/A3 paper or above but nothing underneath. So when the sovereign rating got revised closer to high-yield levels, such funds were forced to sell the bond. The spread on the bond in question moved from 89 basis points over US treasuries as of May 30 to a peak of 530 basis points over on October 28. This was just four days after S&P downgraded Thailand to BBB from A minus, and less than a month after Moody's downgraded it to Baa1 from A3. Since both rating agencies had acted the trustees had no choice but to instruct their fund managers to sell the bonds even in bad market conditions. Little wonder some investors are a little critical.[52]

To translate, the huge movement in the spreads on these bonds had to be deducted from the price they were sold at in this fire sale. Bonds sell at a current market spread over U.S. Treasuries, not the price they were bought at. The gap between 89 basis points and 530 is the loss the sellers experienced in this case.

It was a loss the agencies had not warned investors about in time to avoid, or so the prevailing wisdom suggested. A good illustration of this failure is that the bond markets were already trading Thai debt at 120 basis points over U.S. Treasuries one month after the baht float in July 1997—about the level of a triple BBB credit on S&P's scale. But S&P did not cut Thailand's sovereign rating until *two* months after the baht float, to A– from A.[53]

---

51. Source for the following two paragraphs is ibid., 422.
52. Steven Irvine, "Caught with Their Pants Down?" *Euromoney,* January 1998, 51.
53. Betty W. Liu, "Big Downgrades in Asia Are Criticized," *Wall Street Journal Europe,* October 13, 1997, 12.

Given these huge losses, criticism of the agencies was voluble. The sweeping downgrades of Thailand, South Korea, and Malaysia were, according to some bond traders and investors, "a symptom of inadequate credit analysis": if the "agencies had done their job right, they wouldn't need to adjust ratings as severely as they have."[54] The market perception was that the rating agencies maintained their ratings into the crisis and then downgraded too far. As one analyst put it, the "agencies are basically saying their ratings were too high" before the crisis.[55]

Another sort of criticism suggested that the agencies were ignorant of Asian politics and overestimated how easy it was in these societies to make policy change, like closing insolvent banks.[56] Were the agencies good at analysis in the United States but not in Asia? Are there issues of secrecy and information-gathering in Asia that prevent markets from being transparent there? Had the agencies underestimated the difficulty of doing their job in an environment in which published information can be misleading? Do the agencies have enough resources in their local offices to cope with the level of work involved? Did the agencies find it hard to talk negatively because of Asia's supposed "sensitivity to criticism" and because the market's "conventional wisdom" was that the Asian "miracle was indestructible"?[57]

These questions were repeated over and over in the financial press. Market players started to attack the agencies, as part of a more general backlash against Western financial institutions, including the IMF, that characterized the politics of this period.[58]

If most of the market criticism attacked the agencies for getting Asia wrong and not giving investors the information that would allow them to avoid losses, other comment acknowledged the very difficult situation the contagion provoked and the challenge the agencies faced in trying to assess creditworthiness. Creditworthiness assumes a rationalist world of assets and liabilities with defined values. In a crisis like this one, market sentiment seemed to have been driven at least initially by fears of liquidity problems related to short-term debt, and that sentiment spread by contagion to other countries the market saw as similar. Fundamental issues of assets and liabilities were therefore secondary.[59] How could rating analysts, trained principally

54. Ibid.; on late rating changes, also see Craig S. Smith, "Rating Agencies Turn Cautious on Hong Kong, *Asian Wall Street Journal,* January 14, 1998, 1.

55. Analyst at a North American bank in Hong Kong, quoted in Liu, October 13, 1997.

56. "Risks Beyond Measure," *Economist,* December 13, 1997, 98, 101; Charles Gasparino and Craig Karmin, "Bond Raters Sometimes See No Evil," *Wall Street Journal,* November 28, 1997, C1. The IMF observed that because political variables are less tangible, they may be underemphasized in analysis (Charles Adams, Donald J. Mathieson, and Garry Schinasi, *International Capital Markets: Developments, Prospects and Key Policy Issues* [Washington, D.C.: International Monetary Fund, 1999], annex V, "Credit Ratings and the Recent Crises," 198).

57. Irvine, January 1998, 52.

58. Paul M. Sherer, "Distrust of Western Economics Grows in Thailand Amid Asian Financial Crisis," *Wall Street Journal Europe,* January 21, 1998, 4; Charles Lee, "Ratings Rejected," *Far Eastern Economic Review,* October 1, 1998, 84.

59. Simon Davies and Edward Luce, "Credit Rating Agencies under Fire on Korea," *Financial Times,* December 12, 1997, 30.

to think about these values not as fluctuating social variables but as real, hard numbers, incorporate market risk and its consequences for currency values into their assessments?[60] Could devoting more resources solve a problem analytically if these changes in values are "an inherent problem with market volatility?"[61]

Governments wanted to have their say about the agencies' performance in the Asian crisis. Before the crisis unfolded in the summer of 1997, APEC (Asia-Pacific Economic Cooperation) finance ministers had shown interest in developing domestic bond markets. They wanted a "strong and credible rating agency within each economy," plus a "venue that would allow for the continuous systematic exchange of best practices."[62] Things heated up somewhat when the crisis hit, but finance ministers at another APEC meeting, held in Canada during May 1998, merely noted continuing work on developing rating agencies in the region.[63] Mahathir Mohamad, the Malaysian prime minister, struck out against the global financial markets in general and the rating agencies in particular.[64]

The November 1998 APEC summit in Kuala Lumpur was plagued with disunity, but representatives issued "expressions of concern" about the "role and recent performance of the international credit rating agencies," calling for a "review" of agency practices.[65] Workshops were held in Manila in March 1998 and February 1999, with the goal of developing best practice for domestic agencies.[66] Little substantial work seems to have actually been completed. However, the Asian Development Bank did produce an exhaustive survey of credit rating agencies for the February 1999 workshop.[67]

60. Richard Dale and Steve Thomas, "Different Kind of Risk," *Financial Times*, May 8, 1998, 22.

61. Robin Monro-Davies, chairman of Fitch IBCA, quoted in Edward Luce, "IMF Attacks Credit Rating Agencies," *Financial Times*, September 9, 1999, 4.

62. "Agreements and Recommendations," APEC Financiers Group Meeting, Mactan Island, Republic of the Philippines, April 3–5, 1997, available from www.usinfo.state.gov/regional/ea/apec/cebufin2.htm, accessed February 3, 2001.

63. APEC Finance Ministers Meeting, Kananaskis, Alberta, Canada, May 23–24, 1998; "Joint Ministerial Statement," APEC Secretariat press release 13/98, May 25, 1998, available at www.apecsec.org.sg, accessed May 18, 1999.

64. Mahathir Bin Mohamad, "We Don't Need Manipulators," *Wall Street Journal Europe*, September 23, 1997, 10; Sheila McNulty, "Mahathir Declares Markets Have Failed," *Financial Times*, September 2, 1998, 3.

65. "APEC Leaders' Declaration: Strengthening the Foundations for Growth," Kuala Lumpur, Malaysia, November 18, 1998, available at www1.apecsec.org.sg, accessed May 18, 1999; on the meeting and APEC disunity, see Peter Montagnon and Sheila McNulty, "APEC Assails Credit Rating Agencies," *Financial Times*, November 19, 1998, 4.

66. "APEC's Response to the Financial Crisis: A Stocktaking by the APEC Secretariat," updated May 18, 1999, available from www.apecsec.org.sg, accessed May 18, 1999.

67. *Development of Credit Rating Agencies: Background Paper for the Second Workshop on the Development of CRAs in the APEC Region* (Manila: Asian Development Bank, 1999), available at www.adb.org/APEC?cra/default.asp, accessed August 4, 2001.

Academics have generally avoided outright denunciations of the agencies over the Asia crisis.[68] Ferri, Liu, and Stiglitz have argued that the agencies made the crisis worse first by not detecting the problems and then by downgrading more than the economic fundamentals suggested.[69] But most academics have been too busy criticizing the IMF, the World Bank, and the U.S. Treasury.[70] Some have suggested that other institutions can actually learn from the rating agencies' procedures.[71] Citing the outrage at Moody's downgrade of Thailand in spring 1997, before the Asia crisis, Karacadag and Samuels assert that market euphoria in Asia was very hard for rating agencies (and their analysts) to break through. There were "huge pressures to remain within the mainstream" because "no one wants to spoil the party."[72]

The practice of sovereign rating, as distinct from the rating of corporations or municipalities, has been subject to criticism for its seeming randomness, among other things.[73] Not surprisingly, some researchers who have explored the failure to predict financial crisis have concluded that predicting crises is hard—if not next to impossible—for all relevant parties.[74]

The IMF, with agency agreement, observed that there is scope for improving the analysis that underpins ratings, that the lack of probabilistic tools is "somewhat surprising," and that more analysts are needed. It rejected criticism of the quality of the human resources the agencies recruited.[75] Despite the IMF's defense, Partnoy has suggested that the incorporation of ratings into financial regulation put too much reliance on rating analysts he described as "not—to put it charitably—the

68. An exception is Frank Partnoy, "The Siskel and Ebert of Financial Markets? Two Thumbs Down for the Credit Rating Agencies," *Washington University Law Quarterly* 77, no. 3 (1999): 619–714.

69. G. Ferri, L-G Liu, and J.E. Stiglitz, "The Procyclical Role of Rating Agencies: Evidence from the East Asian Crisis," *Economic Notes* 28, no. 3 (1999): 335.

70. Robert Wade and Frank Veneroso, "The Asian Crisis: The High Debt Model versus the Wall Street–Treasury–IMF Complex," *New Left Review*, no. 228 (March–April 1998): 3–23; also see Richard Higgott, "The Asian Economic Crisis: A Study in the Politics of Resentment," *New Political Economy* 3, no. 3 (November 1998): 333–56.

71. Alan S. Blinder, "Eight Steps to a New Financial Order," *Foreign Affairs* (September–October 1999): 62.

72. Cem Karacadag and Barbara C. Samuels II, "In Search of the Market Failure in the Asian Crisis," *Fletcher Forum of World Affairs* 23, no. 1 (Winter–Spring 1999): 131–43, 135. Samuels subsequently organized a research program on country risk analysis, including credit rating, at the Council on Foreign Relations in 1998 and 1999.

73. D. Johannes Jüttner and Justin McCarthy, "Modelling a Ratings Crisis," unpublished paper available from www.econ.mq.edu.au/staff/djjuttner/, accessed March 21, 2002.

74. Carmen M. Reinhart, "Sovereign Credit Ratings before and after Financial Crises," unpublished paper presented to the Conference on Rating Agencies in the Global Financial System, Salomon Center, Leonard N. Stern School of Business, New York University, June 1, 2001; also see Morris Goldstein, Graciela L. Kaminsky, and Carmen M. Reinhart, *Assessing Financial Vulnerability: An Early Warning System for Emerging Markets* (Washington, D.C.: Institute for International Economics, 2000).

75. Adams, Mathieson, and Schinasi, 1999, 198.

sharpest tools in the shed." Stronger analysts work in better-paying parts of the financial markets, especially banks and funds.[76]

Perhaps the most important IMF finding was that rating agencies can either intensify or moderate boom-bust cycles, to dampen euphoria and subsequent financial crises in emerging markets.[77] Early rating signals can modify euphoria, but only when split ratings between the agencies do not muddy the picture for investors. This finding puts a premium on timely information and early rating changes that add to what markets know.

In this uncomfortable period, the rating agencies responded to the criticism quite differently in public forums. S&P chose to defend ratings as no more than opinions, based on available information.[78] Rating agencies were victims of the data because at the heart of the financial crisis in Asia, S&P suggested, was "a lack of transparency." Subsequently, S&P defended its role in terms of the firm's value to markets, which is independence from government mandates.[79]

Fitch was the most apologetic and confessed to "mistakes we clearly have made" in Asia.[80] After noting how undeveloped sovereign rating analytics are, Fitch observed that "the most significant analytical omission" was to ignore the liquidity implications of short-term debt. The agency also admitted to overestimating the "sophistication of Asian policymakers, who have proved good fair-weather navigators but very poor sailors in a storm," and highlighted the dangers of contagion.

Moody's stuck by its record, producing an elaborate and direct defense of its actions and approach in rating the region.[81] The agency made it clear that it considered itself to have done better than the others and that people placed too much predictive power in ratings. But Moody's was also prepared to acknowledge scope for lessons to be learned and "possible innovations" made in "ratings technology," in relation to short-term debt and contagion.[82]

76. Partnoy, 2003, 385.

77. Helmut Reisen and Julia von Maltzan, "Boom and Bust and Sovereign Ratings," *International Finance* 2, no. 2 (1999): 273–93 [288–89].

78. "Credit Rating Agencies' Power Is Derived Only from Offering Value," letter to the editor from Leo C. O'Neill, president, Standard & Poor's, *Financial Times*, January 8, 1998, 20. O'Neill was reacting to an editorial, "Over-Rated Agencies," *Financial Times*, December 24, 1997, 15.

79. "S&P Chief Dismisses Criticism from APEC Forum," *Asian Wall Street Journal*, December 17, 1998, 5.

80. Fitch IBCA, "After Asia: Some Lessons of the Crisis," January 13, 1998, available from www.fitchibca.com; also see Edward Luce, "Credit Agency Admits It Failed to Predict Asia Woes," *Financial Times*, January 14, 1998, 33.

81. Moody's Investors Service, *White Paper: Moody's Rating Record in the East Asian Financial Crisis* (New York: Moody's Investors Service, May 1998). On Moody's earlier record in the region, see Moody's Investors Service, *The Role of Credit Rating Agencies in the Asian Capital Markets* (New York: Moody's Investors Service, August 1993).

82. Moody's, May 1998, 8; on the rethink, see Eduardo Lachica and Charles Gasparino, "Rating Industry Heeds Asian Lessons, Broadens Its Scope for Danger Signals," *Wall Street Journal*, May 1, 1998, C19.

An example was national ratings. In response to investor demand, Moody's introduced national scale ratings in 1999.[83] The agency had previously strongly defended the necessity of globally comparable ratings. This change brought Moody's into line with other rating agencies.[84] The national scale, which included a special modifying suffix (e.g., AAA.br for Brazil), was intended to allow comparison of creditworthiness within a market but not between markets. The introduction, according to Moody's, acknowledged a large, sophisticated base of local institutional investors, deep local capital markets linked typically to private pension systems, and more professional investment management.[85]

The Asia crisis was a direct challenge to the agencies, although the policy and financial environment had already begun to change during the 1990s. Increasingly, it became apparent that the agencies would have more work than ever in the region.[86] Reports by gatherings of the eminent encouraged longer-term market financing rather than short-term bank lending.[87] Indeed, companies did turn to bond financing rather than the accident-prone banks.[88] Banks were blamed for the crises and were seen as inherently problematic institutions.[89] Reliance on Asian rating agencies was no solution, though.[90] Henry Kaufman even suggested the creation of a combined international rating agency and SEC, along the lines of an international organization.[91] With all the new business, paradoxically, rating agencies never had it so good.[92]

The Asian financial crisis of 1997–98 was a major turning point for rating agencies. Why did the rating agencies not stop this from happening? To ask this question is to assume that the agencies always have a decisive impact on the markets. But the evidence does not support this assumption. In emerging markets, the 1990s were—

83. Moody's Investors Service, *Moody's Introduces National Scale Ratings* (New York: Moody's Investors Service, November 1999).

84. "National Ratings vs. International Consistency," *Development of Credit Rating Agencies* (Manila: Asian Development Bank, 2000), sec. 8.5, 63, available at www.abb.org.

85. Moody's, *Moody's Introduces National Scale Ratings*, 1.

86. On prior change in the policy environment as it affected Asian financial markets and institutions, see Michael Loiaux et al., *Capital Ungoverned: Liberalizing Finance in Interventionist States* (Ithaca: Cornell University Press, 1997).

87. Council on Foreign Relations, *Safeguarding Prosperity in a Global Financial System: The Future International Financial Architecture* (Washington, D.C.: Institute for International Economics, 1999).

88. Marcus W. Brauchli and David Wessel, "Asian Crisis Spawns New Look for Business—Foreign Capital, Concepts Mark Global Approach," *Wall Street Journal*, June 2, 1998, A18; James T. Areddy, "Asia Finds That Banks Aren't Essential Lenders—Postcrisis Economies Turn to Other Resources," *Asian Wall Street Journal*, April 5, 2000, 3.

89. Justin Fox, "First: Blame It on the Banks," *Fortune*, August 3, 1998, 28–29.

90. Betty Liu, "Asian Rating Agencies Come under Fire," *Wall Street Journal Europe*, October 20, 1997, 13.

91. "The Perils of Global Capital," *Economist*, April 11, 1998, 76–78.

92. "On Watch," *Economist*, May 15, 1999, 122, 125.

until the summer of 1997, anyway—when euphoria ruled. In normal times, when the trade-off between risk and return feeds into financial markets, the authority of the rating agencies is more evident. In conditions of market euphoria, the raters are less effective because fewer listen to their warnings. Perhaps the raters themselves do not recognize the euphoria, especially when the market develops in ways not previously experienced.

But the downside of euphoria—financial crisis and collapse—is when rating agencies get blamed for their failure to do their job. Financial markets are dynamic. Hence the question whether the agencies can ever anticipate such events, premised as they are on the fragile confidence of trading desks thousands of miles away from sites of investment, is a vital one for the constructivist IPE perspective. That question leads to consideration of the Enron bankruptcy.

Enron Bankruptcy

Just a few years ago the Texas-based energy-trading corporation, which declared bankruptcy on December 2, 2001, was America's seventh-largest company.[93] At the start of 2001, Enron's market capitalization was $62.5 billion. By spring 2002, Enron stock was worth just pennies.[94] As Partnoy explains, the rating agencies were central to Enron's financial strategy for two reasons.[95] First, given doubts about the company, without an investment-grade rating Enron would be unable to raise new funds at any price. Second, many of Enron's loans contained rating "triggers": if Enron was downgraded below investment grade, these loans would become due immediately in the full amount. This action would impose on the company an instant $4 billion obligation it could have otherwise refinanced for years. For these reasons, "Enron's fate was in the hands of the credit-rating agencies."[96]

Auditing illustrates the nature of the risk Enron posed for the agencies. The "big issue" raised by Enron's demise, according to the *Economist*, was the role played by auditors, who overlooked the exotic financial strategies the firm pursued.[97] The question of who regulates accounting and conflict of interest problems when auditors are also consultants to the same corporation—and the rigor of America's

93. "The Real Scandal," *Economist*, January 19, 2002, 9. For background on Enron, see Mimi Swartz with Sherron Watkins, *Power Failure: The Inside Story of the Collapse of Enron* (New York: Doubleday, 2003); Loren Fox, *Enron: The Rise and Fall* (New York: John Wiley and Sons, 2003).

94. Malcolm S. Salter, Lynne C. Levesque, and Maria Ciampa, "The Rise and Fall of Enron," paper prepared for the Faculty Symposium on Enron Corporation, Harvard Business School, April 10, 2002 (rev. April 23, 2002).

95. Partnoy, 2003, 336.

96. Ibid.

97. Also see Mike Brewster, *Unaccountable: How the Accounting Profession Forfeited a Public Trust* (New York: John Wiley & Sons, 2003).

GAAP standards—were subsequently up for debate and action.[98] The big victim of the public panic about Enron was their auditor, Arthur Andersen.[99] What is interesting about the attack on Andersen is that it demonstrates that a highly regarded institution, whose only real asset is its reputation, can see that asset evaporate if circumstances are right. Enron's experience was not the first time in recent years that Andersen had made significant errors, but the firm had survived these other problems.[100]

> The mounting problems inside Enron's executive suites were missed by many people. None of the watchdogs barked, including the credit rating agencies, who had greater access to Enron's books.[101]

Although subsequently exonerated by a staff report to the Senate Committee on Governmental Affairs, Enron was also a major crisis for the rating agencies.[102] They had got emerging markets "wrong" with the Asia crisis, and now they had got it wrong on a very large scale in America itself. The victims were not unknown citizens of foreign countries, but Americans, who lost their pensions, jobs, and futures. John Diaz, a managing director at Moody's, defended the company before the Senate committee. "Enron was an anomaly," he claimed. "Its responses to our specific requests for information were misleading and incomplete." Moody's rating process "was undermined by the missing information."[103] Ronald M. Barone, the S&P analyst on Enron for several years prior to the bankruptcy, used harsher language. He

98. On accounting reform after Enron, see Michael Peel and Simon London, "The Holes in GAAP: The Collapse of Enron Has Added to Questions about the Adequacy of U.S. Accounting Rules," *Financial Times*, January 17, 2002, 16; Arthur Levitt with Paula Dwyer, *Take on the Street* (New York: Pantheon, 2002).

99. Nicholas Kulish and John R. Wilke, "Indictment Puts Andersen's Fate on Line," *Wall Street Journal*, March 15, 2002, C1; Ken Brown, Cassell Bryan-Low, Carrick Mollenkamp, and Mitchell Pacelle, "Andersen's Foreign Offices Defect," *Wall Street Journal*, March 22, 2002, C1.

100. On the astonishment among Andersen workers about their "death sentence," see Dennis O'Toole, letter to the editor, "Where Is Justice for Andersen Workers?" *USA Today*, March 27, 2002, A12.

101. Sen. Joe Lieberman, statement, "Rating the Raters: Enron and the Credit Rating Agencies," hearings of the Committee on Governmental Affairs, U.S. Senate, Washington, D.C., March 20, 2002, available at www.senate.gov/~gov_affairs/hearings.htm; also see "Rating the Rating Agencies: The State of Transparency and Competition, hearings of the Committee on Financial Services, U.S. House of Representatives, Washington, D.C., April 2, 2003, available at http://financial services.house.gov/hearings.asp?formmode=detail&hearing=201.

102. This report concluded that Moody's delay in downgrading Enron below investment grade on November 8, 2001, was "not based on improper influence or pressure, but on new information" and "that no improper influence was brought to bear by government officials on Moody's." See the report by the staff of the Committee on Governmental Affairs, U.S. Senate, "Enron's Credit Rating: Enron's Bankers' Contacts with Moody's and Government Officials," January 3, 2003, available at http://govt-aff.senate.gov/issues.htm.

103. Testimony of John Diaz, managing director, Moody's Investors Service, before the Committee on Governmental Affairs, U.S. Senate, March 20, 2002, 2–3.

suggested Enron had made "what we later learned were direct and deliberate misrepresentations to us relating to matters of great substance."[104]

Former SEC chairman Arthur Levitt, who had shown little enthusiasm during the 1990s for codifying the rules for rating agencies, called for "greater accountability" by the agencies. He also called for the agencies to "reveal more about how they operate," an assessment of their "impact on the markets," and "new authority" for the SEC to "oversee" their work.[105] Much of the talk from the agencies focused on "speeding up" the rating process in response to the demands for change.[106]

The SEC's role in creating and maintaining the environment in which the agencies operate was noted by White, who suggested the NRSRO designation was anticompetitive and had "lured these rating agencies into complacency."[107] Partnoy also saw the legal environment as granting the agencies a "monopoly lock on the market"[108]

At the Senate committee hearings, Isaac C. Hunt Jr., an SEC commissioner, defended the NRSRO designation as intended "largely to reflect the view of the marketplace as to credibility of the ratings [of an agency] rather than representing a 'seal of approval' of a federal regulatory agency."[109] He noted that the 1997 proposal to codify NRSRO criteria had not yet been acted on by the commission, nor had the commission determined that the NRSRO designation was a "substantial barrier to entry" into the rating business. He further commented that

> growth in the business of several credit rating agencies, not recognized as NRSROs, suggests that there may be a growing appetite among market participants for advice about credit quality . . . and that this makes it possible for new entrants to develop a national following for their credit judgments.

Nevertheless, the commission was determined to examine the competitive impact of the NRSRO designation. If greater supervision of NRSROs was needed, "additional oversight" could become a condition of NRSRO recognition of an agency.

A law professor called to give testimony at the Senate committee hearings attacked the NRSRO designation vigorously. Macey argued that regulation creates

104. Testimony of Ronald M. Barone, managing director, Standard & Poor's, before the Committee on Governmental Affairs, U.S. Senate, March 20, 2002, 2.

105. Arthur Levitt, "Who Audits the Auditors?" *New York Times*, January 17, 2002, A29.

106. Emma Moody, "Moody's Looks at Speeding Ratings," *Ottawa Citizen*, January 19, 2002, H1; Jenny Wiggins and Peter Spiegel, "Enron's Fall May Spark Credit Rating Rethink," *Financial Times*, January 19–20, 2002, 1; Gregory Zuckerman and Christine Richard, "Moody's and S&P, Singed by Enron, May Speed Up Credit Downgrades," *Wall Street Journal*, January 22, 2002, C1; Christopher Mahoney, *The Bond Rating Process in a Changing Environment* (New York: Moody's Investors Service, January 2002); and Jenny Wiggins, "S&P Outlines Ratings Overhaul," *Financial Times*, January 26–27, 2002, 10.

107. Lawrence White, "Credit and Credibility," *New York Times*, February 24, 2002, 13.

108. Partnoy, 2003, 66.

109. Testimony of Isaac C. Hunt, Jr., commissioner, U.S. Securities and Exchange Commission, before the Committee on Governmental Affairs, U.S. Senate, March 20, 2002, 2, 4.

a steady demand. NRSROs, free of competitive forces as a result of their government designation, therefore had incentives to "reduce costs as much as possible" and maximize their profits.[110] Fees paid to the raters were better viewed, he said, as a form of tax rather than a fee for service. Schwarcz, another law professor, claimed that the anticompetitive effect of NRSRO designation, if any, was mitigated by the rating agencies' need to maintain their reputations, with or without regulation. Further regulation would not be likely to materially improve the effects of this reputational incentive.[111]

Another witness at the hearings emphasized that the "cure" should not be "worse than the disease" in considering alternatives to the NRSRO designation.[112] What should change was the quality of analysis, suggested Reynolds, and the fees rating agencies earned were lucrative enough to fund a material improvement. NRSROs should, he advised, be more activist, and quality standards should be imposed on them by regulation.[113] All material risks not covered under public disclosure rules should be reported to the SEC by NRSROs.[114] He feared the agencies had not so much improved the quality of their work as become "trigger happy to overcompensate for Enron," in effect changing the rules of the game.[115]

What is distinctive about the rating agencies' reaction to the crisis is their effort to consult with other parties about improving the rating process to avoid future Enrons. When Moody's announced its intentions in this area, concerns were expressed about a "dramatic increase in the volatility of ratings," which could raise the price of debt as investors started to perceive higher risk.[116] Moody's subsequently said that they would incorporate stock and bond prices in their analyses but would not "let market volatility displace fundamental credit analyses."[117] Nor would they engage in "unannounced multinotch ratings changes."[118] According to Moody's, market analysts were concerned that changes to ratings not disrupt the markets. The markets did expect the agencies to pursue accounting issues and demand undisclosed data, however.

110. Testimony of Jonathan R. Macey, Cornell Law School, before the Committee on Governmental Affairs, U.S. Senate, March 20, 2002, 3.

111. Testimony of Steven L. Schwarcz, Duke University, before the Committee on Governmental Affairs, U.S. Senate, March 20, 2002, 2–3.

112. Testimony of Glenn Reynolds, CEO of CreditSights, Inc., before the Committee on Governmental Affairs, U.S. Senate, March 20, 2002, 1.

113. Ibid., 2.

114. Ibid., 3.

115. Ibid., 6.

116. Louise Purtle, credit strategist at Deutsche Bank in New York, quoted in Gregory Zuckerman and Christine Richard, "Moody's and S&P Singed by Enron, May Speed Up Credit Downgrades," *Wall Street Journal*, January 22, 2002, C1.

117. John Dooley, "Moody's Planned Overhaul of Its Ratings Process Includes Effort to Limit Volatility, Shorten Reviews," *Wall Street Journal*, February 13, 2002, C16.

118. Chris Mahoney, senior managing director, Moody's Investors Service, quoted in ibid.

Although Moody's still expects ratings to be valid through cycles, they are to be adjusted more frequently "in periods of heightened credit stress."[119] This emphasis on going beyond the information issuers formally provided was reinforced in Senate committee hearings chaired by Senator Lieberman.[120] Senator Thompson (R.–Tenn.) questioned whether the agencies added value, asserting that they did not "really go beyond the documents."[121]

Soon after the hearings, the SEC announced a reexamination of the role of the agencies and possible need for greater regulation. Subsequently, the Sarbanes-Oxley Act of July 30, 2002, passed in the wake of the Enron-Andersen scandal, mandated the SEC to study the "role and function of credit rating agencies." The analysis was to include, among other things, impediments to accurate appraisal of creditworthiness, barriers to entry in the rating business, and conflicts of interest in the agencies.[122]

The SEC's report, completed January 24, 2003, drew on work by the staff of the Senate Committee on Governmental Affairs, completed in October 2002, six months after that committee's hearings.[123] The report announced the publication of a concept release, which appeared June 4, 2003.[124] The release suggested possibilities through which NRSRO status could be codified, monitored, and evaluated, to control the problems specified by Sarbanes-Oxley. Comments were invited, to be submitted by the end of July 2003. Moody's, S&P, and Fitch made submissions supporting a more transparent, codified NRSRO system that reinforced independent credit opinion. Moody's suggested eliminating the use of ratings in federal regulation.[125]

119. Ibid.
120. Michael Schroeder, "SEC Weighs Curbs on Credit-Rating Firms," *Wall Street Journal,* March 21, 2002, A3.
121. Sen. Fred Thompson quoted in Schroeder, "SEC Weighs Curbs."
122. Public Law 107–204, "Sarbanes-Oxley Act of 2002," 107th Cong., United States of America, Washington, D.C., July 30, 2002, sec. 702, 797–98; on the subsequent SEC hearings, see Sheila McNulty, "Rating Agencies Get Ready to Defend Role in Energy Meltdown," *Financial Times,* November 15, 2002, 30, and Judith Burns, "U.S. Reviews Credit-Rating Rules," *Wall Street Journal Europe,* November 18, 2002, M6.
123. "Financial Oversight of Enron: The SEC and Private Sector Watchdogs," report of the staff to the Committee on Governmental Affairs, U.S. Senate, October 8, 2002, available at http:// govt-aff.senate.gov/issues.htm; letter from Senators Joseph I. Lieberman and Fred Thompson to chairman, U.S. Securities and Exchange Commission, October 7, 2002; U.S. Securities and Exchange Commission, "Report on the Role and Function of Credit Rating Agencies in the Operation of the Securities Markets," as required by sec. 702 (b) of the Sarbanes-Oxley Act of 2002, January 24, 2003, available at http://www.sec.gov/news/studies/credratingreport0103.pdf.
124. Securities and Exchange Commission, "Concept Release: Rating Agencies and the Use of Credit Ratings under the Federal Securities Laws," June 4, 2003, available at http://www.sec.gov/rules/concept/33–8236.htm.
125. Raymond W. McDaniel, president, Moody's Investors Service, "Letter to SEC re: Concept Release: Rating Agencies and the Use of Credit Ratings under Federal Securities Laws," July 28, 2003; available at www.moodys.com; Standard & Poor's, "Standard & Poor's Supports a New, More Transparent NRSRO Designation Process," July 28, 2003, available at www2.standardandpoors. com; Charles D. Brown, "Letter to SEC re: Concept Release: Rating Agencies and the Use of Credit Ratings under Federal Securities Laws," July 28, 2003, available at www.fitchratings.com.

The SEC has to decide whether to move toward a new draft rule on NRSRO regulation. No decision has been made and the SEC is internally divided on the matter, although some reports see the potential for decisive action.[126] The possibilities the concept release raised did not go beyond managing and developing the current rating regulatory environment, created during the twentieth century.[127] The SEC had published a concept release on NRSROs in 1994 and a proposed rule in 1997 without subsequent implementation. So it remains to be seen whether Enron and the other corporate scandals of the first years of the twenty-first century actually give rise to substantive change in the regulation of bond rating agencies.[128]

Conclusions

In popular accounts, rating agencies are often portrayed as omnipotent, possessing an unlimited power they deploy at their whim. While this has never been true, prior to the 1980s, the agencies were slower moving and yet less vulnerable to criticism. Most of their work was done inside the United States, in markets they knew very well. Since the onset of the junk bond era, things have not been the same for the agencies. Greater international capital mobility has brought greater volatility to markets and greater problems in assigning ratings and adjusting them in a timely fashion that meets the concerns of investors and other parties. This is a problem for everyone in the financial markets and certainly for government regulators and the communities affected. But rating agencies are especially vulnerable to attack. They are supposed to "know better" and to make sure the rest of us are not hurt by these changes. The basis for a substantial response from the aggrieved is considerable, as Arthur Andersen has learned to its cost.

Moody's and S&P have changed greatly since the 1990s as they endeavor to meet these challenges. They defend themselves vigorously. But they are also trying to dispel an image of complacency by developing their relations with market participants and "improving" their rating technology, much like a judge who goes

126. John Labate, "Reining in the Rating Agencies," *Treasury & Risk Management*, June 2004, available at www.treasuryandrisk.com, accessed August 11, 2004.

127. On what the SEC will do after the Sarbanes-Oxley report, see Michael Schroeder and Gregory Zuckerman, "U.S. Officials to Probe Practices of Big Credit-Rating Agencies," *Wall Street Journal Europe*, January 28, 2003, M1.

128. Other reports and investigations have been instigated by IOSCO, The Technical Committee of the International Organization of Securities Commissions, "Report on the Activities of Credit Rating Agencies," (Madrid: 105.0, 2003), and the Committee on Economic and Monetary Affairs, European Parliament, Hearing on "The Role and Methods of Rating Agencies," Brussels, November 24, 2003.

back to law school for a refresher course. The rating agencies have been success-ful so far in avoiding an Andersen-style implosion of their reputational assets and have retained their epistemic authority. The value they are thought to offer seems to shield them from authority decay. But that does not insulate them from the pressures that destroyed Andersen. They remain vulnerable, and with global markets producing surprises at frequent intervals, the question of their survival remains relevant.

CHAPTER EIGHT

A New Constellation of Power

The Masters of the Universe were a set of lurid, rapacious plastic dolls
. . . They looked like Norse gods who lifted weights . . . On Wall Street
he and a few others . . . had become precisely that . . . Masters of the
Universe.

TOM WOLFE, *The Bonfire of the Vanities*, 1988

Tom Wolfe's novel, like the movie *Wall Street,* focused on something
not seen since the late 1920s: unshackled and unapologetic financial capitalism. This
book has examined a central—supposedly technical—support of the financial markets. It argued that rating agencies are changing the norms and practices of commercial and public life around the world, along manifestly American lines. In
support of this position, the book demonstrated that the judgments of the agencies
reflect a particular view of the world—the mental framework of rating orthodoxy.
These judgments are increasingly important in a world of financial globalization.
Moreover, the book examined the static, instrumental form of knowledge the rating
agencies rely on. The rules that govern important dimensions of the world are being
transformed by the work of the agencies, affecting work life and democracy in places
touched by financial globalization. These investigations were informed by contrasting rationalist and constructivist understandings of the phenomena, incorporated
in the analysis via a counterfactual method.

To what degree can the rating agencies be thought to constitute a new constella-
tion of power in the global economy, and what are the limits of this power? The lib-
eral objections to the idea that rating agencies exercise power are discussed, along
with the nature of the relationship between sovereign governments and rating agencies. Subsequently, key features of rating agency power, influence, and authority are
evaluated. Here, the issue of judgment and what this means for different social interests is considered. In addition, the reputation of the agencies and how this is formed
is examined, the significance of competition between agencies is discussed, and the
most important consequences of rating power are identified. The challenges to

rating agencies and the tensions that qualify the power, influence, and authority of rating are also considered. In the concluding section, we discuss how to live with the agencies.

The research presented in this book supports the view that rating agencies represent a new force in the post–Cold War world. In themselves, rating agencies are not new. They have been around since before World War I, but they have changed with the re-emergence of international capital mobility. The policy autonomy of national governments and the choices of municipal governments and corporations have been affected significantly by this development. At the same time as capital was freed from its Cold War shackles—and despite the "war on terror"—the warplanes now stored in Tucson have become less important than they once were. A process of change in how financial capital is organized has taken root. Increasingly, under the spur of financial globalization, banks have become expensive places from which to borrow money, spurring the growth of capital markets. In rationalist terms, these markets needed a way for lenders to obtain reliable information about borrowers. Considered through a constructivist lens, rating agencies do more than merely serve this function. They have become a significant instance of nonstate authority in a post-bipolar world. Rating agencies now need to be incorporated into accounts of global governance, like the IMF or the World Bank. Because they are ostensibly private and operate in the commercial sphere of the capital markets, the rating agencies have power that is camouflaged more effectively than in these higher-profile institutions and are therefore even more deserving of our attention.

Rating agencies do not replace states, even though they represent the shape of newly emerging authority. This authority interacts with pre-existing powers. As I have shown, rating agencies have interesting, complex relationships with national governments. At times, rating agencies wield power against states, corporations and municipalities. Other times, the power of rating agencies is anticipated by these issuers. Political actors use the rating agencies to show how effective they are at management or to justify changes in public policy. National states, especially in emerging markets, enlist the services of rating agencies to encourage the development of their own capital markets, in order to increase transparency and cheapen the cost of lending. This national government-rating agency relationship is a paradoxical one. But in general, the role and influence attributable to rating agencies has grown in the conditions described.

Identifying rating agencies as powerful is difficult for thinkers from traditions in which power is only something that public entities such as sovereign governments can possess. Their view is that rating agencies do not exercise power. Power implies coercion to these critics, who see rating agencies merely as the functional agents of rational market actors. Their position is unconvincing for three reasons. First, this is an impoverished view of power. Power does not merely imply coercion. Consent is also a key element of power, as I have sought to demonstrate throughout this book. The power of rating agencies is certainly as much a product of the success of the rating agencies in generating consent, as it is derived from exercising coercion. Second, as understood in this book, power is not limited to relational power, which is of a behavioral form. Structural power—involving the anticipation of the exercise of power in its relational form—is a feature of the rating world. This latent understanding of power must be deduced rather than counted. Third, any social behavior that has such potentially enormous consequences for hundreds of millions of people can hardly be considered apolitical. Because rating is so consequential, it is not a private affair, just as General Motors, Robert Dahl has observed, "is as much a public enterprise as the U.S. Post Office."[1] Rating agencies are political in these terms, and they exercise power. As much as they would like to deny it, they cannot reasonably be fenced off from politics understood in this wider sense. What they do is simply too important for that to be acceptable.

Let us look a little more closely at key features of the rating agencies' power. It has been argued that at the heart of rating are processes of judgment, premised on the mental framework of rating orthodoxy, introduced in chapter 3. Rating, as it exists today, is not rocket science. It attempts to meld quantitative and qualitative variables that are not commensurate and therefore cannot be placed into an equation. It is crucial to understand this point, for much of the commentary in the financial media passes over the inherent subjectivity of bond rating. Ratings are not deducible. They reflect the application of rules of thumb. What follows from this observation that ratings are judgments is the realization that ratings are actually more contestable than they may appear.

Particular solutions to dilemmas, such as how to fund the construction and maintenance of a bridge, can have very different answers. Some answers, such as funding from general revenue, shift distribution of resources toward certain groups (such as drivers) and away from others. Other solutions, such as the imposition of tolls, target all who drive over the bridge but negatively affect low-income people, whose mobility is reduced accordingly. These distributional impacts are significant political consequences of rating yet they rarely receive acknowledgment. Any critical assessment of rating agencies must acknowledge distributional implications. The social effects are of course unintentional. They are simply the consequences of promoting the interests of creditors. The mental framework of rating orthodoxy is organized accordingly. Rating is not a universal welfare expanding form of expertise. It is a mental technology with an intimate role in generating answers to Lasswell's (and subsequently Susan Strange's) favorite question: who gets what, when, how? Given this observation, rating must be linked to the ascendant social interests that drive financial globalization and policy change.

Another key feature of the new power of the agencies is dependence on reputation. Rating agencies sell the understanding that their judgments are important and

---

1. Robert A. Dahl, *After the Revolution? Authority in a Good Society* (New Haven: Yale University Press, 1970), 120.

accurate or, at the least, that others think so and act accordingly. Through both a rationalist solution to the "information problem" in disintermediated capital markets and a long history of perceived accuracy, rating agencies have constructed for themselves the eminence of an epistemic authority, like a judge. That is, what they say is not so much persuasive as it is widely perceived to be authoritative. The agencies are held to be worthy of being listened to, and in this context it takes a brave individual to go against their judgment. Once made, reputation is a very considerable resource at the rating agencies' disposal. It is resistant to strong assault, much like the stone walls of a castle.

But, paradoxically, just like fortress walls, rating agencies have to be careful they do not allow the basis of their power to be undermined, so precipitating a sudden collapse of their epistemic authority. After all, thousands of once-mighty castles stand idle or in ruins throughout Europe. For this reason, rating agencies are attentive to what is said about them and to presenting themselves in a strong, self-confident way. They never know when the eminence they have established may be fatally weakened. As the executives at Arthur Andersen know, financial globalization throws up more risks of this happening today than in the sedate world of the 1940s and 1950s, when bond rating was institutionalized.

What consequences flow from the power and authority of rating agencies? The agencies and the rating process provide a transmission pathway for the delivery of policy and managerial orthodoxy to widely scattered governments and corporations. In this sense, the agencies are nominally private makers of a global public policy. They are agents of convergence, who seek to enforce "best practice" and "transparency" on the world.

The most significant effect of rating agencies is not their immediate view of a particular budget deficit. It is their implicit promotion of the norms of the mental framework of rating orthodoxy in relation to how all problems, including budget deficits, are to be assessed. This adjustment of the "operating system," or mental schemata, is the most consequential impact of the agencies' work and the least considered elsewhere. Because the United States is already characterized by these schemata, the impact of rating is ultimately less dramatic and conflictual in this country.

Rating agencies face many challenges. The process described above has generated opposition. Newspapers often carry outraged headlines after a rating downgrade. The Japanese government has sought to undermine the system publicly as their creditworthiness has deteriorated since the early 1990s. Rarely do such attempts threaten the agencies. Downgraded entities, it seems, will vent their anger. But what actually corrodes the authority of the rating agencies? What destroys their franchise?

In recent years, the rise of numerous providers of market intelligence and the much greater availability of all manner of economic and financial data have raised the question whether institutions can wield authority. People who possess heightened analytic skills cannot be fooled, we are told.[2] But "fooling people" is not central to rating. The rules of thumb the rating agencies provide become social facts of the market that even the most highly skilled must take into account. Are others using the rating judgments? If they are, then these ratings have a status in the markets, even if an analysis by an individual is divergent. Ratings are part of the environment that even the most skilled need to acknowledge, because they may affect the behavior of others, which in turn can change the market in which all bonds are priced. In other words, even if smart people are not convinced by bond ratings, they must incorporate them to the extent that others do. An authority, even if wrong, still gives rise to all manner of social action because what it does (and how it relates to others) is a "social fact."

Can rating mistakes or crises shatter the rating franchise? For a brief moment in 1997–98, and again in 2002, this was the main question about rating agencies. Had the agencies destroyed their credibility by not providing sufficient or clear enough signals about Thailand, Korea, Indonesia, and Enron? Were they behind the game, and would they lose business because of this failure? Some weaknesses of the rating process—the focus on past performance, the application of Western expectations to the East—plus the euphoria that surrounded the East Asian economies, contributed to a hesitant signaling of risk. Subsequently, the agencies downgraded everything in sight, an action that was similarly criticized.

Curiously, very little has come of all this. Two things seem to have saved the agencies from real disaster. First, "everyone" read Asia wrong. The agencies do not look exceptional when other sources of market intelligence are considered. Just as in the failure to predict the end of the Cold War, the best analytical tools available did not work as intended. Second, the aftermath of the rating debacle in Asia has strengthened the first steps toward disintermediation in that part of the world: banks were the culprits, so the financial system there needs to be reformed along Western (i.e., American) lines and, thus, in the direction of capital markets. In rationalist terms, what these markets need are institutions able to solve the information problems the markets present. Hence the crisis created a greater, not lesser, role for the agencies and therefore the opportunity for the agencies to present themselves as having truly learnt from the Asian experience. Although the crisis showed that the rating agencies are not omniscient, it also provided a long-term opportunity for the agencies to increase their authority. So much for the apparent rating meltdown.

Given the direction of change in capital markets and the agencies' success in surviving the Orange County debacle, Asia, and Enron (much as they survived New York City's crisis during the 1970s), institutions and nations seeking to issue bonds will continue to do business with the agencies. How do governments and corporations engage effectively with the raters, and therefore obtain a rating they can afford?

2. James N. Rosenau, *Turbulence in World Politics: A Theory of Change and Continuity*, (Princeton: Princeton University Press, 1990), 333–87.

Institutions such as the Government of Ontario, which have worked at good communications and transparency about their plans, have been rewarded. In other conditions, they might have anticipated worse ratings than they received during the 1990s. Providing the agencies with timely information and preventing rating analysts from feeling they are the victims of some surprise paid off for the province.

More aggressive strategies have also been developed. The use of third agencies, such as Fitch, and the abandonment of one of the Big Two was the approach taken by the State of New York during the 1990s. But this also encouraged suspicions. Demanding fuller rationales for ratings push the agencies to provide better information that issuers can use to improve subsequent ratings. At the minimum, demands for transparency could increase pressure on the agencies to increasingly think of themselves as accountable, too. Greater competition in the rating industry might develop, although the construction of epistemic authority is a major competitive barrier. After Enron, it is possible that the regulatory environment for rating agencies will become codified in the United States. Initiatives here are likely to be emulated elsewhere. Radical change, however, is unlikely to come from this direction.

Despite its bean-counter image, bond rating is something that stirs great passions, perhaps because it reminds us of the feelings of rejection getting a bad grade in school produced. At a deeper level, some may have an inkling that it is precisely in the seemingly technical, the supposedly objective infrastructural phenomena such as rating that the big questions of today and tomorrow are increasingly being decided. If so, this represents a transformation of the common-sense understandings we have of the things that shape our everyday lives.

INDEX

Cornell Studies in Political Economy
A series edited by
PETER J. KATZENSTEIN